G
302
.J6
1964

640

Jones
Norse Atlantic saga, being
the Norse voyages of dis-
covery and settlement to
Iceland, Greenland and
America

Date Due

D1068895

I. A VIKING

THE NORSE ATLANTIC SAGA

Being the Norse Voyages of Discovery
and Settlement to Iceland,
Greenland, America

GWYN JONES

London
OXFORD UNIVERSITY PRESS
NEW YORK   TORONTO

Oxford University Press, Amen House, London E.C.4

GLASGOW NEW YORK TORONTO MELBOURNE WELLINGTON
BOMBAY CALCUTTA MADRAS KARACHI LAHORE DACCA
CAPE TOWN SALISBURY NAIROBI IBADAN ACCRA
KUALA LUMPUR HONG KONG

First published 1964
Reprinted 1964

Printed in Great Britain
by Ebenezer Baylis and Son, Limited
The Trinity Press, Worcester, and London

Preface

THE theme of this book is the Norsemen's search for new land, 'habitable and trespassable', westward across the North Atlantic from their homes in continental Scandinavia. It deals with their voyages of discovery and exploration to Iceland, Greenland, and the east coast of North America, and their attempt to colonize all three. It is everywhere a story of hope and high endeavour, in Iceland of stern but rewarded endurance, in Greenland of resolution and long-drawn disaster, in America of venture and forced withdrawal. In all three lands the Norsemen found themselves living near or beyond the limits of medieval European survival, and in two of them they failed to maintain their footing. Yet we must be cautious of using the word 'failure'. The Vinland expeditions demonstrate what we now see to be an obvious truth, that a couple of hundred Europeans of the early eleventh century, with tenuous communications and no marked superiority of weapons, could not conquer a hostile continent; but that they managed to reach it, and continued, however intermittently, to visit it over many centuries, is an impressive witness to Norse resource and daring. That the Icelanders colonized the south-west coast of Greenland and held it for five hundred years before the last survivors perished so mysteriously is a failure only in the sense that Scott's journey to the South Pole with its cost in human lives was a failure. While for Iceland, when we consider the literature and the distinctive culture of the Republic, the verdict must be one of brilliant though not untroubled success.

In general the westward voyages and settlements have been written about in two ways: either entire books, large or small, have been devoted to one country or to a single aspect or segment of one country, or Iceland, Greenland, Vinland have figured as chapters or sometimes paragraphs in books that cover the Viking Age. There therefore seemed to be plenty of room for a presentation of the defined subject, including a continuous narrative incorporating the findings of recent scholarship and a translation of the more important early documents—for whatever the additions made to our knowledge by archaeology, history, geography, and their ancillary sciences, it is to the early literary records we must always return. Also, the time invites such a book. There has been a big increase of interest in the vikings and their manifold achievement during recent years, leading to such publications in English as Johannes Brøndsted's *The Vikings*, 1960, Holger Arbman's *The Vikings*, 1961, and P. H. Sawyer's *The Age of the Vikings*, 1962; while three events in particular have enlivened general as well as scholarly interest in the Atlantic voyages and colonies. First there have been the Vinland journey of Jørgen Meldgaard in 1956 and the sustained explorations of Helge Ingstad in 1960, 1961, and 1962 (renewed even as I write, in July 1963), in search of Norse sites in Newfoundland and Labrador. The precise extent and duration of the Vinland voyages southwards will long remain a subject of conjecture, but that an area in northern Newfoundland was the Promontorium Winlandiæ of Norse geographical tradition and an identifiable part of the original voyages of discovery now appears certain. Second came the discovery of Thjodhild's Church near Eirik the Red's farm at Brattahlid, Greenland, in the autumn of 1961, and its partial excavation in the summer of 1962. The importance to the archaeologist and historian of the first Christian church and churchyard to be built anywhere in the western hemisphere beyond the shores of Iceland needs no emphasis; in our present context it is a welcome confirmation of one particular portion of *Eiríks Saga Rauða*, and of the Greenland-Vinland tradition in general. Third has been the raising of five Norse ships, also in 1962, from the waters of Roskilde Fjord in Denmark, whose black and sodden timbers provide us with our first examples of the different kinds of *knerrir* or ocean-going ships which carried the Norsemen on their voyages of trade and exploration over heaving seas to their known and unknown landfalls on the shores of the 'island countries of the North'. The goodwill of Danish scholars has allowed me a personal acquaintance with Thjodhild's Church and the *knerrir*, while in respect of the Promontorium Winlandiæ I have had the benefit of many conversations with Jørgen Meldgaard of the National Museum of Denmark, and generous communications from the Icelanders Kristján Eldjárn and Thórhallur Vilmundarson, who both took part in the 1962 excavations conducted in the Sacred Bay area of Newfoundland by Helge Ingstad in 1962.

The translations in my volume are newly done and the story newly written, save for some of the paragraphs on pages 32–36 which deal with the old Icelandic literature, and the Appendix on '*Njála*: Greatest of Sagas'. In their case I must thank the *Times Literary Supplement*, the American-Scandinavian Foundation, and the Oxford University Press for allowing me to repeat or adapt words first written in a different but related context.

In story and translation I have used the customary anglicized forms of the names of saga places and persons, i.e., Gudbrand, Thorhall, Reykjavik; for more recent reference I have used modern forms, i.e., Guðbrandur, Thórhallur, Reykjavík. Complete consistency in nomenclature is in theory desirable, but is not to be attained except at heavy cost to all save the specialist reader, who is in any case catered for by the original texts. As to the translations, I hope that they will convey to the English reader not only the subject matter but the strong human interest of the works they seek to render.

I have received much kindness during the writing of this book, including hospitality, gifts of published and unpublished information, and grants of time and money. I owe thanks to several institutions: the University of Wales for sending me to Iceland once more in 1961; the National Museum of Denmark and its Director for inviting me to join its party at Qagssiarssuk-Brattahlid in 1962; the Leverhulme Trustees for the research grant which made it possible for me to spend the late spring and summer there and in Denmark and Norway; my own College for releasing me at a difficult time. I have numerous personal obligations, two of them outstanding: to Museumsinspektør Jørgen Meldgaard who, with the other members of his party, made my stay in Greenland as instructive as it was happy, and at all times let me draw freely on his knowledge of the Norse and Eskimo civilizations; and to Dr. Kristján Eldjárn, Director of the National Museum of Iceland. Others who have shown me courtesies of various kinds include Dr. Harald Andersen, Professor E. G. Bowen, Professor Norman Davis, Dr. H. D. Emmanuel, Museumsinspektør Bent Fredskild, Professor Anders Hagen, Frú Guðrún P. Helgadóttir, Mr. Isak Heilmann, Mr. Helge Ingstad, Arkitekt Knud Krogh, Professor Sigurður Nordal,

Museumsinspektør Olaf Olsen, Dr. Aage Roussell, Sir Graham Sutton, Professor Einar Ól. Sveinsson, Sir Ben Bowen Thomas, Museumsinspektør C. L. Vebæk, Professor Thórhallur Vilmundarson, and Pastor Michael Wolfe, O.M.I., of Godthaab. *Gott ey gǫmlum mǫnnum, gott ey ærum mǫnnum!* The artists and institutions to whom I owe my illustrations are listed in the appropriate place; here I offer them my thanks and appreciation. Finally I express my greatest obligation of all, to my wife Alice, for encouragement and assurance, and for wise counsel and practical help at every stage of my book.

GWYN JONES

Contents

Part One THE STORY

Illustrations

LIST OF PLATES

LIST OF TEXT FIGURES

THE MAPS

Part One

THE STORY

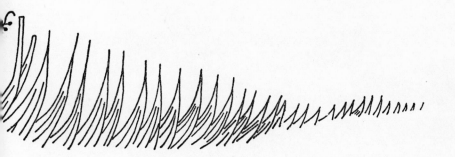

I

Iceland

I. BEFORE THE NORSEMEN

W HO first saw Iceland, and whether god-impelled, mirage-led, wind-whipt and storm-belted, or on a tin-and-amber course laid north to roll back trade horizons, we do not know. But he was a brave man, or an unlucky, and it was a long time ago.

The dragon prow of a Norse adventurer made the first recorded circumnavigation of the island about 860; the curachs of Irish anchorites had reached its south-eastern shore in the last years of the eighth century; but it is probable that Iceland's story starts in a remoter past than this. We have learned in the last thirty years that man's early knowledge of the sea and willingness to venture out upon it resulted in voyages undreamt of by nineteenth-century historians; and that this is as true of the northern as the southern hemisphere, of the Atlantic as the Pacific. By 2500 B.C., and maybe much earlier, the sea was man's highway, and already the funerary ritual of the megalith builders of Spain, Portugal, and France was being spread by sea throughout the islands and peninsulas of the west, and from these northwards through the Irish Sea and Pentland Firth. The western sea-routes have been frequented ways ever since, for though profit and policy have often led peoples to stow knowledge under hatches, as did the Phoenicians in respect of Africa and the Cassiterides, or the merchants of Bristol in respect of their illegal fifteenth-century trade with Greenland, such mind-cargo is rarely lost to human memory. Someone knows, or confusedly recalls, that far out on the ocean's bosom lies a Land of Promise, Eternal Youth, silent refuge, stockfish profit. There is therefore nothing improbable in the notion that the Greek astronomer, mathematician, and geographer, Pytheas of Massalia, acquired in the purlieus of Britain as much news of Thule as he is thought to have bequeathed to it. Unfortunately Pytheas's account of his voyage of exploration to Britain and further north in 330–300 B.C. has not survived. We have to rely instead on pieces of not always consistent information, at times derived from careless intermediaries, embedded in the writings of later and often derisory Greek geographers. In this shadowed way we first meet the name Thule, though it is far from certain that by Thule Pytheas meant the country we now know as Iceland. It lay six days' sail north of Britain (Strabo and Pliny), and one day's sail beyond it lay a congealed, curdled, or frozen ocean (Pliny). At the time of the summer solstice the sun was visible there for twenty-four hours of the day (Cleomedis), or at least the night was very short, lasting in some places two hours, in others three (Geminos), all of which is consonant with Iceland. But Pytheas speaks of Thule as a country inhabited by barbarians, of whom he offers credible intelligence. They have little in the way of domestic animals, he says, but live on millet and herbs, together with fruit and roots. Those who have grain and honey make drink from them. This grain, when it was cut, they brought into large covered barns and threshed indoors, because the sunlessness of the climate and its downpours of rain made threshing floors in the open impracticable. Of any such habitation the archaeological record of Iceland is bare, while the little we know of the cold recession in the climate of the northern hemisphere in Pytheas's day makes the identification still less likely. The west coast of Norway has stronger claims to be this early 'farthest north', and those of Shetland and even Orkney are not easily dismissed. If we can trust Strabo, Pytheas said of these high latitudes that here was a region where earth, sea, and air existed not as distinguishable elements, but inchoately as a congelation of all three, a 'sea lung' heaving with the rhythmic breath of Demogorgon, not to be journeyed on or sailed through. This he saw for himself. But what it was that he saw, whether fog-bank and slush-ice, or some legitimately powerful effect of the imagination upon the massed phenomena of a bad sub-arctic day, we fail to see it after him, our recognition of Thule is stayed, and Iceland does not enter the historical record.[1]

---

[1] For Pytheas see Gaston-E. Broche, *Pythéas le Massaliote*, Paris, 1935; V. Stefánsson, *Ultima Thule*, 1941; and *Pytheas Von Massalia*, Collegit Hans Joachim Mette, Berlin, 1952 (contains the literary remains, pp. 17–35).

If not the Phoenicians and Greeks, were the Romans able to reach Iceland? The likeliest time for such an exploit would be during the bull-necked Carausius's control of the Classis Britannica, whether as admiral in the Low Countries or emperor of Britain (*c.* A.D. 286–93); but there is no literary evidence, and that of archaeology is slight and inconclusive: just three well-preserved Roman copper coins from the period 270–305 (these dates embrace the entire reigns of the emperors whose effigies they bear) discovered this present century, two at Bragðarvellir in Hamarsfjord, the other in the Hvalnes district of Lon, all in the south-eastern corner of Iceland. This area is the likeliest landfall of ships from the south. But we need not believe that so few and such low-valued coins came north with their first owners whether Roman or Scottish; it is likelier that they were brought to Iceland by a Norseman who had picked them up abroad, as part of a plundered hoard, as keepsake or curio, or for any of the thousand and one arbitrary reasons why a man has such things in his possession. Certainly, if a Roman vessel came so far north, by design or accident, there is no record of her return; the three copper coins are the sole memorial of her voyage, and when we weigh the hazards of the ocean and the land's inclemency we incline to add, of her crew.[1]

Meantime the western sea-routes were endlessly busy. When the day of the megalith builders was over, Celtic invaders of the Bronze Age took their place as voyagers by sea as well as land. For a further thousand years there was a continuous movement of peoples and cultures between the Continent and the islands and promontories of western Britain, till finally in the early Christian period the missionary fervour of the Celtic saints united Ireland and Brittany, Cornwall, Wales, and Strathclyde in a close cultural unity.[2] By the fifth and sixth centuries A.D. it was along these western routes alone that the peoples of Britain and Ireland could maintain contact with the shrunken Roman civilization in Gaul and the western Mediterranean. Sea-going activity was unending, so that when the Irish saints and peregrini sought for ever more

---

[1] Kristján Eldjárn, *Gengið á Reka*, Reykjavík, 1948, pp. 10–24; *Kuml og Haug fé úr Heiðnum Sið í Íslandi*, 1956, pp. 13–24; *Viking Archaeology in Iceland*, Þriðji Víkinga-fundur, 1956, pp. 27–8; Einar Ól. Sveinsson, *Landnám í Skaftafellsþingi*, 1948, pp. 2–3.

[2] For an attempt to set this 'Celtic thalassocracy' in a European context, see A. R. Lewis, *The Northern Seas*, Princeton, 1958, Chapter II, 'The Invasion Period' *passim*, and particularly p. 64.

distant isles and hermitages they had in aid an almost immemorial habit of ocean-travel in addition to well-found ships and a rich navigational lore. These ships were curachs, made of hides (*coria*) over a wooden frame, some small as that constructed of two and a half hides in which three Irish pilgrims came to England to visit king Alfred in 891, others vessels of a good size and burden, able to transport at least a score of men with their gear and provisions. In these curachs, from monasteries such as Aran, Bangor, Clonfert, and Clonmacnoise, Irishmen by oar and sail reached every British coast (Columba was in Iona by 563), then turned their prows to the northern ocean. Between Scotland and Orkney lies a narrow sound whose frequent storms and sudden changes from smooth water to a broken sea did nothing to daunt, though sometimes they drowned, early seafarers. From Orkney it is a bare 50 miles to Shetland, and from Shetland less than 200 to the Faeroes. Here, to Iceland, the ocean gulf is wider, 240 miles; while from Malin Head in the north of Ireland the direct sailing distance is some 600; but the continued northward progress of the peregrini seems inevitable, particularly when we allow for the well-attested effects of the northern *hillingar* or *fata morgana*, which may easily double the distance at which land grows visible to the hopeful traveller. Even the unhopeful was into soundings 400 miles from the Butt of Lewis.

It is often difficult to distinguish truth from fiction in the lives of Celtic saints, and never more so than when the saints are Irish. Which is a pity, because in their *Imrama* or travel-tales are to be found passages which seem to record, or rather reflect, experiences in high latitudes, with blowing whales and belching volcanoes. No pains were too severe for those who like Cormac ua Liathain sought their desert in the ocean, though for most who found it, in caves and huts on lonely islands, there remained only prayer and worship, solitude and self-mortification.

> Eager wailings to cloudy heaven, sincere and truly devout confession, fervent showers of tears.
> A cold anxious bed, like the lying-down of the doomed, a brief apprehensive sleep, cries frequent and early. . . .
> Alone in my little hut, all alone so, alone I came into the world, alone I shall go from it.

Others, true, sound a happier note, as in the anonymous twelfth-century poem on St. Columba's island hermitage:

Delightful I think it to be in the bosom of an isle, on the peak of a rock, that I might often see there the calm of the sea. . . .

That I might see its splendid flocks of birds over the full-watered ocean; that I might see its mighty whales, greatest of wonders.

That I might see its ebb and its flood-tide in their flow; that this may be my name, a secret I tell, 'He who turned his back on Ireland.'

For most of these God-committed men *peregrinari pro Christo* permitted no return. Starvation or violent death, all terrors of earth and ocean were for God's sake welcome. The peregrini had embraced the white martyrdom of a heroic renunciation.[1]

The best known of the Irish *Imrama*, and the most relevant to the story of Iceland, records the travels of St. Brendan. On one occasion, at no great distance north of them in the ocean, the saint and his companions beheld a high mountain, its summit wreathed in cloud and smoke; and as their ship was borne closer to the island it was to find a coast so immensely towering that they could hardly see the top of it, steep as a wall, and glowing like coals. Ashore they lost one of their number to the devils who dwelt here, and when by divine favour they were enabled to sail away, they saw as they looked back the mountain now freed from smoke, first spewing its flames into the heavens, then sucking them back again, so that the entire mountain down to the sea's edge had the appearance of a blazing pyre.[2] This certainly looks like the description of an erupting volcano near the southerly shore of a mountainous island, and one is tempted to think it not so much a new location of hell as a word-picture of a flaming Hekla, Katla, or some crater in Oræfi, with its attendant lavaflow; but the Mediterranean had its volcanoes too, and classical literature many references to such, so we are still short of a full assurance. In fact, for reliable literary evidence that the Irish religious not only knew of Iceland but actually lived there for 60 to 70 years before its

---

[1] The two verse translations, the first of an eighth–ninth century original, are from K. B. Jackson, *A Celtic Miscellany*, 1951, pp. 307–10. For the peregrinus see J. F. Kenney, *The Sources for the Early History of Ireland*, New York, 1929, Vol. I, Ecclesiastical, p. 488: ' "peregrinus" as used in Ireland of the early Middle Ages (Irish *deórad*) meant not one who goes on pilgrimage to a shrine and then returns home, but one who departs his homeland to dwell for a space of years or for the rest of his life in strange countries.' For *baanmartre* see Thurneysen, *Old Irish Reader* (translated by Binchy and Bergin), Dublin, 1949, p. 36. The O.E. *Guthlac* has a moving passage (lines 81 ff.) on those who 'dwell in deserts, seek and inhabit of their own will homes in dark places, await their heavenly mansion'.

[2] O. O. Selmer, *Navigatio Sancti Brendani*, Notre Dame, 1959, p. 64; Plummer, *Vitæ Sanctorum Hiberniæ*, 1910, I, 130; Kenney, *op. cit.*, pp. 409–12.

discovery by Norsemen, we must look not to the wonder-tales of
the hagiographers, nor yet to the witness of Bede[1] (reminiscent
as this last is of the Pytheas fragments, and readily adopted by the
Icelandic authors or redactors of *Landnámabók*), that six days'
sailing north of Britain lay the island whose name was Thule
where for a few days in summer the sun was never lost to view
below the horizon—not to these, for all their tantalizing interest,
but to the sober testimony of the *Liber de Mensura Orbis Terræ* of
the Irish monk Dicuil, written in A.D. 825, in which he sets down
information about the islands that lie north of Britain taken by
word of mouth from priests who in their turn spoke not by
hearsay but from an exact and first-hand knowledge.

All round our island of Hibernia [says Dicuil] there are islands, some
small, some tiny. Off the coast of the island of Britain are many islands,
some big, some small, some middling; some lie in the sea to the south
of Britain, others to the west; but they are most numerous in the north-
western sphere and the north. On some of these islands I have lived,
on others set foot, of some had a sight, of others read. . . .

It is now thirty years since priests [*clerici*] who lived in that island
[i.e., Thule] from the first day of February to the first day of August
told me that not only at the summer solstice, but in the days on either
side of it, the setting sun hides itself at the evening hour as if behind a
little hill, so that no darkness occurs during that very brief period of
time, but whatever task a man wishes to perform, even to picking the
lice out of his shirt, he can manage it precisely as in broad daylight.
And had they been on a high mountain, the sun would at no time have
been hidden from them. . . .

They deal in fallacies who have written that the sea round the island
is frozen, and that there is continuous day without night from the
vernal to the autumnal equinox, and vice versa, perpetual night from
the autumnal equinox to the vernal; for those sailing at an expected
time of great cold have made their way thereto, and dwelling on the
island enjoyed always alternate night and day save at the time of the
solstice. But after one day's sailing from there to the north they found
the frozen sea.[2]

---

[1] In his *De Ratione Temporum: In Libros Regum Quæstionum xxx liber.*
[2] Ed. Walkenaer, Paris, 1807, pp. 27–30. Dicuil continues: 'There are many other
islands in the ocean to the north of Britain which can be reached from the northernmost British isles in two days' and nights' direct sailing, with full sails and an un-
dropping fair wind. A certain holy man [*presbyter religiosus*] informed me that in two
summer days and the night between, sailing in a little boat of two thwarts, he came
to land on one of them. Some of these islands are very small; nearly all of them are
separated one from the other by narrow sounds. On these islands hermits who have
sailed from our Scotia [Ireland] have lived for roughly a hundred years. But, even as

Some of the puzzles inherent in these fascinating sentences could not have been puzzles to Dicuil. Were these priests on a first and isolated voyage of exploration, confirmatory of Pytheas and Pliny? Or were they part of an established, if occasional, traffic of Irish anchorites to Thule, as we may believe in the light of the *De Ratione Temporum* (if we further believe Bede's Thule and Dicuil's to be the same)? How many were they, these anchorites, and with what resources? And how account for the precise dating of their stay from the first day of the Irish spring to the first day of the Irish autumn? Whatever our answers, or even our cavils, they can hardly cast doubt on a conclusion that towards the end of the eighth century Irishmen, priests among them, reached Iceland where they spent the more clement part of the year and observed the midnight sun. Which is conclusion enough for the pre-Norse stage of Icelandic history.

From now on our concern is with Icelandic and Norwegian sources of information. *Íslendingabók* and *Landnámabók*, as well as the Norwegian History of Theodricus, record that when the first Norse settlers arrived in Iceland there were already Irishmen resident there, Christians who refused to live with heathens, so betook themselves off, leaving behind them Irish books (that is to say, devotional books in the Latin tongue but written in Irish script), bells and croziers, by which their nationality and character were established. These were the papar (sing. papi, Irish *pab(b)a*, *pob(b)a*, from Latin *papa*), monks and anchorites. From the evidence of placenames it is clear that there was a sprinkling of these papar over much of south-eastern Iceland, especially between the island of Papey and Papos in Lon. Much further west, beyond the ice-spurs of the Vatnajokul and the desolate sands of Skeidara, in the beautiful and fertile countryside of Sida, there was a cluster of papar at Kirkjubœr; and such was the sanctity of the site that it was not granted to heathen men ever to dwell there. The first settler was Ketil the Fool (so styled because he was a Christian), a Hebridean Norseman and grandson of the great Ketil Flatnose, and life sped well for him. After his day

they have been constantly uninhabited since the world's beginning, so now, because of Norse pirates, they are empty of anchorites, but full of innumerable sheep and a great many different kinds of seafowl. I have never found these islands mentioned in the books of scholars.'

It is generally accepted that Dicuil is here speaking of the Faeroes, the Færeyjar or Sheep Islands. For Dicuil in general see Kenney, *op. cit.*, pp. 545–8.

Hildir Eysteinsson presumed to show that a heathen *could* dwell at Kirkjubœr; but as he reached the boundary of the homefield God's wrath was visited upon him, there he bowed, he fell, and where he bowed he fell down dead.

Of the economy of these papar we know nothing. The caves, byres, cells, and houses at various times ascribed to their habitation have all proved to be the work of later comers. Whether they succeeded in raising any variety of corn is not known, but it is likely that from no farther afield than the Faeroes they shipped flocks to provide them with milk and wool. They were certainly fishermen, and their numbers would be tiny, hardly a hundred all told. But this little said, we have said our all. We do not even know how this thin and temporary Christian occupation ended. Were the papar solitaries? Or does the placename Pap(p)yli point to a cell or cloister? Did the same fate whelm them all, and what fate was it? 'Later they went away (*Þeir fóru síðan á braut*)': a laconic, unrevealing epitaph. And how came they to leave behind their precious books, their church or hand-bells, crooks and croziers? Either their going was sudden and bare, in the same curachs which had fetched them to Iceland; or maybe these treasures came into Norse possession after their flight into the inhospitable and deathly abodes of lava, rock, and ice so plentiful in Iceland. Not that one normally associates priests and Irishmen with flight. In any case, wherever they went in Iceland, a male community vowed to chastity, their days were numbered.

In one way only they and their like were to influence Icelandic history. They had discovered the Faeroes by about the year 700 and lived there till perhaps 820. The first Norse settler Grim Kamban arrived about that time and maybe dispossessed them of Sudero. Since his nickname appears to be cognate with Irish *camm*, bent or crooked, he is more likely, despite the witness of *Færeyinga Saga*, to have come by way of Ireland or the Hebrides than direct from Norway, and may even have been a Christian. The Norse pirates who followed him must quickly have gained control of all the islands, but despite Dicuil's statement that the Faeroes were thereafter empty of hermits, some of them and something of their lore must have remained behind and helped prepare men's minds for Iceland. Similarly, knowledge of the Iceland hermitages must have spread throughout Ireland and Scotland, Orkney and Shetland, and every windswept corner of the

Hebrides, so that Norse immigrants, traders, pirates, and adventurers—all and everything implied by the word viking—would receive intelligence, even of distance and direction, as to new land for the taking this side the frozen sea.

II. THE NORSE DISCOVERY AND FIRST SETTLEMENT

THE papar went away when the Norsemen came, and the Norsemen came about 860. We need not suppose that the papar took themselves off immediately after the discovery. It was the wave of settlement rising fourteen years later which loosed them from their rock-holes in the south-east, then swept them to oblivion.

Our main source of information about the Norse discoverers is *Landnámabók*, the Book of the Landtakings or Settlements. According to one of its recensions, *Sturlubók*, the first of them was Naddod the Viking. According to another, *Hauksbók*, it was a Swede named Gardar Svavarsson, and this we must accept, for three reasons: that *Hauksbók* seems here to rest upon the authority of the original text of *Landnámabók*; that it is confirmed by the two earliest Norse sources (written in Latin) which treat of the subject, the anonymous *Historia Norwegiæ*, of uncertain date but appearing to derive from an original of about 1170, and the *Historia de Antiquitate Regum Norwagiensium* of Theodricus Monachus, of about 1180,[1] and by *Brennu-Njáls Saga* too; and third, if we can trust to the story (and its disparate versions agree in this particular), that it was Gardar's son Uni whom king Harald Fairhair hoped to use as a catspaw to bring Iceland into subjection to Norway, presumably on the ground of his right to inherit the entire country after his first-come-first-served father. He was a true explorer, this Swedish Gardar, and having reached land east of the Eastern Horn he sailed on past the ice-mountains and bursting rivers of the Vatnajokul and the long, flat, melancholy reaches of the harbourless south coast. To a mariner under sail the prospect here is uninviting, and he would stand right out from the land, till at last the purple tusks of the Vestmannaeyjar and the long sweep of the Landeyjar conducted him to the inhospitable peninsula of Reykjanes, past Skagi its northern extremity, where there would open up before him the noble

[1] Both published in G. Storm, *Monumenta Historica Norvegiæ*, 1880.

expanse of Faxafloi, shining-watered, mountain-rimmed, and
northwards, sixty miles away, the perfect cone of the Snæfellsjokul. Past Snæfellsnes a second wide entry would appear before
him, Breidafjord, Broadfjord, with its uncountable islands, reefs
and skerries, and the white snail-tracks of its quick-drowning
currents. Then the Vestfirthir, their glimmering waters webbed
between the bony fingers of that contorted hand whose wrist lies
back in Laxardal and Haukadal. He would pass Isafjardardjup,
Icefjord Deep, with the seven axe-clefts in its southern shore
backed by the desolation of snow-pocked Glama, and at the
northern end of the Deep, Kaldalon, where the ice-falls of the
Drangajokul meet the sea. The man-rejecting wall of Snæfjalla-
strand comes next, and then the bitter entries of the Jokulfirthir.
Soon now Gardar would round Hornbjarg, the North Cape, and
along a rocky coast sail south and a little east into Hunafloi. Here
he would find lands flatter and richer, long valleys running inland,
but behind them always peaks, bluffs, broken ranges, and sometimes the glint of ice. He must have been tempted to put ashore
here, or in the neighbouring fjords eastward, Skagafjord and
Eyjafjord, and since the end of summer was at hand he would
have done well to beach his ship and build winter quarters in the
kindly head-reaches of this last; but he pressed his luck round one
more promontory and came into Skjalfandi, the Trembler, where
he built a house at the place called Husavik, House Bay, on a steep
cliff face, by a bad harbour, open to invasion of the arctic ice.
When he put out the following spring he was forced to leave
behind one of his crew, Nattfari, with a thrall and bondwoman.
Just how this happened we do not know, but Gardar's need to get
away when the chance presented itself may well have seemed
imperative, and get away he did. Certainly Nattfari survived his
abandonment, if such it was, for his name makes a modest
appearance later in *Landnámabók's* account of the North Quarter
settlement.

So there is Gardar now, sailing north-east to the Arctic Circle
and the headlands of Melrakkasletta, and on across Thistilfjord to
the narrow peninsula of Langanes, where he must wait for a more
northerly wind to carry him south to Vapnafjord. Soon thereafter
he would be back in fjord country, this time the Austfirthir, the
arms of water penetrating less deeply the riven plateau behind,
and the spurs of land somewhat less formidable, but from Beru-

fjord southwards the interior most daunting, as Gardar came back within sight of the Vatnajokul. Past Berufjord, too, he would be sailing off the papar country, and who can doubt with what dismay the anchorites of Papey and Papafjord beheld his high prow and striped sail before their eyes again, a grievous token that the decades of their seclusion were for ever over. When he reached the Eastern Horn again Gardar knew that he had circumnavigated an island, so called it Gardarsholm after himself, and when he returned home spoke warmly of it.

The second arrival, the viking Naddod, was not in search of Iceland, and stayed no longer than he had to. As he sailed out of Reydarfjord a heavy snowstorm enveloped the land, so he renamed it Snæland, Snowland.

The third, Floki, is a more intriguing character, with his sacrifices and ravens. Presumably he had settlement in mind, for he took livestock with him. From his landfall at Horn he followed Gardar's course westward off the surfy southern shore, crossed Faxafloi, which he named after one of his shipmates, and built a hall at Brjanslœk on the far side of Breidafjord. From this favoured spot he and his crew surveyed their blessings, fine pastures on land, islands for summer grazing, a fjord teeming with fish and seals, and myriads of seabirds. Sheltered by natural ramparts from cold northern winds, they were misled like many who followed them by the blue skies and pricking sun of summer, and spent their time at the easy harvest of waters never fished since the world began save by gulls and puffins and salmon-hunting seals. For as a colonizer Floki was a greenhorn. Suddenly winter was upon him, with snow and frost; the pastures vanished, and while the men need not go short their livestock perished. Spring, when it came, was cold, and when Floki got himself up on to a hill to the north his reward was the cheerless sight of a southerly arm of Arnarfjord choked with drift ice. So to Thule, Gardarsholm, Snæland, he added yet another name, *Ísland*, Iceland, the name the land has borne ever since. The bad season lasted long, they were late getting to sea, and their troubles, had they known it, were far from over. Gales from the south-west stopped them rounding Reykjanes, they were driven back into Faxafloi, to the Borgarfjord area, where they spent an unwilling second winter. Home in Norway, Floki, having given the land a bad name, did his best to hang it; his shipmate Herjolf, who must have made a hair-raising

passage over Faxafloi in his parted tow-boat, found both good and
bad to report; while Thorolf, whom the Icelanders would have
needed to invent had he never existed, swore that butter dripped
from every blade of grass in the island, for which reason he was
nicknamed and has been known as Thorolf Butter ever since.

In the stories of these three men, Gardar, Naddod and Floki,
as they are related with various inconsistencies by the different
versions of *Landnámabók*, every circumstance cannot be true. But
two things appear certain; that there were various exploratory
voyages to Iceland in the decade or so preceding the settlement
of Ingolf and Hjorleif; and that these voyages cannot be disso-
ciated from the Norsemen in the West, that is, in the British Isles
and the Faeroes. Also, there is a marked pattern of maritime mis-
adventure in the voyages, ships blown off course and boats parting, which appears to conform to the motifs of story as much as
to the realities of life.

By the late 860's Iceland would be a word in many men's
mouths in Norway. It must have fallen joyfully enough on the
ears of the fosterbrothers Ingolf and Leif, who by virtue of their
feud with earl Atli of Gaular, two of whose sons they had slain
and thereafter paid for out of their estates, were in need of land
and sanctuary. They promptly set off on a well-prepared recon-
noitring expedition, reached the classic area of landfall in the
south-east, sailed past Papey, then nosed their way through sand-
reefs into the protected waters of the southern Alptafjord, on
whose shores they spent the winter prospecting, and then returned
to Norway in order to wind up affairs at home. Ingolf laid out
what money they still had on goods useful for their voyage and
settlement, while Leif took warshields aboard for a last raid on
Ireland. He returned with a sword from which he was to get his
nickname Hjorleif (Sword-Leif) and ten captives from whom he
was to get his death. But Ingolf's auguries said nothing of this
last—Hjorleif was no concern of Thor's—and away they sailed,
each in command of his ship. As soon as Ingolf sighted land he
flung his high-seat pillars overboard, a god-fearing man seeking
a god's direction where he should make his new home. Like
Hjorlief and his crew the pillars were borne west, but Ingolf
brought his ship in by Ingolfshofdi, and somewhere near the Head
spent his first winter. The Head is so compelling a landmark on
this dangerous coast, so dramatically situated where the land after

a long run south-west from the Horns bends abruptly west, and by reason of some violent disruption in distant times is so lonely and commanding a fortress promontory, that it is tempting to believe that the ancient remains on its eastern side are the remains of Ingolf's house there. But this is unlikely. All probability favours the notion that so canny and resourceful a leader would have looked for a kindlier site back in Oræfi, where still today, after many cruel convulsions of nature, there are delightful and sheltered farmsteads thriving between the talons of the jokul.

It was on another such head or land-isle, 60-odd miles further west, that Hjorleif built his home. Hjorleifshofdi today stands up on the seaward edge of the black Myrdal Sands, perpendicular, green-topped, its sides eroded since 894 by nine deluges of ice and water from the ice-capped volcano Katla; but when the first settlers saw it it must have looked a safe and genial home amidst its plenitude of pastures and birch woods. Hjorleif set to build in earnest, to clear the ground and plough. But his Irish thralls, all fighting men with a hot brew of hate in their breasts, detested these menial tasks, and with their tale of a forest-bear contrived to destroy their masters.[1] They then made off with the womenfolk, movable goods, and necessarily the ship's boat, to certain precipitous islands they had observed from the brow of the Head, about fifty miles to the south-west, where they lived in their fools' paradise till Ingolf hunted them down and slew them in their turn. Their prodigious leaps to death still shadow a sunny passage through the Vestmannaeyjar, the Isles of the Irishmen. If the Settlement required an inaugural sacrifice, in both senses they provided it. Iceland had been blooded.

Ingolf had still not found his pillars. He spent his second winter at his dead brother's, then moved west, exploring coast and countryside as far as the river Olfus. So far it had not been too difficult for his thralls Vifil and Karli to hug the water's edge, keeping a look-out for the sea's rejections; but past the Olfus are wide lavafields, mud springs, and much desolation, so Ingolf, a practical man, turned inland with his main party, got himself across the river, and lay up for the winter under the benign flank of Ingolfsfell. Meantime his two thralls were making a progress round Reykjanes, west, then north, then east, till by luck or good

[1] Hjorleif was not to know that the only bears ever found in Iceland are polar bears, drifted over on floes from Greenland, normally to the north coast.

judgement, or Thor helping, before the end of summer they found his high-seat pillars where Reykjavik stands today. So in the spring Ingolf made his third journey west, climbed up on to the heath, and one imagines not without misgiving skirted the crater-studded, lava-strewn, ash-littered hinterland of Reykjavik. Remembering like Karli the 150 miles of often attractive country they had traversed on their way there, one can sympathize with his grumble: 'We travelled past good country to bad purpose if we must live on this stuck-out limb of land!' The land, that is, beyond Hellisheidi and the Sulphur Mountains, the land beyond the landscape of the moon.

But Thor had not misled his worshipper. He had brought him west to the well-spring of Icelandic history, of her law and constitution, and there endowed him with a patrimony ample as a homeland kingdom. With Ingolf in his high-seat at Reykjavik (and its pillars were still in the living-room there when *Landnámabók* was compiled), the settlement of Iceland was auspiciously under way.

III. THE STRIPLING REPUBLIC

THE process of settlement begun with such vicissitude by Ingolf in the south-west was completed throughout the island some sixty years later. There would still be latecomers seeking Iceland's coasts, among them men as famous as Eirik the Red and Ketil Gufa with his death-dealing thralls; far-reaching estates would be hewn or refashioned, and residences splendid as those at Helgafell, Hjardarholt, and Reykholt were still to arise at a chieftain's bidding, but by *c.* 930 all the habitable land was taken. The lifeless sands, the lavafields, the wastes and moraines would remain for ever empty; the sculptured mountains and glittering jokuls would be left to trolls and giants; of mortal men only lone-going outlaws, deathly and sterile, would attempt the central desolation, break out again, be hunted down, and perish. Some five-sixths of the country offered no support to human life. But wherever there was grass, the glint of leaf and berry, there would be found a farm. Along leagues of the sea's edge, lining the fjords, softening the long valleys that penetrate inland, in nooks and hollows everywhere, there was pasture and birchwood, and it was with an eye to these, fresh water, freedom from snow and shelter from wild

weather, a creek or ship's haven or land-route manageable by the
small, tough, gallant, handsome Icelandic pony,[1] that the first
settlers planned their homes. Often too with an eye to the beauty,
splendour, or oddness of the site, so frequently reflected in Icelandic placenames: Ale-force River, Angelica Bank, Smoky Bay,
Clearwater Pass, Glassriver Shaw and Cold Cheek, Red Dunes and
Holy Mountain. Some felt the land breeze sweeter than the sea's,
some smelled honey in the grass; and to some a god said, 'Leave
here. Go there.' From the beginning the land-takings showed
style and imagination.

The nation-to-be was spectacularly fortunate in its founding
families. They had ambition, independence, energy, an aristocratic tradition, and an aesthetic appreciation of character and
conduct, and the dominant Norse strain was generously leavened
with Celtic blood. The literary and historical sources play down
the Swedish and Danish share in the settlement, whereas the
grave-findings tend to exaggerate it, particularly the high proportion of chapes (which may point to Sweden) and the absence of
any evidence for cremation (which possibly points to Denmark);
and it is reasonable to think that there was a bigger infiltration of
Swedes and Danes into Iceland by way of south-west Norway
than native writings allow. Still, the Icelandic homeland was
Norway, more particularly the south-west, Sogn, Hordaland, and
Rogaland, though there were immigrants from the entire coastal
area between Agdir and southern Halogaland. Iceland took not
only men but law and language from the Norwegian west, and of
all Scandinavia it was for Sogn and Hordaland that Icelanders of
later generations felt the strongest emotional attachment. Also it
was this area which most actively opposed Harald Fairhair's
attempt to make one kingdom of Norway, and it was from ports
and anchorages between Hafrsfjord and the Sognsjo that vikings
first sailed west-over-sea to Scotland and her adjacent isles, to the
Orkneys, Faeroes, and Ireland, with all this signified for Iceland
in its turn.

Landnámabók records the names of roughly 400 settlement-men,
and of these maybe one-seventh had a connexion with the Celtic
countries. Effective viking action there dates from the last decade

---

[1] The horse in Iceland should have a saga to himself. More than two-thirds of
Icelandic Viking graves contain the remains of horses buried with their masters. The
Sílastaðir grave (Plate 16) contains two horse skeletons in their separate chamber.

of the eighth century, when in the three ominous years 793–4–5 Norse freebooters not only pillaged Lindisfarne in Northumbria and Morganwg in South Wales, but struck at Lambey Island north of Dublin, and the sacred isle of Iona. After 830 a pattern of conquest emerges in Ireland, Scotland, and the Isles, and various ambitious leaders from Norway hacked temporary domains from these distraught and mangled kingdoms, among them Turgeis and Olaf the White, Ivar the Boneless and Ketil Flatnose, Onund Treefoot, Eyvind Eastman, and Thorstein the Red. The predominance of men from the south-west is suggested by the linguistic evidence too: ninth-century Norse loanwords in Irish came mostly from that area. Finngail and Gall-Gaidhill, White Foreigners (Norwegians) and Foreign Gaels (at first Irishmen who had renounced their faith and nation, later a mixed Norse-Celtic strain in both Ireland and western Scotland) roamed, fought, made and dissolved alliances, commanded, served, wed and bred throughout these Celtic lands, from time to time reinforced by new viking crews from home, by malcontents, rebels, adventurers, and great lords grown hungry for fresh lands in place of those they had forfeited to king Harald back in Norway. But during the last third of the century the times grew less propitious for Norse adventurers not only in Ireland but in England and the rest of western Christendom. Harald Fairhair's victory over the vikings at Hafrsfjord in 885 ushered in a bad thirty years abroad. In 890 the Bretons heavily defeated the viking army then plundering the Western Empire, and the following year king Arnulf smote them anew on the Dyle near Louvain. The forces of Hastein and the Great Horde then moved over to England, but in a four-year campaign were so hammered by Alfred and his martial son that their army fell to pieces. In Ireland the initiative was back again in the hands of the native kings, and the capture of Dublin in 902 by Cearbhall king of Leinster gave the country comparative peace for twenty years. In Scotland Thorstein the Red was killed by guile or treachery about the year 900, and earl Sigurd of Orkney, by now master of Caithness and Sutherland, Ross and Moray, fulfilled his strange destiny of being destroyed by a dead man. He had killed the Scottish earl Melbrigdi and set his head to dangle at his saddle; but Melbrigdi had a protruding tooth, or tusk, which punctured the skin of his leg, the leg festered, and the earl sickened and died. At much the same time

2. NORSE TOOLS

Anvil, tongs, rasp, shears, hammer-head, and nail-block of iron.

3. NORSE WEAPONS

Swords, axe-heads, spears, shield and helmet.

Onund Treefoot was prised out of the Hebrides. Ingimund who after the loss of Dublin in 902 thought to find land and wealth in Wales was promptly dispatched from Anglesey. Odo and Arnulf, Alfred and Edward and Ethelfleda lady of the Mercians, Cearbhall king of Leinster and the Welsh of North Wales and Anglesey, without knowing it were all making a contribution to the settlement of Iceland, which stood ready and waiting for adventurous but dispossessed men. And in Norway, most formidable contributor of all, there ruled Harald Fairhair.

To the Icelandic historians of the Middle Ages there was one over-riding reason why men sought homes and estates in Iceland. They came *fyrir ofríki Haralds konungs*, because of the tyranny of king Harald. It was this which drove Thorolf Mostrarskegg from Most to Thorsnes, uprooted Kveldulf and Skallagrim from the Firthafylki and sped them to Borgarfjord, brought Baug to Hlidarendi, and Geirmund Heljarskin from a prince's seat in Hordaland to a lord's estate in north-western Iceland. Some of the settlers had opposed Harald's attempt to unify (or as they saw it, seize) all Norway, some had fought against him at Hafrsfjord and suffered the bitterness of unrelieved defeat; others had merely held aloof from the struggle and so incurred the royal displeasure. They resented the loss of their titles, saw no reason why they should hold their estates of the king, regarded taxes as robbery and oaths of allegiance as the diminution of a free man's dignity. Some chose of their own accord to leave, while some among them were forcibly driven out:

Once he had established possession of these territories which were newly come into his power, king Harald paid close attention to the landed men and leading farmers, and all those from whom he suspected some rebellion might be looked for. He made everyone do one thing or the other, become his retainers or quit the country, or, for a third choice, suffer hardship or forfeit their lives; while some were maimed hand or foot. King Harald seized possession in every district of all odal rights [i.e., rights in land hitherto inalienable from the owner-family] and the entire land, settled and unsettled, and equally the sea and the waters, and all husbandmen must become his tenants, and those too who worked in the forests, and saltmen, and all hunters and fishers by sea and land—all these were now made subject to him. But many a man fled the land from this servitude, and it was now that many desert places were settled far and wide, both east in Jamtaland and Helsingjaland,

3

and in the western lands, the Hebrides and Dublin district, Ireland, and Normandy in France, Caithness in Scotland, the Orkneys and Shetland, and the Faeroes. And it was now that Iceland was discovered.

This picture presented by Snorri Sturluson in *Egils Saga* of Harald's oppressive measures and personal ruthlessness even before the battle of Hafrsfjord is overdrawn, but it was the picture accepted by most informed persons in Iceland. In Norwegian tradition Harald appears as a wise, paternal ruler who gave Norway the peace and order she so badly needed, but to small nations struggling for their independence an external tyrant is an emotional necessity, and an unjust, relentless Harald was the most impressive of the many Norwegian candidates. That some chieftains left Norway because of him is not to be doubted. That their number was exaggerated, and the manner of their going dramatized, is certain.

Among them would be some of the vikings whose lairs enlivened the south-west coast. These were men to whom the warlike pursuit of wealth and glory was an established way of life, forced on them by personal desire, family tradition, their social and economic system, and the geographical compulsions which made the sea the highway of a coast-dwelling aristocracy. For a century before the battle of Hafrsfjord they had been raiding east in the Baltic, west in the British Isles, and sailing the protected leads and water-alleys of Norway, then a land of petty kingdoms and jealous lordships. The vikings of Sogn and Hordaland were well placed for voyages abroad and for intercepting the southern traffic in hides and furs and sea-ivory with Halogaland and Finnmark, and their subjugation was a necessity to a strong ruler like Harald Fairhair or earl Hakon. Many vikings though were not just pirates. They did not despise the profits of trade, and their innumerable sea-crossings opened up much-needed routes and widened Norse horizons. Their subsequent conquests and piracy owed much to their created needs. The merchant-venturers who first brought cargoes of wine, honey, malt, and wheat, and English clothes and weapons from the west roused demanding appetites at home. Likewise these fjord-dwellers of the south-west were more vulnerable than most to the increase of population in Norway and the shortage of land which this increase made more and more pinching. So their main outpourings, whether from Norway direct to the Celtic lands or to Iceland, or to Iceland by way of the Celtic lands, were an inevitable phase of the great Viking Movement itself. There were compulsions other than Harald's real or fancied tyranny. Ingolf and Hjorleif had made the land too hot to hold them and left for Iceland twelve years before Hafrsfjord, and among those who travelled there soon after the battle were friends and loyal supporters of the king, like Ingimund the Old who settled Vatnsdal in the north and Hrollaug, son ·of earl Rognvald of Mœr, who controlled all Hornafjord in the east. The sea-passages west over the open Atlantic demanded good ships and good men to sail them. Throughout the viking age the Norwegians had both, and had them in plenty. They had the best ships of any European people, such exquisite calm-water vessels as the Oseberg ship, fit sepulchre for a northern queen, the more seaworthy *karfi* for coastal voyages, whose prototype for us today is the Gokstad ship, so seaworthy that a copy of her under Magnus Andersen crossed the Atlantic without mishap in 1893, and the ship of all work, the true ocean-goer, the *hafskip* or *knörr*.[1] By

---

[1] The classic account of viking ships and seafaring is that of Brøgger and Shetelig, *Vikingeskipene. Deres forg jengere og etterfølgere*, Oslo, 1950: English version, *The Viking Ships—their Ancestry and Evolution*, Oslo 1953. The chapter on 'Seafaring' (by Hjalmar Falk) in Shetelig and Falk, *Scandinavian Archaeology*, 1937, is a valuable and compact summary for the English reader. Falk had earlier written extensively on the subject in *Altnordisches Seewesen*, Heidelberg, 1912. The most recent discussion, summarizing the views of Harald Åkerlund ('Åss och beitiåss', *Unda Maris*, 1955–56; 'Vikingatidens skepp och sjövåsen', *Svenska Kryssarklubbens årsskrift*, 1959), is in P. H. Sawyer, *The Age of the Vikings*, 1962, Chapter IV, 'The Ships'. For a convincing reconstruction of a Norse ocean voyage from Bergen to Greenland see C. Sølver, *Vestervejen*, Copenhagen, 1954, pp. 18–34 (a briefer account in 'Leiðarsteinn, The Compass of the Vikings', in *Old Lore Miscellany*, No. 75, 1946, pp. 293–321); Magnus Andersen described his stormy but triumphant crossing from Bergen to Newfoundland in the 'Viking' (27 days) in *Vikingfærden*, Kristiania, 1895. See too E. G. R. Taylor, *The Haven-Finding Art*, 1956, especially pp. 35–88; G. J. Marcus, 'The Course for Greenland', *Saga-Book* XIV, 1953–55, and 'The Navigation of the Norsemen', *The Mariner's Mirror*, XXXIX, 1953; Björn Landström, *The Ship*, 1961 (Landström thinks the *knörr* had a cutwater). The Gokstad ship, presumably of the mid-ninth century, is 76½ feet from stem to stern, with a beam of 17½ feet; from the bottom of the keel to the gunwale amidships is a little over 6 feet 4 inches. She was clinker built, of 16 strakes, and though designed as a sailing ship had provision for 16 rowers a side. The mast, not all of which was found, seems to have been between 37½ and 41 feet tall, the squarish sail was of heavy woollen cloth, in all probability strengthened by a rope net, and could be shortened. She could sail across and even near the wind. She was steered by a siderudder fastened to the starboard quarter. The *knörr* or *hafskip*, in which the voyages to Iceland, Greenland, and America were made, was in its general construction similar to the Gokstad ship, but broader in the beam, deeper in the water, and of a higher freeboard. Save when becalmed or when manœuvring in narrow waters it relied still less on oars and more on sail, and was a faster traveller. It would normally carry two ship's boats, one stowed on board, the other towed behind. Like other Norse ships it could be tented for sleeping quarters by night. Five ships of more or less

sail, and when necessary by oar, this last could go anywhere, to the Atlantic islands, to Iceland, Greenland, and the north American coast. The ocean-goers were sailed with immense courage and skill by men without compass or chart but inured to hardship and learned in the sea's ways. They sailed by latitude and the sun and stars, by landmarks and the flight of birds,[1] by the evidence of marine creatures and the colour of water, by rough or dead reckoning, by currents, driftwood and weed, by the feel of a wind, and when need be by guess and by god. They used the line to search the ocean's bottom. In a good day's sailing of 24 hours they could cover 120 miles and more.[2]

Among the settlers of Iceland was a high proportion of land-hungry, wealth-hungry, fame-hungry men, their native vigour and inventiveness quickened by their sojourn in the Celtic countries. There were three main sources of Celtic, and more specifically Irish, influence upon early Iceland. First there was the importance of settlers like Helgi the Lean, born of the marriage between a Norse nobleman and a princess of Ireland, and reared in the Hebrides. He did not stand alone. As late as the fourth generation in Iceland one of its foremost chieftains was Olaf

this type, but showing variation of size and build, were in the summer of 1962 raised from the waters of Peberrenden in Roskilde Fjord, Denmark, where they had been filled with stones and sunk to block the deep-water channel, presumably as a precaution against a seaborne attack on Roskilde town. They appear to be of the period 1000–1050. Wreck 2, which is about 65 feet long, and Wreck 1, which is somewhat longer, are undoubted medium or large-sized *knerrir*, and the first examples of their kind recovered in modern times. There is a preliminary account of all five ships, with illustrations, in Olaf Olsen and Ole Crumlin-Pedersen, *Viking-skibene i Roskilde Fjord*, Nationalmuseet, Copenhagen, 1962–63. Eventually they will be housed in Roskilde.

[1] The use of land birds for navigation goes back far beyond Floki Vilgerdarson's voyage to Iceland. The daily and seasonal flights of different birds would be closely marked by the mariner. It may well have been the annual flights of geese migrating to their Icelandic breeding grounds which first convinced men in Ireland that somewhere north of them lay the land they would eventually discover and use for hermitages.

[2] The problems connected with the term *dægr sigling*, 'a day's sailing', are many and have been much discussed (notably by G. M. Gathorne-Hardy, *The Norse Discoverers of America*, 1921, and Almar Næss, *Hvor lå Vinland?*, 1956). For the early coasting voyages it seems to have meant twelve hours' sailing. When the Norwegian Ottar (Ohthere) tells us that it was over a month's journey from his home in Halogaland down the coast of Norway to Skiringssalir he makes it clear that he sailed with a following wind by day but went ashore every night. But for sea crossings it as certainly often meant a sailing of twenty-four hours. Thus Wulfstan, the second sea-captain whose narrative was incorporated by king Alfred in his translation of Orosius, tells us how he sailed from Hedeby to Truso in seven days and nights, and that 'the ship was the whole way running under sail'. The sagas often leave the matter in doubt, and *dægr sigling* seems at times to convey nothing more precise than that 'it takes a day to get there'.

Peacock of Hjardarholt, the son of Hoskuld Dalakollsson (of the line of Aud the Deep-minded) and Melkorka (Mael-Curcaigh) daughter of the Irish king Muircertagh. There seems to have been no bar to Norse-Irish and Norse-Pictish marriages at any social level. In addition there must have been a great deal of concubinage, for the Norsemen abroad (and for that matter at home) were notoriously addicted to the use of women. Consequently among the immigrants into Iceland from the lands west-over-sea there were many of mixed Norse and Celtic descent, including some who by blood were predominantly Celtic. Second there were the Celtic slaves brought out by Norse warriors—often warriors themselves, prone to revolt and violence, and some of them great men in their own country. There were women slaves too, though their number is not known. Third there was the influence of Irish civilization, its literature and religion. One of the most famous of all settlers, Aud the Deep-minded, was so devout a Christian that she gave orders for her burial in the salty no-man's-land between high and low water, so that she might not lie in unconsecrated ground like any heathen. There were even more like Helgi the Lean, Christians who reached for Thor in a tight corner. Soon the faith of their kinsfolk went awry, their chapels became heathen shrines; but they probably helped produce the climate of tolerance which made the conversion of Iceland in the year 1000 the comparatively bloodless and worldly affair it proved to be. Among saga heroes stand the Irish-named Njal, Kormak, and Kjartan; there are Irish place-names in most parts of Iceland; there have been attempts to relate Icelandic literary forms to those of Ireland; and while the thesis is in its nature unprovable it is hard not to believe that it was the Irish blood flowing in Norse veins which distinguished the Icelanders from all other Scandinavian peoples ethnographically and contributed in large measure to their literary achievement in the twelfth and thirteenth centuries.

Even so, the colonization of Iceland was a Norse viking undertaking. They sailed round the nesses, threaded the islands, penetrated the fjords as far as their ships would carry them, those sturdy *knerrir* with twenty or thirty men aboard, women and children, animals, food and timber. Sometimes they left their landing to fate or a god, threw their high-seat pillars over the side, and made their homes where these came drifting in. They hallowed land to themselves with fire, with the flighting of spears and arrows, by setting up peeled wands and weapons, by marking the trees. And they explored. Skallagrim Kveldulfsson's land-taking in Borgarfjord was typical of many. He came ashore at the headland of Knarrarnes in the west, carried his cargo to land, and at once began to explore the countryside. 'There was extensive marshland there and spacious forest, with plenty of room between mountains and sea, ample seal-hunting and good fishing.' Keeping close to the shore they moved southwards to Borgarfjord itself, and found there their comrades who had sailed in a second ship, who led Skallagrim to where his dead father's body had come to land in its coffin—as old Kveldulf had promised it would. 'Then Skallagrim took land in settlement between mountains and sea, the entire Myrar out to Selalon and inland to Borgarhraun, also south to Hafnarfjall—the whole area marked out by its rivers falling seawards. The following spring he brought his ship south to the fjord and into the inlet nearest to the spot where Kveldulf had come ashore. Here he established house and home, calling it Borg and the fjord Borgarfjord; and the countryside inland from there, that too they named after the fjord.' Much of this immense estate he distributed among his shipmates and kinsmen-at-law, so that in a year or two a dozen homesteads starred this delectable river-veined wilderness. And now they explored further afield, proceeding inland along Borgarfjord till the fjord became a river white with glacial silt, then still onwards through the virgin territory traversed by Nordra and Thvera, and found every river, stream, and lake filled with trout and salmon. He was a master of work, this big, black-visaged, bald-headed manslayer from the Firthafylki, a skilled raiser of crops and beasts, fisherman, sailor, and boat-builder, and a resourceful worker in iron. In short, a born pioneer. 'He always kept a lot of men on hand, and sought busily after such supplies as might be found thereabouts which could prove useful to them; for at first they had little livestock in comparison with what was needed for the number of men they had with them. However, what livestock there was found its own food in the forest throughout the winter. Skallagrim was a fine shipbuilder, nor was there any shortage of driftwood west off the Myrar. He had a farm built at Alptanes, and had a second home there, from which he had men go out rowing for fish and seal-hunting and egg-collecting, for there was abundance of all these provisions, and also driftwood to be fetched back home. At that time too there were numerous whale-strandings, and harpooning them was free for all. And all creatures were at their ease in the hunting-grounds, for men were unknown to them.'

So it came about in a short space of years that Skallagrim's estate 'stood on more legs than one'. He now bred two wonderful sons, Thorolf fair and handsome, Egil black and ugly. Nature's horn of glory had been tilted over Thorolf at his birth; he became a traveller abroad, the friend of king Eirik Bloodaxe of Norway, and the darling of Gunnhild, his amorous sorceress of a queen. But her love for him turned sour, he fled from her hate, and died a hero's death at Brunanburh in England, fighting for king Athelstan. Egil was a viking adventurer over many seas and lands,

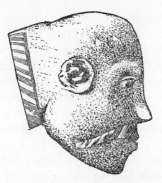

2. NINTH-CENTURY NORSEMAN
A carving in wood from the Oseberg wagon.

and the greatest poet of medieval Scandinavia. Egil's son was Thorstein the White, and Thorstein's daughter was Helga the Fair, the loveliest woman Iceland ever saw, for whom Gunnlaug Wormtongue and Hrafn the Poet strove in love and battle and slew each other in distant Norway. No family could be more bravely representative of the settlers and the early generations, Skallagrim the viking-farmer and breaker of new ground in the west, Egil the viking-poet, passionate, cunning, greedy, remorseless in his love and hate, the *Hávamál's* disciple, and Odin's man to his eyelash-ends. High-stomached yet pragmatical, at once hardhanded and creative, they and their like shaped the history, culture, and institutions of their new island home; their fame survived their bones; and centuries later the generations of the

Myramen would be a subject of story in *Egils Saga*, the foremost historical and viking saga, while *Gunnlaugs Saga Ormstunga* preserves for posterity the doom-laden tale of the wooing of Helga the Fair.

All in all the settlement of Iceland and the development of the infant Republic is the best documented of medieval *völkerwanderungen*. There are recorders of history like Ari Thorgilsson and the redactors of *Landnámabók*, and there are recreators of history, the saga-men. Between them they tell us with much picturesque embellishment the full course of events from 870 to 1262, from the arrival of the first settlers to the end of the independent Republic. And to history and saga we may now briefly address ourselves.

When the settlement men reached Iceland the country was theirs to do as they liked with. There was no need to subjugate a native population: the land was empty; nor were they in fear of attack 'from kings or criminals' abroad. They had the opportunity for a unique experiment in nationhood, and after two generations during which they came to terms with the physical problems of colonization they set to work at it. They were intensely self-reliant and conservative, and for a while were content to live on their estates, distribute land, exact obedience, dispense justice, defend their own and their followers' interests in patriarchal aristocratic fashion. From the first they were devoted to their feuds. They met as friends and clashed as enemies, and soon the strategy of living among men as resolute as themselves made them feel the need for a form of government and the institutions that go with it. Their approach to these, as with most other things in Iceland, was distinctive. Secular power and religious authority, united in the person of one and the same man, were to dictate the growth of the nation.

It is hard to know just how religious the Icelanders were. What Christianity there was soon came to an end, and though Njord, Tyr, and Balder, even Odin, had their followers, the gods who counted most in Iceland were Thor with his hammer and the phallused Frey. The worship of a god requires ceremonial and festive seasons, and a place to worship him in; and from the sagas rather than archaeological discovery we can learn about these. Thorolf Mostrarskegg, than whom Thor had no more fanatical worshipper, built such a temple at Hofstadir in Breidafjord, with timber fetched from his old temple on Most in Norway. He brought out likewise, for continuity and consecration, earth from under the pedestal on which Thor's image had stood.

He had a temple built—and a mighty edifice it was. There was a doorway in the side wall, nearer to the one end, and inside stood the pillars of the high-seat, with nails in them which were called the gods' nails. The area inside was a great sanctuary. Further in was a room of the same shape and order as the choir in churches today, where in the middle of the floor, like an altar, stood a pedestal, with an arm ring

3. Norse Temple

The temple at Hofstaðir (Templesteads), near Mývatn, Iceland, seen from the north. Nearest is the 'chancel', and beyond it the hall. Approximate measurements, 44 × 6·8 metres.

without a join lying on it, twenty ounces in weight, on which men must swear all their oaths. The temple-priest was required to wear this ring on his arm at all public assemblies. On the pedestal too must stand the sacrificial bowl, and in it a sacrificial twig, like an aspergillum, by means of which the blood, which was called *hlaut*, shall be sprinkled from the bowl. The blood, that is, which was shed when animals were slaughtered as a sacrifice to the gods. Around the pedestal in this same room were set the images of the gods.[1]

[1] *Eyrbyggja Saga*, 4. This was the kind of ring on which the Danish leaders swore oaths to king Alfred in 875, 'which before this they would never do to any nation.' They went back on these oaths and Thor exacted his penalty: a hundred and twenty of their offending ships were lost at sea off Swanage. *Anglo-Saxon Chronicle, sub. anno.*

Clearly, to build a temple and maintain its structure and sacrifices (oxen and horses, and occasionally men) would be beyond all save the wealthy. To the end of the Commonwealth a priesthood (*goðorð*) meant 'power but not wealth'. It followed then that those among the settlers whose means did not run to it but who wanted, whether their emphasis was on worship or festivity, to attend the temple ceremonies must be prepared to pay for the privilege with money and regard. Soon it became obligatory for them to pay a temple-tax and accompany the temple-priest (*goði*, godly one) to public assemblies. The priest exerted increasing authority over his followers and temple-worshippers; he was their leader in matters spiritual, and with secular reinforcement was destined to become their sole lord and master.

Of the four hundred chief settlers and their families less than one-tenth were the real rulers of Iceland. *Landnámabók* is a shade prodigal of royal genealogies, but among the priests were men of royal descent, both Norse and Celtic, lords and lordlings, captains of ships and leaders of men. Queen Aud came out with twenty freemen and many thralls; Skallagrim with sixty able-bodied followers; Geirmund Heljarskin made an almost royal progress between his four farms with an escort of eighty. When in 927–30 legislative and judicial power was placed in the hands of thirty-six *goðar* it was the descendants of such as these who inherited. The chosen thirty-six constituted the Althing or General Assembly of Iceland. The law administered there applied to the whole of the country, and had been adapted by Ulfljot of Lon from the Gulathing law of south-west Norway. The *goðar*, the temple-priests, elected a President or Lawspeaker for a renewable term of three years, whose duty it was to recite one-third of the law to the assembled congregation every year. Many, perhaps all, of the temple-priests had been long accustomed to hold Things or gatherings for law in their own districts. Thorolf Mostrarskegg had established such a Thing at Thorsnes, and Thorstein Ingolfsson one at Kjalarnes. Under Ulfljot's law there would be twelve such throughout Iceland, each managed by three priests. The system was less democratic than it sounds. The Althing was unquestionably an assembly for law of all free men who chose to attend it; it was an excellent place to meet your friends, buy a sword, sell land, marry off a daughter, wear your best clothes, and share the excitement of a national occasion; but all power lay

with the *goðar*. The Constitution was anti-State. The Althing did
not control the *goðar*, but they it; and within their home-districts
their rule was absolute. Going to law was a chancy business, and
success in it impossible without the backing of one or more
priests. Many of the famous lawsuits described in the sagas were
a deployment of strength rather than a submittal to justice. Still
it was better than nothing, and there were attempts to make the
system more workable in 965, by establishing an apparently
useless Quarter Thing and very successful Spring Thing for each
quarter of the land and increasing the number of priests to thirty-
nine, and in 1005 by instituting a Court of Appeal, the so-called
Fifth Court, and increasing the number of priests to forty-eight.
It was a Fifth Court because as part of the reform of 965 the legis-
lature and the judicature had been separated, and instead of one
court or *Alþingisdómr* there were four courts corresponding to the
four Quarters of the country. All power remained with the *goðar*,
and no further reforms were attempted before the capitulation of
the Republic in 1262.

And yet with all its imperfections Iceland owed much to the
Althing. Its site was magnificent, the huge sunken plain of
Thingvellir in south-west Iceland, lying between bold rifts and
chasms and the biggest and second loveliest lake of the island, surrounded in the further distance by mountains of differing shape
but constant beauty. It was created by fire, by earthquake and
volcanic action, and a more impressive setting for national
ceremony is hardly to be imagined. During the debate which
established Christianity as the religion of Iceland men were
dividing into two hostile camps there, when a man came running
to the Althing to announce that fire was coming up out of the
earth in Olfus. Said the heathens, with the Christians' argument in
mind: 'No wonder the gods are angry at such talk!' But, 'At what
were the gods angry, pray,' asked Snorri Godi in reply, 'when the
lava we now stand on burned here?' Even in Iceland there are
few more striking demonstrations of divine (or infernal) power
than the riving of Thingvellir. It quickly established itself as a
meeting-place for the nation. Indeed for part of every June it *was*
the nation. Here from 930 on a man could know himself an
Icelander and not a Norwegian at one or two removes. To travel
the long, hard, but hospitable roads to the Althing, to share for a
fortnight the bustle and business there, was to be at the hub of

the wheel, the heart of the body legal, economic, political, and social.

The strength of the temple-priests as a ruling class ensured that medieval Iceland was never in any acceptable sense of the word a democracy. It would have been highly unnatural if it were. Still less was it a theocracy, for the authority of the *goðar* even in heathen times and still more emphatically after the adoption of Christianity rested less and less on their priestly office. Its enduring basis was secular strength, without which it was nothing. Normally the office descended from father to son, but it could be disposed of by gift, sale, or loan. It could also be divided and shared. By this possibility of transfer and acquisition, and an absence of controlling power above and over the *goðar*, the peculiar Icelandic form of autocracy bore within itself from the beginning the seeds of its decay, and the political disasters of the thirteenth century followed logically from the constitutional advances of the tenth.

IV. LIFE AND LITERATURE

In other respects too the Icelanders did not show themselves the most prudent of colonists. Many of them, for example, started off in Iceland by building big long-houses of the kind they were used to at home, but whose construction and upkeep required more timber and heating than their riven, barren, cold, wet island could supply. There was no native oak or beech or conifer, and in this land of 'stones, more stones, and all stones' by cosmic irony there is practically no stone suitable for building. Even a man's gravestone must be shipped in from abroad. So the houses were turf-built, with walls three to six feet thick, or thicker, and roofs on which a springy ewe could graze. But their inner construction and sometimes their inner lining was of timber, and the big hall of the viking age, sixty or even a hundred feet long, required big pillars and cross-beams. So already by the eleventh century the Icelandic house was changing shape, with the big hall divided into two parts, sometimes with the addition of other rooms at right-angles to the main structure, and by the end of the Commonwealth the smaller passage-house (*gangahús*) was a belated recognition of cold reality. Again, the Icelanders never learned how to clothe themselves against cold and rain. Their foot-gear was particularly ill-

suited to their climate and terrain, and it is the witness of their
foremost modern geographer that, 'In times of starvation they
did not even learn to eat several of the edible things found in the
country, and their fishing tackle was not anything to boast of.'[1]
Worst of all, they were improvident farmers. In a country where
the balance between soil erosion through the rapid alternations of
cold and thaw and soil building by glacial and volcanic action was
at best precarious, they lived like prodigals, destroying the pro-
tective birch-scrub by intensive grazing, fire-wood felling, and
accidental forest fires. Without realizing it, they were living on
their soil's capital; it lasted them for the best part of three centuries
before its decline became disastrous and led to the denudation of
whole districts. Except for his home-field the Icelandic farmer,
primarily an animal husbandman, was something of a despoiler.
For one reason or another, bad siting or a tale of bad seasons,
about a quarter of the 600 farms named in Landnámabók were
subsequently abandoned; but the index to spoliation is clearest in
the farm register for 1703, when farms occupied numbered 4059
and farms abandoned 3200. It would however be unfair to argue
that all of these were lost through human mismanagement. The
land and later the climate were formidable.

But while the sixty thousand inhabitants of the island, especially
its leading families, were laying up this store of assorted troubles
for themselves by the thirteenth century, they were concurrently
preparing for an almost miraculous triumph in the art and practice
of literature. The first generations were the fortunate inheritors,
sustainers, and transmitters of a strong and distinctive culture,
whose literary remains back home in Scandinavia have largely
disappeared, but whose ships, tools, weapons, sculptures, carv-
ings, inscriptions, buildings, and patterns, as they are displayed in
the museums of Oslo, Stockholm, and Copenhagen provide overwhelming evidence of Norse craftsmanship and artistic power.
But for the Icelanders limitations were at once imposed upon that
culture. The visual arts had flourished in both Ireland and Scandinavia, but in Iceland there was practically no stone to hew, no
native wood to carve (though a number of splendid things like
the door from the church at Valthjofsstadir show how the craft
persisted), and little metal to mould; architecture and illumina-
tion were in the nature of things beyond their reach; and there is

[1] Sigurður Thórarinsson, Iceland in the Saga Period, Þriðji Víkingafundur, p. 23.

small evidence that they were a musical people. Their distinctive artistic expression must be in words, and by a singular stroke of fortune many of these words could be preserved. The long dark winters and certain quirks in the developing national character provided all the time in the world, the need to kill off most of their cattle ensured a large supply of week-old calves' skins for vellum, and the coming of Christianity and an acquaintance with books provided a practicable alphabet and a conventional format. Beginning on the estates of the wealthy chieftains and bishops and in the monasteries south and north, but spreading later among the farmers over the whole island, transcription took place on an unprecedented scale. There still exist in European libraries some 700 Icelandic manuscripts or fragments of manuscripts on vellum, and these, in Sigurður Nordal's words, are 'like the poor wreckage from a proud fleet', which on a cautious estimate must have been ten times as numerous.

The substance of many of them is known far beyond Iceland's shores. There are those precious repositories, Codex Regius 2365 4to supreme among them, which contain the Eddic poems, the Lays of Gods and Men, a treasure of all Germania; there are the two undisputed works of Snorri Sturluson, the Prose Edda, in which a consummate artist recreates the heathen Norse mythology, tells how the gods have lived and how they shall die, and *Heimskringla*, those brilliantly narrative 'Lives of the Norse Kings' of which it has been said that they presented Norway with her national history; and there are the family sagas and tháettir, perhaps 120 of them in all, together with the skaldic verses and other poems they preserve embedded in their prose. Less familiar but still blessed with northward-looking readers are such foundations of Icelandic history as the *Libellus Islandorum* of Ari the Learned, the 'Father of Icelandic history', and *Landnámabók*, with its record of the landtakings, the settlers and their sons and grandsons; the mythical and legendary sagas of Old Time, the *Fornaldarsögur*, laden with marvels and adventures, the glory of the Skjoldings and the sorrows of Sigurd and Gudrun; the Bishops' sagas, and that dramatic sequence of twelfth- and thirteenth-century history whose title is *Sturlunga Saga*. But there is an immense literature besides, much of it hardly to be discerned in the shadow of these works of native, national impulse. The Icelanders were earnest translators and adapters of foreign works. They rendered into their own tongue histories from Sallust to Geoffrey of Monmouth; there exist voluminous collections of story and lore concerning Our Lady, the Saints, and the Apostles; there is a full homiletic literature in Icelandic; and the treasuries of southern Romance were ransacked for 'sagas' of Tristan and Yvain, Erec and Blancheflor. The general impression is one of intense and unending activity, a broad, strong river of words, creative, informative, derivative, flowing from eager and acquisitive minds to the haven of the vellums.

The sagas, then, are written literature. Conditions in medieval Iceland, it is true, were unusually favourable for the development of story-telling and oral tradition, and we hear a good deal about the practice of reciting stories before kings abroad and at entertainments, marriages, and all kinds of gatherings at home. But the sagas as we have them, and know them, are written. It is certain that oral tales, oral tradition, including old verses, form a considerable part of the raw material of the saga-writers, but it would be misleading to consider the sagas as the mere writing down of such tales or tradition. Modern scholarship is making us more and more aware of written sources for the sagas, both native and foreign, historical, legendary, homiletic and exemplary. Among the sources drawn on by the author of *Eiríks Saga Rauða*, a singularly well-informed man, were not only the oral traditions of Thorfinn Karlsefni's descendants, but possibly *Grœnlendinga Saga*,[1] and certainly *Sturlubók* and the Life of Olaf Tryggvason written by Gunnlaug Leifsson the Monk; while the influence of ecclesiastical and geographical writings and, in the case of *Hauksbók* especially, of family pride and genealogy are easily discernible. The saga-men were in general of serious purpose and well-stored mind; they were organizers of material, both oral and written; and to think of them as mere transcribers by ear does them scant justice.

The word *saga* (plur. *sögur*) means something said, something recorded in words, and hence by easy transition a prose story or narrative. Specifically it is the term used to describe, or rather distinguish, the prose narratives which were Iceland's main contribution to the medieval literature of Europe, above all the *Íslendingasögur* or Sagas of Icelanders, which relate the lives and feuds of individuals and families during the so-called Saga Age,

---

[1] As is argued by Jón Jóhannesson, 'Aldur Grœnlendinga Sögu', in *Nordæla*, 1956, pp. 149–58.

which lasted from 930 to 1030. The Family Sagas, as they are also called, are the very heart of Icelandic literature; they have been described too as the 'last and finest' expression of the heroic age of the Germanic peoples. They are the prose (and sometimes homespun) counterparts of Germanic heroic poetry, as that poetry survives in the Old English poems *Beowulf* and *The Battle of Maldon*, the Old High German *Hildebrandslied*, the Latin fragments concerning Waltharius and Bothvar Bjarki, and the (Icelandic) Eddic lays of Helgi and Sigrun and Sigurd the Dragonslayer. This is because the saga-men's conception of character and destiny was heroic in the same way as the poets'. Fate, they say, is all-powerful and implacable. Man is at its mercy. But in this harsh dilemma lies the assurance of man's greatness, for it is open to him to accept his destiny without surrendering to it. If he so accepts he is full man. If he surrenders, complains, or evades, he is slavishly diminished. There is a right way to act: the consequences may be dreadful, but the conduct is more important than its consequences. In *Brennu-Njáls Saga* a good and noble man, Flosi from ice-girt Svinafell down in the Vatnajokul, burns the good and noble Njal and his sons (and with them an ageing woman and child) alive in their home, not because he wants to; he loathes the task, but fate has put him in a position where it is the only thing he can do. So he does it. In part, this is the familiar tragic dilemma of the Germanic hero: he has a choice not between right and wrong, but between wrongs, and cannot renegue. In part, it is a saga reading of character and destiny: to see one's fate and embrace it, with this curious aesthetic appreciation of what one is doing—it was this that made one a saga personage, a person worthy to be told about. We know the name of Bjarni Grimolfsson in *Eiríks Saga Rauða* not so much because he sailed to America as because he gave up his place in a boat to a man more concerned to live than he. Certain death was the price of his gesture, but the name of the survivor was not worth remembrance. He was merely the occasion of Bjarni's moment of destiny. One need not be a lord or prince's son to be a saga hero. But one must be a man of unbreakable will. For the unbreakable will, as with Flosi and Bjarni, triumphs over the blind injustice of all-powerful Fate, and makes man its equal.

That Icelandic society during the Settlement and Saga Age was a heroic society had consequences for both life and literature. The

4. THE OSEBERG SHIP IN ITS MOUND

The carved stern seen from the port side.

5. THE VALTHJÓFSSTADIR DOOR

Probably the door of a chieftain's hall, later used as a church door. The lower circular field (not illustrated here) contains a device of four interlacing dragons. The upper circular field shows three scenes from the story of 'Le Chevalier au Lion': the knight on horseback saves the lion from a dragon (*below*); the lion accompanies the knight; the lion mourns on the knight's tomb. The runic inscription may be translated: '[Behold] the burial place of the mighty king who slew this dragon'.

Icelanders were wedded to feud. This could be conducted by law or the manipulation of law, or could proceed along well-charted channels to private or public arbitration; but ideally feud was blood-feud, and its solution (or more often its progression) was by blood-vengeance. An unappreciative (and unacceptable) summary of the Icelandic sagas is 'peasants at loggerheads'. 'Farmers at feud' would be harder to rebut. For more than anything the sagas tell of the quarrels, killings, counter-killings, victories, defeats, reconciliations, and general manœuvres of individuals or families in a state of feud with a neighbour. One hears of the peace-loving, law-abiding Scandinavian of our own day that if he feels himself driven to the point of murder he murders himself, commits suicide. Not so the medieval Icelander. He was blood-brother to the Normans, and the energy and insight they in their European context devoted to the arts of war and statecraft, he in his stonier province gave to the arts of literature and feud. Admittedly the sagas include much more than feud. Together they provide not only a composite history of Iceland's heroic age; they are its epic, and the fullest expression of the nation's soul. Without them the Icelandic ethos is not to be comprehended, neither the complex of ideals and beliefs nor the qualities of mind which led to the best years of the Republic, the Greenland-Vinland adventure, and to Icelandic literature, and on the other hand to blood-feud, civil war, the loss of independence and the disasters that ensued. The greatest of sagas is *Brennu-Njáls Saga*, the Saga of the Burning of Njal, composed about 1280 by an unknown master in the south-west of Iceland. To reduce its narrative riches to a sentence, it tells how the hero Gunnar of Hlidarendi was brought to his death by fate and his own character; how the sage Njal was in the same fashion brought to destruction with his entire family; and how at last the man who burned him and the man who avenged him grew reconciled. Written about 1280, some twenty years after the loss of national independence, it is both pæan and elegy for the great days of the Republic. From *Brennu-Njáls Saga* or, to give it its title of affection, *Njála*, we shall learn more of medieval Iceland and the Icelanders than from any other single source. It is also Iceland's supreme work of art. On both counts it challenges our close attention.[1]

But if *Njála* is the greatest of sagas it is not a lonely giant, and

[1] For *Njála* see Appendix I, '*Njála*: Greatest of Sagas.'

it is permissible to have a favourite elsewhere. The chivalric and
sentimental reader may respond more warmly to the fine feeling
and noble situations of *Laxdœla Saga*; those who love high poetry
and fierce adventure must always find *Egils Saga* irresistible; while
the passionate regard of many Icelanders for the saga of the
crossed and outlawed Grettir is a moving revelation of how a
people may find its soul mirrored and its fate expressed in the tale
of one man. Among shorter pieces the saga of Hrafnkel Priest of
Frey is almost flawless, a magnificent study of chieftainship in
action; while the tale of Authun the Westfirther who bought a
bear in Greenland and gave it to king Svein in Denmark is
perfect. The list of good things can be extended at pleasure, but
in our present context it will be wiser to touch on one aspect of
saga literature relevant to the documentation of this book. Are
the sagas true? Are they faithful histories? If not, to what extent
can they be relied upon as evidence for, among |other things, the
settlement of Iceland and the Greenland and Vinland voyages?

The beginning of the sagas was in history. The first Icelandic
'school' of writing was that located in the south, at Oddi and
Haukadal, with which were associated the glorious names of
Sæmund the Learned and Ari Thorgilsson. This was an aristocratic school, scholarly in its interests, and productive of formal
histories, genealogies, annals, and summaries of biographical fact
which were later to be used extensively by writers of sagas. In
Ari's *Libellus Islandorum* (*c.* 1122–33) the emphasis is so strongly on
tested historical truth that for a thing to be mentioned in the
Libellus is in general a guarantee of its veracity. Ari, we remember,
according to Snorri Sturluson, was the first author to write
scholarly works in the native language. But by the time of *Víglundar
Saga* and similar compilations of the fourteenth century the historical element has disappeared. Between these extremes there can
be traced a development of Icelandic narrative writing having its
origin in historical scholarship, severe and exact as at Oddi and
Haukadal, or more romantic and legendary as at Thingeyrar in
the north, but soon compelled to take notice of an audience's
desire for entertainment as well as instruction, for what would be
popular as well as historically reputable. At first slowly, and then
with some rapidity, the creative artist gains on the historian, till at
length artistry and history are in equipoise in *Egils Saga*, 1220–25;
in *Njála* some fifty years later the untrammelled artist achieves his

greatest triumph, though his narrative rests on the bedrock of historical and antiquarian scholarship; by the time of the latest recension of *Grettis Saga*, about 1310–20, the author is treating his material even more freely, and the bone of history is much less discernible under the tissue of romance and wondrous tradition; and finally, in *Víglundar Saga*, history has died into an absurd pretence of historical colouring.

It follows that in most good family sagas, those whose compilation and writing down was undertaken in a serious and responsible way, there is a firm foundation of history and antiquarian knowledge. Remembering always that we are dealing with history as it was known to the medieval and not the modern mind, and remembering too that the saga-men were dealing with events which had taken place some two or three hundred years ago. It follows further that the historicity of every saga must be established in a positive way by checking it with every known source of information, where possible with the archaeological record, and in a negative safeguarding way by distinguishing between the reasonable and the incredible elements in its narrative. Remembering further that though fiction or the recasting of material in the crucible of the creative imagination was an essential element of all the best family sagas, there would be no sagas but for the saga-men's interest in history and regard for contemporary historical method. Of all this the sagas of Eirik the Red and the Greenlanders are excellent examples. Underlying them is a sound historical tradition about the discovery and settlement of Greenland and the attempted colonization of a coastal area in North America. In the course of centuries this tradition has collected various accretions and confusions, but its soundness has always been discernible, and in these last two years it has been dramatically confirmed by the discovery at Qagssiarssuk-Brattahlid of the original turf-built Thjodhild's Church, 'not over near' Eirik's main farm, and by increasing evidence that the northern extremity of Newfoundland and the area of Sacred Bay were the scene of early Norse habitation in the ancient Promontorium Winlandiæ.

V. THE REPUBLIC ENDS

THE first Icelandic Republic lasted for almost 400 years, if we date its inception from the arrival of Ingolf Arnarson; and no fewer than 330 if we regard the Age of Settlement, 870–930, as its preliminaries rather than its first chapter. As to its last, no nation worked harder at its own destruction, or was worse served by those to whom it had a right to look for leadership and example, and consequently, of all the periods of Iceland's history the Age of the Sturlungs, the last century of independence, has come in for most polemic, most abuse. It was an age of greed for wealth and power, of selfishness and pride, leading to civil war and national exhaustion, and its many betrayals ended in the greatest betrayal of all: the handing over of the nation to a foreign power. Even so we must guard against an over-righteous verdict and an over-simplified picture. The so-called 'betrayers' were as much the victims of history and circumstance as those they betrayed, and among their number were some of the most gifted and famous men the island has ever known.

No one cause, still less one event or person, led to the loss of Iceland's independence in 1262–64, and the slackening of national life that ensued. The Icelanders' heritage of heroic individualism was in its nature perilous to political unity; but even had that unity been attained Iceland would have found it hard to remain a nation on her own. The settlers and their sons' sons were fine seamen whose ships carried them viking, trading, poetizing, exploring, to known and unknown lands. But already in the eleventh century fewer and fewer chieftains owned their own ships. Those belonging to their forefathers were by now lost or grown unseaworthy, and there was no native timber, no strong oak, with which to lay down the keels of new. In trustworthy sources of the twelfth century there are surprisingly few references to Icelandic-owned sea-going vessels; in the thirteenth century they are hardly to be found at all. A native-owned ship was becoming a rarity.[1] For a people inhabiting a mostly infertile island far out in the North Atlantic this was at best a dangerous development. Overseas trade and travel were now becoming possible only by the grace of others, which in the thirteenth century meant the Norwegians. This was the greatest danger of all, for in Norway both monarchy and church had plans of their own for Iceland, and these postulated the loss of her independence.

These plans were much helped by changing conditions in the

[1] See in particular the sub-chapters on ships and seagoing in Jón Jóhannesson, *Íslendinga Saga*, I and II.

island, where while heroic (which means excessive) individualism remained constant, family ambition intensified. During the twelfth century power came increasingly into fewer sets of hands, as a small number of energetic and unscrupulous chieftains acquired the ownership of many godords or were allowed in return for reward and protection to exercise the privileges and controls that went with them. It followed that the old relationship between godi and thingman, chieftain and retainer, changed: it became less personal, more feudal. In theory a thingman could still transfer his allegiance, and so express his opinion of old master and new; but in fact his freedom of action had become circumscribed. Even in quarrels which did not touch him close he was forced to take sides. There had been noteworthy trials of strength between chieftains in the old days: armies of three or four hundred men twice confronted each other in the 960's after the burning to death of Blund-Ketil, and in 1012 almost the entire congregation for law was locked in battle on the sacred Thingfield after the burning to death of Njal; by 1121 Haflidi Masson (in whose home, ironically enough, the civil law of Iceland had four years earlier been amended and for the first time written down) could prosecute his quarrel against Thorgils Oddsson with a force of almost 1500 men. A pattern was now established whereby levies drawn from entire Quarters replaced those bands of kinsmen and friends who rode out with the old-time protagonists of feud. Lesser men, and many chieftains with them, must throw in their lot with the Sturlungs, who controlled the Dales, Borgarfjord, and Eyjafjord, or with the Asbirnings of Skagafjord; with the Vatnsfirthings of the north-west or the Svinfellings of the east; with the Oddaverjar of the south whose star was setting, or the Haukadalers whose delayed and murky triumph would precede and ensure that of the Norwegian king. Loyalties drained away like water on sand, for the rending feuds and quasi-dynastic wars of the thirteenth century were made worse by struggles for supremacy within the contending groups, by disconcerting shifts of alignment, and by the ambiguous relationship of so many Icelandic chieftains to the Norwegian king. Many of Iceland's leading men who visited the court of king Hakon Hakonsson became his liegemen and promised him obedience; but of all the king's chosen instruments, Snorri Sturluson, Sturla Sighvatsson, Thord Kakali, Thorgils Skardi and Gizur Thorvaldsson, only Thorgils wholeheartedly served

the royal cause. Snorri, wise beyond his time and not enough the
man of action, brooded and procrastinated and zealously accumu-
lated estates and wealth and worries till Hakon wearied of him
and he was murdered in a night raid on Reykholt in 1241. Sturla,
too much the man of action and abusing the king's authority in
order to square private accounts and forward personal ambitions,
had already perished in 1238, cut down with two of his brothers
after the battle of Orlygsstadir, in which his father, old Sighvat,
died grim and reluctant of seventeen bloody wounds. Sturla's
brother Thord Kakali by a skilled use of force and diplomacy
became overlord of all Iceland, and might have become its king,[1]
but his personal ambition showed so nakedly that king Hakon
had him recalled in 1250, and he never set foot in his homeland
again. Thorgils Skardi (another Sturlung), whose unquestioned
loyalty to the king was enhanced by his intelligence and magnanimity, was treacherously murdered in 1258, while still a young
man of thirty-two. Gizur alone survived the royal commission,
to emerge as the most important man in Iceland and an earl. But
the price he paid hardly bears thinking on. His wife and three sons
and more than twenty of his household and friends died when his
enemies burned Flugumyr, and his heart died with them. All that
was good in his nature grew corrupted in those faithless times, and
a man sensitive, intelligent, and deep-rooted in his country's past,
grew cunning and merciless, and destroyed his country's freedom. The coldest reading in *Sturlunga Saga* is his reply to Thord
Andresson whom he seized in 1264 while under a pledge of safe
conduct. The wretched Thord asked Gizur to forgive him. 'I
will,' said Gizur, 'the minute you are dead.' No wonder Thord
Kakali told king Hakon, when the king had asked him whether he
would consent to live in heaven if Gizur were there too: 'Gladly,
sire—so long as we might be far apart.'[2] Hatred pursued him at
home, and suspicion abroad, and though the only earl in Iceland
he died lonely and desperate as a fox in a stone trap. To Norway's
king all these men were expendable. The more so because Hakon
knew how divided were their loyalties and how enigmatic their
purpose.

But his success was inevitable. Time, the spirit of the age, and
the church were all on his side. By definition the Republic was an

---

[1] See Appendix II, 'The only King who rests in Iceland'.
[2] Einar Ól. Sveinsson, *The Age of the Sturlungs*, p. 94.

anachronism, pagan and anti-monarchic. The Icelanders *must* give allegiance to king Hakon, pronounced Cardinal William of Sabina, 'for he thought it against all reason that this country should not serve a king even as all other countries in the world'. Not only Norwegian bishops like the arch-intriguer Heinrek, but Icelanders like Brand, Arni, and Jorund were among the most determined underminers of the old Constitution. They stood for the monarchy because the monarchy stood for the church, and both before and after the loss of national independence they fought for the ecclesiastical control of church property, including church buildings and their revenues, which had always been, like the heathen temples which preceded them, the personal property of the chieftains who built them. Their success in securing these rights impoverished families as wealthy as the Oddaverjar and beggared beyond recovery many lesser godar. By these and other means the old way of life was being broken in pieces, and the old culture destroyed in its foundations. Also the Icelandic farmer, who more than any chieftain was the nation's prop and stay, grew sick to death of war and disorder. He wanted peace, and after 1250 and the recall of Thord Kakali saw no hope of it save by favour of the Norwegian king. When Thorgils Skardi offered himself as chieftain over Skagafjord after his victory at Thvera in 1255, it was a farmer, Broddi Thorleifsson, who made answer not only for himself, but for all his kind. If one must serve a chieftain, he said, very well, let it be Thorgils. 'But it would be better to serve none, if only a man could be left in peace.' Rule by chieftains was in discredit and men's minds were open to the only alternative: rule by a king. So it came about that between 1262 and 1264 the four Quarters of Iceland made submission to king Hakon. Soon they had a new civil and constitutional law from Norway, and a new church law. Within a decade they had peace and thereafter stagnation. For by an unforeseeable misfortune they had committed their future into the hands of Norway just as Norway entered upon a period of rapid decline. From now on the parent country would have more than enough to do to help herself, much less Iceland, which after enjoying a brief increase in her exports of fish was to suffer cruelly from lack of trade and communications. The number of independent farmers declined, householders became tenants and cotters, and, as always in hard times, the poor grew ever poorer. Many turned beggar and tramped the countryside.

But much of Iceland's misery was not man-made. It came from
the forbidding nature of the land. Geologically Iceland was still
in the making, and its people shared in its growing-pains. For
a start, the climate was becoming colder and bad ice-years in-
creased in number after 1270, blocking the coasts and prolonging
the already long winter. But worse tribulation was in store. The
year 1283 ushered in a period of plague and famine: seven of the
next ten years saw men and cattle die of cold, epidemic, or starvation. The turn of the century was marked by the eruption of
the volcano Hekla, with violent earthquakes, and in 1301 as many
as 500 people died by epidemic in the north. Between 1306 and
1314 only two years were free of volcanic action, earthquake, or
plague, with their resultant loss of life and destruction of the means
of existence. Periodically throughout the rest of the century the
fire-mountains of the south would explode with terrifying force
and devastate wide areas of the countryside. Farms vanished,
pasture was erased, man and his beasts alike perished of blast,
avalanche, flood, and fire, and wherever the pall of ash and
pumice blackened Iceland's skies the birds as they flew fell dead
to the poisoned ground. The eruption of Oræfajokul in 1362 with
its attendant *jökulhlaup* or glacier-burst was 'in all probability the
biggest explosive eruption in Europe since Pompeii was destroyed
in A.D. 79'.[1] The whole area of Oræfi was temporarily abandoned,
and two parishes were extinguished for ever. Even more
notorious was Hekla, *mons perpetuo ardens*, recognized by an awed
Europe as the Mouth of Hell itself. Here in time of eruption might
be heard the gnashing of teeth and shrill lamentation, while the
souls of the damned fluttered round like black ravens. It was Iceland's bitter distinction that it fulfilled the requirements of both
the viking and the christian hells, the first cold and icy, the
second endlessly aflame. And when at last these conceptions were
combined, Hell's worst horror was seen to be Iceland's too, where
the doomed alternate hopelessly between tartarean fire and
numbing glaciers and drift ice.

With it all, Iceland survived, though necessarily in herself and
for herself. Her political dependence and maritime impoverish-

[1] Sigurður Thórarinsson, *The Thousand Years Struggle against Ice and Fire*, Reykjavík,
1956, p. 46. The glacier-burst from Katla in 1918 may serve as an illustration of the
destructive power of this phenomenon. Its discharge has been estimated at 200,000
cubic metres of water a second, roughly three times the discharge of the Amazon.
The lifeless waste of the black Myrdal sands is Katla's enduring memorial.

ment, her natural catastrophes and the mere stark act of endurance would make it impossible for her to succour her neighbour Greenland when Greenland in turn felt the remorseless pressures of geography and history. There the Norsemen would be lost beyond knowledge or redemption in a dark, impenetrable night; but Iceland would come safely through the fourteenth century, and however distant, however obscured, a fresh dawn lay ahead.

2

Greenland

I. DISCOVERY AND SETTLEMENT

THE early history of Greenland is the life story of Eirik the Red. He was its first explorer and settler; he gave it a name and took out shiploads of Icelanders to make their home there; he brought its western coast firmly within the confines of late tenth-century Norse geography. Yet he was not the first to sight it. About the Norse discovery of Iceland blew the winds of accident and chance. Ships blown off course and storm-driven about the western ocean made landfalls unknown or unexpected. So with Greenland. Late in the period of settlement, between 900 and 930, a man named Gunnbjorn, sailing from Norway to Iceland, was driven headlong past his destination to sight a new land and its attendant islands in the west. These islands, or skerries, were henceforth known by his name, Gunnbjarnarsker, but it is a very long time since they were last satisfactorily identified. In the middle of the fourteenth century Ivar Bardarson said the skerries lie half-way between Iceland and Greenland; and since by Greenland he presumably meant the Norse settlements on its western coast, it seems reasonable to identify them with the islands east of Sermiligaq, near Angmagssalik, due west of Snæfellsnes.[1] In any

---

[1] So Gustav Holm, *MGr.* 56, 1918. But nothing is certain, for their number, nature, and position were the subject of speculation rather than geographical knowledge. Thus in the *Grænlandsannáll* of Björn Jónsson of Skardsa (*c.* 1625) we read of the *Gunnbjarnareyjar* which lie off the mouth of the Isafjord, to the north-west. A decade or so later Joris Carolus's map shows 'I. Gouberma' as eight islands due west of the Vestfirthir, but Joris was a congenital inventor of islands. The learned Arngrímur Jónsson at different times, in his *Gronlandia* and *Specimen Islandiæ*, thought of them as west, north-west, and north of Iceland. They were inhabited and uninhabited. Jón lærði Guðmundsson attempted a summary in his *Um Íslands aðskiljanlegar náttúrur*, shortly after 1637. 'Gunnbiarnareyjar. Gunnbjorn Ulf-Krakason, a Norwegian, who sailed the whole way round Iceland after Gardar in order to discover what lands would lie most adjacent to Iceland, first lighted on these islands, which appeared to him to be as it were skerries off Gardarsholm, full of birds and

case, the land Gunnbjorn saw was Greenland. He made no descent upon its shores, undertook no survey, but his news was to bear good fruit back in Isafjord and under Snæfellsnes, where his sons and his brother had earlier taken land in settlement.

Eirik the Red, a red-headed, red-bearded, and on occasion red-handed man, was born on a farm in Jaeren, some thirty miles south of Stavanger in Norway, but in his middle teens was forced to leave the country along with his father Thorvald, by reason of a feud which ended in manslaughter. The Age of Settlement was over, the good land taken, and father and son could do no better for themselves than a farm on the harsh, rocky coast which runs south from Hornbjarg, Cape Horn. This ice-prone area must have struck young Eirik as a hard exchange for the green fields and early harvests of his boyhood home, so when his father died, and he himself was married and collecting a father's responsibilities, he abandoned Drangar and cleared land south in Haukadal, then as now an area of gnarled birchwood and pleasant grazing. Soon he was involved in heavy blood-feuds, thrown out of Haukadal by men with more bone in their fist than he, drawn into new manslayings in the islands of Breidafjord, and finally banished overseas for a period of three years. Still, he had a gift for friendship, and his friends stood by him manfully, but they were probably relieved to hear his resolution to rediscover the land Gunnbjorn Ulf-Krakason had sighted the time he was storm-driven into the western ocean and discovered Gunnbjarnarsker. This need not have been a sudden resolution: Gunnbjorn's family had lived in Eirik's corner of Iceland, and the notion of new land for those brave enough to take it must have been often canvassed in the Vestfirthir. Besides, in the Iceland of 982 there was simply no room for Eirik's out-stuck elbows. On all his farms he had been strongly contained by more influential families, and by now must

herbage and amply endowed with produce of the sea. Of these it would be too long to give an account. Master Juris tréfótur Hollendski [= Joris Carolus] is now the latest claimant to have landed there, and saw two churches. These [islands] will be six in number and all of them of a good size. Whether the English and Dutch ply their trade there I cannot say. They lie in the sea to the north-west off Isafjardardjup and Adalvikur-rytabjarg, as the old poem recounts (ed. Hermansson, *Islandica* xv, p. 3).' This old poem would appear to be Styrbjorn's prophetic verse about the fate of Snæbjorn Galti (see p. 129, below), in which case we are back where we started, and little the wiser. A legend on a map by Ruysch in the 1507 edition of Ptolemy reads '*Insula hæc anno Domini 1456 fuit totaliter combusta*' (O'Dell, *The Scandinavian World*, p. 359), which would dispose of island(s) and problem alike if we could accept it—which we cannot. *Gunnbiarne Skær, Goubar Schoer*, and the like, persist on maps till well into the eighteenth century.

have realized that if he was ever to attain full stature it must be elsewhere. But where? In Norway as in Iceland the avengers of blood stood waiting. For a man of Eirik's temperament, resolute and ambitious, adventurous yet canny, and born to captain men, it made sense to sail west through the islands, west past the Snæfell jokul, west for the glimpsed cloud-hackles and ice-shirted mountains of Greenland.

From his hideout in Breidafjord he had the best part of 450 miles to go. Sailing on the 65th parallel with the prevailing easterly of early summer behind him, he would be near enough to the Greenland coast in four days (assuming that he hove-to in the brief hours of darkness) to discern its inhospitable nature. He would then head south by south-west along the land, still conning an iron landscape of mountain, nunatak, and the glittering desolation of the ice-cap, till after long sailing he would start threading the southern fjords and by way of Prins Christians Sund feel his way to the western coast, then follow the bent of the land north-west.[1] Soon thereafter he would know his hunch had been right and that his hopes would be gratified. For as he sailed in the warm bright days northwards beyond Hvarf he quickly reached the southern extremity of the most habitable region of Greenland. Inland, as ever, was the daunting majesty of the ice-cap, but here it was hidden, and instead of the contorted face of the eastern coast, rock-browed and glacier-tongued, medusa-like to man and ship, he found himself navigating an archipelago of bird-haunted islands, with a shore to starboard fissured with deep, life-teeming fjords. The country was most beautiful, and to a seaman's eye the fjords and island-channels, with their good sailing and innumerable anchorages and harbours, were altogether more attractive than the exposed coasts of Iceland. While best of all for a man who whatever else he was was still a farmer, he found at the inner extremities of these fjords emerald grass, flowery hillslopes, dwarf willow, birch, and juniper. Edible berries grew there in profusion, angelica, bog-cotton, and the mosses of home. Above all, the land was empty of inhabitants, though various house-ruins,

[1] It was Otto Pettersson's view that Eirik would sail through Prins Christians Sund and not need to round Cape Farewell, and he is likely to be right. If so, this would support the notion sometimes expressed that during his third summer Eirik explored the *east* coast of Greenland as far north as the latitude of the head of Eiriksfjord, and that it was on this coast that he found relics of the Eskimo. The Dorset Culture Eskimo had disappeared from the south-west coast some 800 years before the Norsemen arrived there. But the detail of Eirik's movements is quite uncertain.

fragments of boats and stone implements bore witness to an earlier, and as they judged, non-European occupation. And as he probed these fjords and explored the islands during the three summers of his exile, for the first time in his life Eirik was free of constrictive neighbours. We cannot doubt that his ideas expanded accordingly, for when he returned to Iceland it was to sing the praises of his new found land, named not too unfairly, when we think of the luxuriant pastures of the southern fjords, *Grænaland*, The Green Land, or *Grænland*, Greenland. The connotations of this happy title, *green, grass,* and *grow,* were a joyous augury to land-hungry men, and richly redolent of pastures new. He prepared at once for its permanent colonization. He would have returned too with a cargo of bearskins, reindeer, seal and walrus hides, and sea-ivory, as an earnest of the country's riches, and with a full crew to witness to its clemency. For throughout those three years we hear of not one casualty among his men, an astonishing tribute to Eirik's resolution and prudence. Hoping for the best, he had clearly prepared for the worst, and so evaded it.

At home he found many ready to listen to him. Ten years earlier Iceland had suffered the worst famine of her history, so terrible that some killed the old and helpless out of the way, and many starved.[1] So there were plenty with nothing to hope for at home, great householders fallen on evil times like Thorbjorn Vifilsson, and poor farmers overshadowed by such new-rich upstarts as the hateful Hen-Thorir. Even so, the response to Eirik's preaching must have surprised him. When he returned to Greenland early in the summer of 986 it was as leader of an armada of twenty-five ships, of which fourteen arrived safely. Some perished, more were forced back, but the effective colonization of Greenland must have begun with hardly less than four hundred people taking possession of land after the Icelandic fashion in the inner reaches of the hundred and twenty miles of fjord country extending north from Herjolfnes to Isafjord.[2] Practically all these people were Icelanders.

[1] 976 was a famine year throughout north and north-western Europe. After Iceland, Norway and England were among the worst sufferers.
[2] The locations of settlement were as follows. Herjolf took in settlement Herjolfsnes (the modern Ikigait), and Herjolfsfjord (Amitsuarssuk). Ketil took Ketilsfjord (Tasermiut). Hrafn took Hrafnsfjord (Agdluitsoq, or possibly its inner northern arm, up to Foss). Solvi took Solvadal (probably a valley running up from Kangikitsoq). Helgi Thorbrandsson took Alptafjord (Sermilik), named after his home fjord in Iceland. Thorbjorn Glora took Siglufjord (Unartoq), which according

Eventually the so-called Eastern Settlement of the modern Julianehaab district would number by contemporary record 190 farms, a cathedral at Gardar, on the neck between Eiriksfjord and Einarsfjord, an Augustine monastery and Benedictine nunnery, and twelve parish churches. Concurrently there were hardy spirits pressing further north three hundred miles and more to found the Western Settlement, Vestribyggd, in the district where Godthaab stands today. This was smaller but still substantial, with its 90 farms and four churches.[1] That the twenty or more farms round Ivigtut (with no church) should be regarded as a Middle Settlement is doubtful; they seem rather to belong to the Eastern Settlement. Between Eystribyggd and Vestribyggd (we should probably describe them today as the Southern and Northern Settlements, for their bearing one from the other is north-west and south-east) the coastal strip was too narrow for animal husbandry, and inland of the mountains lay nothing but ice. 'Men,' says the author of the *King's Mirror*, in his mid-thirteenth-century description of Greenland, 'have often tried to go up into the country and climb the highest mountains in various places to look about and learn whether any land could be found that was free from ice and habitable. But nowhere have they found such a place, except what is now occupied, which is a little strip along the water's edge.' Where that strip failed them, they had nothing.

The uninhabited and uninhabitable parts of Greenland were the Obyggdir, most of them good for little or nothing, but some providing the two settlements with excellent hunting and fishing grounds and with their best supply of driftwood. In these last hunters and skippers like the ogreish Thorhall in *Eiríks Saga* or the gallant Sigurd Njalsson in *Einars Tháttr* reaped a rich and

to Ivar Bardarson had the home comfort of hot springs. Einar took Einarsfjord (Igaliko). Hafgrim took Hafgrimsfjord (Eqaluit) and Vatnahverfi (the inner half of the peninsula between Igaliko and Agdluitsoq, and the largest area of inland settlement in the Norse colonies). Arnlaug took Arnlaugsfjord (not entirely identifiable, but in the northern reaches of Eystribyggd). Eirik himself first lived on Eiriksey (Igdlutalik) off the mouth of Eiriksfjord (Tunugdliarfik), and thereafter at Brattahlid (Qagssiarssuk), near the northern inner extremity of the fjord, west across the water from the modern airstrip at Narssarssuaq.

[1] *Det gamle Gronlands beskrivelse* (1930); GHM, III, 228. In all some 400 Norse ruins have been discovered in Greenland, almost 300 of which are farms of varying size and different periods. The standard account of Norse findings to the beginning of World War II is Aage Roussell, *Farms and Churches in the Mediaeval Norse Settlements of Greenland*, MGr. 89, 1941. For a recent summary see Michael Wolfe, O.M.I., 'Norse Archæology in Greenland since World War II' in the *American-Scandinavian Review*, xlix, 4, pp. 380–92, 1961–62.

recurrent harvest by land and sea. The best hunting grounds lay north of Vestribyggd; Disco and its environs in latitude 70° N was a favourite resort for men whose skill matched their hardihood, and here they built huts to serve them in summer and sometimes in winter too on their far thrusts north. From the modern Holsteinsborg northwards to the Nugssuaq peninsula lay the *Norðrsetr, –seta*, the Northern Hunting Ground(s), and men who came sojourning here were said to 'go on, or into, Nordseta (*fara í norðsetu*)' for narwhal, walrus, and the esteemed white bear of Greenland. Nor was this their northern limit. In 1824 the eskimo Pelimut discovered in one of three cairns on the island of Kingigtorssuaq, just north of Upernavik, and a little short of latitude 73° N, a small stone inscribed with runes which recorded that, 'Erling Sighvatsson and Bjarni Thordarson and Eindridi Jonsson on the Saturday before the minor Rogation Day [April 25] piled these cairns and . . .' The inscription, whose ending is unclear, dates from the beginning of the fourteenth century, and presumably these men had spent the winter on Kingigtorssuaq. Some fifty years earlier, in 1267, we hear of an expedition which sailed almost to the 76th parallel, right into Melville Bay, a startling 'farthest north', saw traces of Skrælings up in Kroksfjardarheid (Disco Bay), and then got itself back to the Eastern Settlement. That men died of cold and hunger, sickness and shipwreck, and all the accidents attendant on high latitude exploration, is as certain of these half-glimpsed expeditions of the Middle Ages as of the elaborately documented expeditions of the last two hundred and fifty years. The fate of Arnbjorn's crew in the later 1120's, as recorded in *Einars Tháttr*, is one example. There are others. We read of a shipwreck on the east coast in *Flóamanna Saga*, followed by Thorgils Orrabeinsfostri's desperate journey to safety in the south-west. This is not without its trappings of magic, mutiny, and murder most foul; but the account of the survivors dragging their boat over the glaciers and ice-floes, and when possible rowing through the open leads; the wounded bear at the water-hole with Thorgils hanging on to its lugs that it might not sink; the dead men covered by the fallen snow; these look like the white bone of truth for many besides Thorgils.[1] The saga of

---

[1] At the end of his travels Thorgils wound up with Eirik the Red at Brattahlid. From the first his welcome was a cool one (Thorgils was a Christian), and his chief exploit that winter did nothing to warm it. 'It happened there that winter that a bear

Gudmund the Good (*Resenbók*) has a grim little anecdote of a
ship's crew fighting over provisions and the last three survivors
dying a day's journey short of safety. In 1189 a ship named
Stangarfoli was wrecked in the Obyggdir with the priest Ingimund on board: the bodies of seven men were recovered fourteen
years later. From the shaky evidence of *Tósta Tháttr* it would
seem that such mishaps were common enough for one Lika-
Lodinn, Corpse-Lodinn, to find employment ransacking the
northern Obyggdir for the dead bodies of shipwrecked mariners
which he would bring back south for church burial.

But to return to the Settlements. The men who sold their homes
in Iceland and brought their families, wealth, or merely their
services out to Greenland, were most of them not hunters or
explorers, but solid settlement-men, and in everything save their
choice of a homeland strongly conservative. They were husbandmen, concerned to raise stock, and for that they required, as the
canny Eirik had foreseen, good grazing lands. These were to be
found in fair profusion not on the outer coast but well up the
fjords, sometimes close to the permanent ice, and it was along
these inner reaches, in magnificent and challenging situations,
that they built their houses and byres of stone and turf, roofing
them with driftwood, and in their structure following or re-
developing the changing fashions of Iceland, or at times ringing
such changes on these as to produce a Greenland style of their
own. The heart of Norse Greenland was the thirty miles from the
head of Eiriksfjord by way of the head of Einarsfjord to Vatnahverfi, and it was here that living conditions were easiest. The
summer though short was warm and pleasant, and it is noticeable that the richest herbage in Greenland is still to be found on

made inroads on men's stock and did severe injury to many. Meetings were held
about this, whether some remedy might be found, and what emerged was that a price
was set on the bear's head. The people of both settlements agreed to this, but Eirik
did not like it one bit. Then as winter drew to a close men came to trade with
Thorgils and his foster-father Thorstein. There were a lot of men in the storehouse
which contained their goods, and the boy Thorfinn Thorgilsson was there too, and
this is what he said to his father: "There is such a lovely dog come outside here,
father. I never saw one like him before, he is so big." "Leave it be," said Thorgils,
"and don't be going outside." Even so the boy went running out. It was the bear
who had come there, strolling down off the glacier. It caught up the boy, who cried
out. Thorgils rushed outside, and had his drawn sword in his hand. The bear was
playing with the boy. Thorgils smote it between the ears with all his strength and
passion, splitting the beast's skull right through, so that it fell down dead. He picked
up the boy, who was hardly hurt at all . . . Eirik was not overjoyed at this deed . . .
Some maintained that Eirik was displeased that Thorgils had the good fortune to
achieve this deed, because he himself put an evil trust in the creature.' (Cap. 25).

6. HVALSEY, GREENLAND

The Church, *c.* 1300, is to the left, and the Great Hall right. In between are the farm buildings, and in the foreground is the enclosure.

7. HVALSEY: THE OLD HALL

Looking west to the Great Hall. On the right the gravel bench inside the rear wall, in the middle the long fire-trench and ember-pit, on the left the south row of post holes. Measurements 14×4 metres.

8. THE CATHEDRAL
GARDAR (IGALIKO)

The Cathedral ruins are in the foreground. Behind stand houses of
modern Greenlanders, constructed
in large measure of stones taken
from the ruins.

the sites of these old Norse farms. The situation of the Hill Farm at Brattahlid is positively idyllic, with its dark and sparkling stream, its luscious dark green pastures, and the low ramparts of hills which protect it on all sides. 'It is reported,' says the author of the *King's Mirror*, 'that the pasturage is good, and that there are large and fine farms in Greenland.' And again, 'The earth yields good and fragrant grass.' The North and River farms at Brattahlid could support twenty-eight and twelve cattle respectively, and

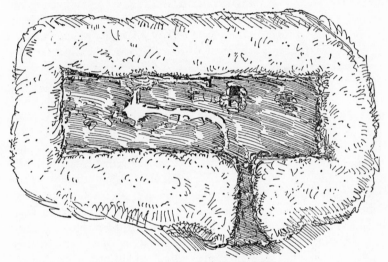

4. BRATTAHLID, THE GREAT HALL

The interior measures 14·7 × 4·5 metres. The walls, part stone, part turf, were between a metre and two metres thick. The entrance faces south-east, with a commanding view of the fjord. Opposite it, indoors, is the main fireplace, and a stone-covered channel conveyed fresh water through the house.

the Bishop's establishment at Gardar no less than seventy-five; and in addition there were the horses they brought with them from Iceland, sheep, goats, and a few pigs. 'The farmers', says our same source of information, 'raise cattle and sheep in large numbers, and make butter and cheese in great quantities. The people subsist chiefly on these foods and on beef; but they also eat the flesh of various kinds of game, such as reindeer [caribou], whales, seals, and bears. That is what people live on in that country.' And, of course, fish, in great variety and avid of the hook.

5

On favoured sunny slopes a little corn grew and ripened; later
in the colony's history a little iron was worked; but of neither was
there enough. Timber too was in short supply, with no native
growth worth mentioning and only scanty driftwood brought on
a long rounding course from Siberia. Trade was therefore a
necessity of life for the Greenlanders, and for a while this prospered well enough. Among the early settlers were men who
owned their own ships and plied the seas as merchant-venturers.
From Greenland they carried furs and hides, ropes and cables so
strong that the heaving of threescore men could not part them,
with walrus and narwhal ivory, and white falcons of such exquisite rapacity that in 1396 'the Duke of Burgundy sent to Bayezid
as a ransom for his son twelve Greenland falcons'.[1] There were
bears too, the white ice-bears of Greenland, esteemed throughout
Europe as gifts for prelates and princes, the most endearing
account of which will be found in the Icelandic tale of Authun
the Westfirther. Greenland woollen was in demand too. Leif
Eiriksson, the first white man to set foot in America, thought a
cloak of this, together with a belt of walrus ivory, a ring for her
finger, and a baby for her cradle, a suitable gift at parting for his
Hebridean sweetheart Thorgunna. In addition the Greenlanders
had seal-oil and similar commodities for export. In return they
needed, and needed badly, timber, iron for all purposes, made
weapons, corn, clothes of continental style, and such further
amenities of existence as malt, wine, and church vestments.
Timber, iron, and corn could not in the nature of things be obtained from Iceland. They came from Norway instead, and for a
while came sufficiently. So long as this balance of trade could be
maintained, in theory the life of the white man in Greenland could
go on for ever. Like the Eskimo they had hunting and fishing
with all their products, and in addition animal husbandry to
provide them with meat, milk, and wool. They lived in a hard
world, but a world filled with hope and promise, and time must
have seemed their friend. So:

> They on that sunlit morning
> Heard not the ice-floe's warning.

Their lives were too busy for omens and foreboding. Hardly was

[1] So Vilhjálmur Stefánsson, *The Three Voyages of Martin Frobisher*, 1938, p. xliv,
with a footnote reference to E. Müller-Röder, *Die Beizjagd und der Falkensport in alter
und neuer Zeit*, Leipzig, 1906, p. 15.

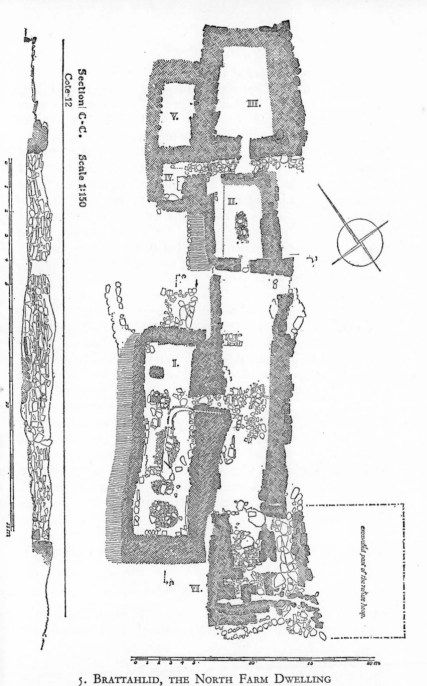

Section C–C.
Cote 12   Scale 1:150

5. Brattahlid, the North Farm Dwelling

I, the oldest part of the complex, probably the site of Eirik the Red's
great hall; II–V, later extensions northwards, by way of a fire-house,
sleeping-house, and store-rooms; VI, the roofed well-house. Outside
were byres, store-houses, and other buildings.

the settlement completed at Eystribyggd than men were moving
north, and before the last roof was sodded at Vestribyggd there
was a new religion in the land.[1] Thereafter for twenty-five years
men's mouths were full of news from Vinland the Good. There
was oral story-telling and a literature in prose and verse, with the
'Greenland Lay of Atli' as its most notable survival; and for a
craftsman there was all the walrus ivory and whalebone his hands
could hope to use. Also they had to shape a constitution under
which to live, and a legal system by which they could live together. The part played by Eirik the Red and his sons in all this was
considerable, and probably decisive. Eirik's exact position in the
colony has not been defined for us, but that he was its patriarch
and first citizen is clear, and probably the authority with which he
is credited in the sagas rested on some office analogous to the
allsherjargoði, the priest or leader of the Congregation, or the
lögsögumaðr, or lawspeaker, of Iceland. He was followed by his son
Leif, and Leif by his son Thorkel; and a full hundred years after
Eirik's death we read how Sokki Thorisson and his son Einar,
who lived at Eirik's Brattahlid, 'had great authority in Greenland,
and stood head and shoulders above other men'. Probably Sokki
was a descendant of Eirik's by blood or marriage; according to
Ivar Bardarson, Greenland's laugmader or lawman was always
domiciled at Brattahlid; but we lack evidence to prove what in its
nature seems unlikely, that the chief office of the colony was
hereditary. Like so much else the constitution of Greenland was
on the Icelandic model, with a national assembly through which it
could function. So the Republic, like the white man in Greenland,
could in theory go on for ever. In fact it lasted till 1261, when the
Greenlanders accepted the sovereignty of the king of Norway,
and in return for various unrealized trading concessions sur-
rendered their independence one year ahead of their kinsmen in
Iceland.

II. DECLINE AND FALL

THE Greenland colony, as distinct from the Greenland state or
nation, survived till the beginning of the sixteenth century, and

[1] The notion that Leif was responsible, under king Olaf Tryggvason, for the
conversion of Greenland, goes back to Gunnlaug Leifsson the Monk and his Life of
Olaf Tryggvason. Early sources such as the *Historia Norwegiæ* and *Ágrip* do not
name Greenland among the lands converted by Olaf. The *Historia* gives the credit of
the conversion to the Icelanders.

the nature of its passing has greatly exercised men's minds. The Greenland colony was the remotest northern outpost of European civilization, and its extinction on a far strand, in an almost forgotten country, in worsening conditions of cold, and with much macabre circumstance, has been thought by many of its students the most poignant tragedy ever played out by a Northern people. And it remains one of the unsolved mysteries of history.

We see now, wise after the event, that everything about the Norse settlements in Greenland was marginal. They could survive only if nothing altered for the worse. In Iceland the medieval European had staked the furthest claim north he could without abandoning a Scandinavian mode of life. Iceland lay on the outer fringe of the habitable world. Greenland lay beyond it. 'The church at Gardar,' wrote Pope Alexander VI in 1492, 'is situated at the world's end,' and the way there was notoriously *per mare non minus tempestuosissimum quam longissimum*. It was therefore a first requisite of the Greenlanders, if they were to control their destiny, that they should have sea-going ships of their own. But soon they had at their disposal neither the wealth nor the materials for these; after their submission to Norway they were expressly forbidden to use such; and from there on the conditions for survival were not at their own dictation. Political and economic changes abroad, without fault or offence of their own, could destroy them, and neglect would prove as deadly as assault. Second, their numbers were dangerously small, probably never more than three thousand souls. The population of Iceland in the year 1100 was roughly 80,000. Fire, ice, pestilence, and neglect reduced this to 47,000 by 1800—a murderous wastage in a fast-breeding race. Greenland had no such reservoir of human sacrifice. And third, of all European communities they were the most vulnerable to climatic change. For the rest of European man a run of cold winters and bad summers is a grievance and vexation; for the Greenlanders they sounded a death knell.

Throughout the north Atlantic area the ninth to the twelfth centuries were a comparatively warm period.[1] Had they not been,

---

[1] The immense and deserved authority of Fridtjof Nansen (see especially *Klimatsvekslinger in Nordens Historie*, Oslo, 1925; *Klimatsvekslinger i historisk og postglacial Tid*, Oslo, 1926) and Vilhjálmur Stefánsson has helped inhibit many students of literature and history from accepting the picture of climatic change here set forth. On the other hand, archaeologists, geographers, oceanographers, zoologists, palaeobotanists, and, most important of all, climatologists are overwhelmingly (though sometimes

we should be troubled to account for the Greenland voyages of
Gunnbjorn and Eirik the Red, and to a lesser extent the Vinland
voyages of Bjarni Herjolfsson, Leif Eiriksson, and Thorfinn
Karlsefni. In modern conditions of ice (by no means the severest
on record), it would, for example, have been impossible for Eirik
to make the journeys we hear he made, at the time of year and in
the directions in which we are told he made them. He *must* now
meet with ice, both off Greenland's east coast and off Eystribyggd
on the west. He seems however to have moved about with complete freedom, and though only fourteen of the twenty-five
settlement ships of the 986 armada reached Greenland, there is no
mention of ice turning the others back. The Icelandic Annals
(*Konungsannáll*) for 1126 have a short entry, *Steingrímr í ísum.*
'Steingrim in the ice,' and no doubt this Icelander is the Isa-
Steingrim who threw in his lot with the Norwegian merchants up
in the Western Settlement in the year 1130 (see p. 196, below).
Einars Tháttr also records how in this same summer of 1130 ice
drove into the south-western fjords and prevented the Norwegians getting away. However, their beleaguering was a brief
one, for the ice soon swept out again. Apart from this, saga
accounts of the Greenland and Vinland voyages make no mention
of ice at sea. In the case of Thorgils Orrabeinsfostri's shipwreck
on the east coast already mentioned, it is worth noting that it was
a shipwreck on the coast itself, *í vík nökkuri við sandmöl,* in a certain
bay on a sand-dune or hillock, and it happened just one week
before winter. Without pressing for too favourable a conclusion,

in individual cases diffidently) in its favour. My own convictions I owe primarily to
the writings, though not always to the conclusions, of Otto Pettersson, 'Climatic
Variations in Historic and Prehistoric Time', *Svenska Hydrografisk-Biologiska Kom-
missionens, Skrifter V*, Göteborg, 1914; Lauge Koch, *The East Greenland Ice, MGr.*
130, 1945 (Koch sums up: 'Thus it seems that the Norsemen were troubled by the
deterioration of the climate in the 13th century . . . however, before the extermina-
tion of the Norsemen an amelioration of the climate set in [after 1400 (p. 354)], so
the Norsemen did not die out owing to a fall in the temperature, but more probably
on account of a failing communication with Europe and the advance of the Eskimos
from the north,' (p. 349); C. E. P. Brooks, *Climate Through the Ages,* revised ed., 1949;
H. H. Lamb, 'Climatic Variation', 1960; 'On the Nature of Certain Climatic Epochs
which differed from the Modern (1900–39) Normal', Rome Symposium on changes
of Climate with special reference to the Arid Zones, 1961. The writings, comments
or summaries of Poul Nørlund, Jón Jóhannesson, Hans Ahlman, E. Bull, Andreas
Holmsen, G. Manley, William Hovgaard, Mads Lidegaard, C. L. Vebæk (Data
presented to the Conference on the Climate of the 11th and 16th Centuries, Aspen,
Colorado; Anthropological Section: 'The Climate of Greenland in the 11th and
16th Centuries (and the Time in Between)', 1962, typescript privately communicated
by C.L.V.), Johannes Iversen, Knut Fægri, Jørgen Meldgaard, and Sigurður
Thórarinsson have fortified them.

it would appear from the saga evidence that around the year
1000 a latitude sailing west from Snæfellsnes to the region of
Angmagssalik presented no problem to seamen, either because
there was no drift ice off the east coast in early summer or, more
likely, because such ice as there was was not formidable. In other
words, East Greenland had nothing like the drift ice of later
centuries. This is confirmed by the sailing directions preserved in
Landnámabók, by Ivar Bardarson, and by the *Navigatio Vetus* of
the Holar map of bishop Guðbrandur Vígfússon.

It is confirmed too by modern research into the history of
European climate. There is a wealth of evidence of various kinds
which allows modern scientists to conclude that during the
'Climatic Optimum' of 1000 to 1200 the mean summer temperature of western and middle Europe was higher by at least 1° C
than it is at present; that in southern Greenland annual mean
temperatures were 2° C to 4° C higher than now, and that sea
temperatures in the northernmost Atlantic were of the same order
of increase, with all that this must mean for the Canadian Archipelago and the area of Baffin Bay. The area of permanent ice lay
north of 80° N, drift ice must have been rare south of 70° N, and
very rare indeed in troublesome quantities south of the Arctic
Circle. There is therefore no reason rooted in climate for dis-
believing the Norse voyages to Greenland and the mainland of
North America.

But in terms of the Greenland settlement the important thing
to establish is not that the Climatic Optimum was somewhat
warmer than our own warm period, but that it was succeeded by a
period decidedly, and in the event fatally, colder. Here too
literary, historical, archaeological, and (in the widest sense)
meteorological and climatic evidence leads to the same conclusion: that after 1200 the climate of the northern hemisphere
fell progressively for two hundred years or more, and that by
c. 1430 Europe had entered a 'Little Ice Age'. Over much of
Europe the glaciers were beginning to advance, the tree-line fell
lower, vegetation and harvests were diminished by the cold; and
worst of all for the Greenlanders (though Iceland was a fellow
sufferer) the sea temperatures sank, causing an immense increase
in the drift ice which comes south with the East Greenland
Current to Cape Farewell and then swings north-west so as to en-
close first the Eastern and then the Western Settlement. For ice

conditions by the middle of the thirteenth century we have the
testimony of *Konungs Skuggsjá*, the *King's Mirror*.

As soon as one has passed over the deepest part of the ocean, he
will encounter such masses of ice in the sea, that I know no equal of it
anywhere else in all the earth. Sometimes these ice fields are as flat as if
they were frozen on the sea itself. They are about four or five ells thick
and extend so far out from the land that it may mean a journey of four
days or more to travel across them. There is more ice to the north-east
and north of the land than to the south, south-west and west; consequently, whoever wishes to make the land should sail around it to the
south-west and west, till he has come past all those places where ice
may be looked for, and approach the land on that side. It has frequently
happened that men have sought to make the land too soon and, as a
result, have been caught in the ice floes. Some of those who have been
caught have perished; but others have got out again, and we have met
some of these and have heard their accounts and tales. But all those
who have been caught in these ice-drifts have adopted the same plan:
they have taken their small boats and have dragged them up on the ice
with them, and in this way have sought to reach land; but the ship and
everything else of value had to be abandoned and was lost. Some have
had to spend four or five days upon the ice before reaching land, and
some even longer.

These ice floes have peculiar habits. Sometimes they lie as quiet as
can be, though cut apart by creeks or large fjords; at other times they
travel with a speed so swift and violent that a ship with a fair wind
behind is not more speedy; and when once in motion, they travel as
often against the wind as with it. There is also ice of a different shape
which the Greenlanders call icebergs. In appearance these resemble
high mountains rising out of the sea; they never mingle with other ice
but stand by themselves.[1]

The more obvious consequences of these ice conditions for
the mariner are set out in Ivar Bardarson's sailing directions a
hundred years later (*c.* 1360).

Item from Snæfellsnes in Iceland, where there is the shortest crossing
to Greenland, the course is two days' and two nights' sailing due west,
and there lie the Gunnbjarnarsker, half-way between Greenland and
Iceland. This was the old course, but nowadays ice has come down

---

[1] L. M. Larson (Translator), *The King's Mirror*, New York, 1917, pp. 138–9. The
brief quotations from the *King's Mirror* on p. 48 and p. 51 are also from Larson.

from the north-east out of the gulf of the sea[1] so close to the aforesaid skerries that without risk to life no one can sail the old course and be heard of again. . . . Item when one sails from Iceland one must take one's course from Snæfellsnes . . . and then sail due west one day and one night, then slightly south-west [*variant* then steer south-west] to avoid the aforesaid ice which lies off Gunnbjarnarsker; and then one day and one night due north-west, and so one comes right under the aforesaid elevation, Hvarf in Greenland, under which lie the aforesaid Herjolfsnes and Sandhavn.[2]

We are not asked to believe that there were no bitter spells during the good centuries, and no genial ones during the bad. That is not the way of the world's weather. But, reverting to the marginal position of the Greenland settlements, we may remember that conditions decidedly less severe than those that eventually obtained would quickly maim and finally destroy them. In high latitudes the formation of sea ice in falling temperatures is an ineluctable process, by nature's law. The calculated fall of temperatures in all waters north of 50° N in the 'Little Ice Age' is from 1° to 3° below those of today, which means from 3° to 7° below those attendant on the first two centuries of the settlement. The most conservative of these figures will explain the deadly mantle of drift ice off the east Greenland coast, as the *King's Mirror* describes it, the subsequent choking of the fjords of the Eastern Settlement, and the reappearance on the west coast of the Eskimo or Skræling.[3]

---

[1] It was long believed that there was a continuous land-bridge between Greenland and the north of Europe. Its eastern conjunction was with Bjarmaland, beyond the White Sea. This continuous land, sometimes with a Giant-home legend, is to be observed on many maps, including those of Skalholt and Holar, and it must have figured prominently on the two maps of the world sent in 1551 by Burgomaster Grip of Kiel to King Christian III of Denmark—'from which your majesty may see that your majesty's land of Greenland extends on both maps towards the new world and the islands which the Portuguese and Spaniards have discovered, so that these countries may be reached overland from Greenland. Likewise that they may be reached overland from Lapland, from the castle of Vardöhus'. The existence of this well-charted un-land in the minds of men led to notable fantasies, not least that the Hafsbotn or Polar Gulf extended from longitude 20° W to beyond 40° E. The land-bridge, happily, was not impassable for man or beast. One Hreidar is reputed to have crossed it with a goat. The goat fed on pockets of grass, and Hreidar on the goat's milk. Inevitably he became known as Goat-Hreidar.

[2] *Det gamle Grønlands beskrivelse*, p. 19. The *King's Mirror* and Ivar accord well with Abbot Arngrim Brandsson's description of Iceland and her surrounding waters, written some time before 1350. See *Guðmundar Saga Arasonar*, cap. 2 (ed. Guðni Jónsson, *Byskupa Sögur* III, Íslendingasagnaútgáfan, 1948).

[3] The name *Skrælingar* was applied by the Norsemen to the natives (Eskimo: Greenlandic *Kaláleq*, plur. *Kalátdlit*) they encountered in Greenland and (Eskimo or Indian) in Markland and Vinland. It is not certain what it means. 'It may be related

When Eirik the Red and his fellow colonists established the Eastern and Western Settlements towards the end of the tenth century, they found traces of earlier occupants at both places. These were Eskimo of the Dorset culture who by now had either perished or migrated elsewhere. When the Norsemen came into direct contact with Skrælings in the second half of the thirteenth century, well north of the Western Settlement, these were a new wave of Eskimo, people of the Thule culture, who moving across Canada from Alaska entered Greenland towards 1200 and then, as the Inugsuk folk, proceeded to occupy its habitable areas. Some moved down the west coast. They reached Vestribyggd early in the fourteenth century, and were off Eystribyggd's seaward limits by 1350–1400,[1] so pressed on to Cape Farewell, leaving Eystribyggd as a lonely and anxious Norse outpost far behind them. Others, journeying north out of the environs of Thule, with the passing of the generations reached the regions now known as Nansen Land and Peary Land, whence they headed south in the direction of Scoresby Sound. But with this twofold saga of exploration and endurance we are concerned only in so far as it affected the Norse colonies on the west coast, and the Skræling inheritors of the east coast affected them not at all.[2]

Presumably the growing cold and drier conditions after 1200 helped draw the Eskimo south. As the ice spread further and further down the west Greenland coast the seals followed it, and in their turn the Skrælings followed the seals, for their whole way of life depended on this creature. Walrus and whale, caribou and

to modern Norwegian *skræla* "scream", or to Icelandic *skrælna*, "shrink". In modern Icelandic *skræling* means "churl", "coarse fellow", in modern Norwegian "weakling". Connexion with *skræla*, "scream" seems more natural, but the modern forms point rather to the other etymology.' *An Introduction to Old Norse*, revised by A. R. Taylor, Oxford, 1957, p. 218. The Eskimos' name for themselves was *Inuit* (sing. *Inuk*), 'human beings' or 'men'.

[1] The basic studies of these movements were those of Therkel Mathiassen, Erik Holtved, and Lauge Koch, all published in *MGr* at various dates since 1927. In general they place the Eskimo re-entry into Greenland some two centuries earlier, while Koch, *The East Greenland Ice*, p. 310, thinks 1350 too early a date for Eskimo encroachment on the fjords of the Eastern Settlement, perhaps by as much as a hundred years. The most recent information about these complicated problems will be found in the writings of Helge Larsen, J. Meldgaard, and Kaj Birket-Smith.

[2] It has not seemed worth while entering into any discussion of Svalbard, where it was, and what this particular 'Cold Edge' meant to the Icelanders who discovered it in 1194 and may have rediscovered it or some land adjacent in 1285. It is probable almost to the point of certainty that the Icelanders made expeditions to various parts of the east coast of Greenland, which lay so near to them, and Svalbard is probably to be placed in the region of Scoresby Sound. The remote and unprofitable Jan Mayen is an unlikely and Spitzbergen a next-to-impossible claimant to the name.

bear, ptarmigan and char, all were welcome in their season, but to the seal the Skræling was tied as with a birthcord. So what with the Norseman drawn north for good hunting and driftwood, and the Eskimo drawn south after seals, encounters between them were inevitable. How many of these left blood on the snow we cannot say, for both Norseman and Eskimo had much at stake, and must have known it. Yet the changing climate would ensure that the future lay with that people which could best come to terms with it. The Eskimo, made self-sufficient by the seal, warmly clothed against the cold, mobile without being nomadic, with his summer tent and winter house and flashing kayak, was admirably equipped for survival. The Norseman, conservatively European in his dress to the end of the settlement, dependent upon iron, wedded to his flocks and herds and his wasting pastures, could not survive his *fimbulvetr*, that long and awful unremitting winter whose present onset, had he but known it, heralded the ending of his world.

It must have taken the white Greenlander some time to realize this. His natural reaction towards the short, dark, smelly, fur-enclosed bundles of humanity he encountered in the northern hunting grounds would be not unlike that displayed towards the Skrælings of Vinland by the Greenland explorers of America. He would judge himself their superior, treat them as 'natives', and seek to exploit them. It would seem natural for him to covet their agreeable little women, but so far no trace has been found of a mingling of Norse and Eskimo stock anywhere or at any time during the settlement. Emphatically he would start by thinking himself top dog here as in so many other lands. But (to continue the metaphor) he was the wrong breed of dog for the country, and when the cold came to pinch him he must learn new tricks, cross-breed for a heavier coat, or die out.

The Western Settlement was at an end by 1342. Evidence as to how this came about is scanty and debatable. Under that year the Annals of Bishop Gísli Oddsson state that 'The inhabitants of Greenland of their own will abandoned the true faith and the Christian religion, having already forsaken all good ways and true virtues, and joined themselves with the people of America (*ad Americæ populos se converterunt*). Some consider too that Greenland lies closely adjacent to the western regions of the world. From this it came about that the Christians gave up their voyaging

to Greenland.'[1] To the Bishop the 'people of America' were almost certainly the Eskimo, just such Skrælings as the Greenlanders
had long before encountered in Markland and Vinland; and his
statement must be interpreted as meaning that by 1342 the Norse
Greenlanders were by some considered to have gone native in
custom and religion. Presumably it was to examine the nature and
extent of this apostasy that a year earlier, in 1341, Bishop Hakon
of Bergen had dispatched the priest Ivar Bardarson on his celebrated expedition. It is a pity that Ivar's account of his subsequent
visit to the Western Settlement is preserved in late manuscripts, at
second or third hand, and in translation, and is couched in terms
which have lent themselves to unending debate.

Item from the Eastern Settlement to the Western is twelve sea-
leagues and all uninhabited. Up there in the Western Settlement stands
a big church which is called Stensnes [=Sandnes] Church. This church
was for a while a cathedral and the see of a bishop [*sic*]. At present the
Skrælings hold the entire Western Settlement. There are indeed horses,
goats, cattle, and sheep, but all wild, and no people, either Christian or
heathen.
Item all this that is recorded above was told us by Iffuer bort [Ivar
Bardarson], a Greenlander who for many years was steward of the
bishop's household at Gardar in Greenland: how he had seen all this,
and was one of those who were chosen by the Laugmader [*lögmaðr*,
lawman, chief officer] to go to the Western Settlement against the
Skrælings, in order to expel them from the Settlement. But when they
arrived there they found never a man, either Christian or heathen,
merely some wild cattle and sheep. They made use of these cattle and
sheep for provisions, as much as the ships could carry, and with this
sailed back, and the aforesaid Iffuer was of their party.[2]

These seeming-simple sentences have been interpreted in
various ways: as meaning that the Western Settlement had been
forcibly exterminated by Skrælings; that the white population,
man, woman and child, had gone off fishing or hunting, with the
grisly consequence that their would-be rescuers from Eystribyggd
by carrying off their stock ensured their death by starvation the

---

[1] *Annalium Farrago*, Islandica X, p. 2. The Annals were written in Latin *c.* 1637.
It is assumed that they were based on documents lost in the fire which destroyed the
Cathedral at Skalholt in 1630. The 'parallel' lines in Lyskander's *Grönlandske Chronica*
of 1608 are a somewhat dubious confirmation of this annal.
[2] *Det gamle Grønlands beskrivelse*, p. 8 and p. 29.

following winter; that the whites had become so blended with the Eskimo as to have abandoned animal husbandry and a fixed settlement; that the whites either by themselves or in company with the Eskimo had migrated to Baffin Island or Labrador, so giving a literal meaning to Bishop Gísli Oddsson's words, *ad Americæ populos se converterunt;*[1] that Ivar Bardarson was a coward, a liar, or an ass, who took one perfunctory glance at one western fjord, or even one homestead, then sped home 'by sail and oar' to the safety of Eystribyggd, where with the connivance of the entire expedition he maintained for over twenty years his easily disprovable story.

Some of its details are troublesome enough. If Sandnes Church was ever the see of a bishop this is as much as we hear of it: it appears a most unlikely circumstance. The presence of domestic animals in a settlement devoid of human beings has been held inexplicable: yet it is probable that they could survive for a year or two without human aid. But if we allow for garbling and inaccuracy in the existing unsatisfactory versions of Ivar's report we are left with a conclusion which there is nothing to disprove and a good deal to support: that by the time of his visit the Western Settlement was extinct. For we know that the pastures of the Western Settlement had been affected before this time by an invasion of the pest *Agrotis occulta*, and so reduced in quality and extent as to make animal husbandry much more difficult. Again, in the early fourteenth century Greenland trade was seriously injured by the development of the trade in furs and hides out of Russia, the growth of the English and Dutch cloth trade as against Greenland woollens, and the preference of French workshops for

---

[1] This view has been developed forcibly by Vilhjálmur Stefánsson in many of his writings and by Helge Ingstad, *Landet under Polarstjernen*, pp. 356–61, and has received the cautious approval of C. Gini, 'On the Extinction of the Norse Settlements in Greenland', The Institute of Economics, Bergen, Paper 10, 1958. Gini stresses the marked disequilibrium of the sexes in Vestribyggd graves, argues from that a similar disequilibrium in life, and puts forward the curious and untenable suggestion that it was mainly on the initiative of the Norse women that the whites went over to the Skrælings. This too is perhaps the place to mention the extensive collections of material and sometimes reckless speculations on the Norse Atlantic settlements of Jón Dúason, *Landkönnun og Landnám Íslendinga í Vesturheim*, Reykjavík, 1941–48. The migration theory has its merits and disposes of various harassing difficulties; unfortunately it creates others, and the evidence for it is both thin and strongly debatable. The natural place of refuge for the hard-pressed Norsemen of the Western Settlement was with their fellow countrymen and kinsmen back in Eystribyggd. See Jørgen Meldgaard, 'Om de gamle Nordboer og deres Skæbne (Betragtinger over Helge Ingstads bog *Landet under Polarstjernen*)', in *Tidsskriftet Grønland*, 1961, pp. 93–102.

ivory from Africa or Asia over the inferior walrus tusk. The
Western Settlement was no longer a viable economy. And as the
climate grew colder its effects were more serious up there than in
Eystribyggd. The colony must have been considerably weakened
for decades before its end, and the arrival of the Skrælings was
decisive. First the outlying farms were abandoned; the colony
drew in upon itself; small groups would depart for Eystribyggd
laden not only with their worldly goods but with grim news of
the relentlessly advancing little men who were making life impossible for the people of the northern hunting grounds first, and
then for the cruelly tried homesteaders from Lodinsfjord to
Lysufjord. Some of this news, not always understood and often
darkly embroidered, would filter back to Iceland, Norway, and
remoter Europe, and convince its hearers that something very
queer and unpleasant was taking place out in Greenland, that
the Norsemen were 'going over to' the Eskimo and abandoning
the Christian faith, and that something must be done about it. But
by the time Ivar Bardarson arrived in Greenland one of two things
had happened: either the last survivors of the Western Settlement
had drawn back south to safety, or they had been overrun and
exterminated by the Skrælings. In either case, 'At present the
Skrælings hold the entire Western Settlement,' and Ivar's expedition did little more than confirm the fact. The distinctive culture
of Scandinavia disappeared everywhere beyond latitude 62° N.
After *c.* 1350 the record of the Norse colonies is confined to
Eystribyggd.

The historical and archaeological record shows that the Eastern
Settlement fought for its life tenaciously. Most of the Norse
population lived there, and there too was most of the good land.
Yet the loss of the Western Settlement was an irreparable afflic-
tion. For one thing it involved the loss of the Nordseta, the best
hunting grounds of Greenland, which lay beyond it; and though
the trade demand for Nordseta products was falling off this was a
sharp diminution of the colonists' resources. Still worse would be
the feeling that a similar fate threatened them too. Certainly the
Eskimo were reacting strongly to the white man's presence in the
south, and under the year 1379 we read in the Icelandic Annals
(*Gottskálksannáll*) that 'The Skrælings attacked the Greenlanders,
killed eighteen of them, and carried off two boys, whom they

made slaves.'[1] Yet strangely enough, there was no compelling reason for head-on clashes between the south-moving Eskimo and the stationary Norsemen. The middens of the Eastern Settlement show that the Norsemen relied greatly on the seal for meat, but they were primarily farmers and their homes lay far back in the fjords, for the compelling reason that there was the best grazing. Eirik's splendid and extensive farm at Brattahlid, with its heavy concentration of neighbours, lay sixty miles from the outer limits of the skærgaard; the strong settlement in Einarsfjord and the numerous farms of the Vatnahverfi some forty to fifty. But these inner extremities of the fjords were of little interest to the Eskimo; they froze comparatively late in the year, and their ice was rarely safe. They were thus less attractive to hunters than the headlands, islands, and sea-ice outside where seals and other marine animals were more abundant. Encounters between the two peoples could not be entirely avoided (contemporary pieces of Eskimo sculpture and carving show with what curiosity the Skrælings observed their huge white neighbours, and some of their folk-tales collected by Rink record other than peaceful meetings); but so long as the Norsemen decided to keep to themselves, the two races had elbow room enough and need not prove deadly to each other's way of life. In theory, that is, for who can doubt the stress and dismay under which the Eastern Settlement laboured, with the Western Settlement gone, its own northern spur around Ivigtut (the 'Middle Settlement') subsequently abandoned, and the Skrælings in kayaks and umiaks plying the fjord-mouths down to Herjolfsnes.

Nor did they fear for their physical survival only. The Eastern Settlement was now the sole custodian of the Christian faith in the further reaches of the West Atlantic. Helluland, Markland, Vinland, still languished under their blight of heathendom; and

[1] We do not know where this clash took place. Somewhere on the edge of the Eastern Settlement, as is commonly assumed, or were the victims a hunting party still trying their luck in the Nordseta? The reference to slavery is unreal in an Eskimo context, but perhaps the Norsemen were not to know this. Direct evidence of strife between Norsemen and Eskimo is slight, whether literary (as here) or archaeological. The burned farm at Nipaitsoq in the Ameragdla Fjord (Western Settlement), sometimes thought to provide such evidence, does not necessarily do so, for the antler arrow-heads found in the ashes there have not as yet been firmly identified as Eskimo types. For the most relevant of the Eskimo folk-tales collected by Rink, 'Ungortok the Chief of Kakortok', see Appendix III, where it is reproduced. It is a safe assumption that the Eskimo of the Middle Ages, whether in Labrador or Greenland, were as warlike, or at least as prepared to fight, as any of the peoples they came into contact with.

now at home men of Norse stock, Christian for three and a half
centuries, were under suspicion of having abandoned themselves
to the pains of hell-fire. Shafts of uncertain light pierce the
descending darkness. In 1355 king Magnus Smek commands Poul
Knudsson to sail his ship to Greenland (there is no evidence that
Poul did so): 'We do this for the glory of God and our soul's
salvation, and for those forefathers of ours who brought Christianity to Greenland and have upheld it to this present time, and
which we will not let perish in our day.'[1] In 1407 Church and Law
joined hands to burn one Kolgrim at the stake for having carnal
knowledge of Steinunn, daughter of lawman Hrafn the Icelander,
by means of his black art (*með svartakonstur*).[2] The often-quoted
'papal' letter of 1448 from Nicholas V to the self-appointing pair
of Iceland bishops, Marcellus and Mathæus, looks like a forgery,
but the pleas of the impudent are notoriously drafted for the
maximum of appeal and effect, and the letter speaks with sad and
anxious heart of the doleful situation of the Greenland Christians.[3]
Clearly the fifteenth century was not lacking in pious prayers and
heartfelt ejaculations for Greenland: what will be found wanting
is any readiness to back these with action. The record of the
Church in all this was deplorable. After the death of Bishop Alf in
1377 no bishop set foot in Greenland.

Even before 1261 a European and Christian way of life in the
Greenland colonies depended on the maintenance of pasture and
the balance of trade. As to the first, there was a native improvi-
dence in both Iceland and Greenland.[4] As to the second, this
meant trade with Norway. The precise terms of the treaty between
the two countries (if Greenland ever was a sovereign state: the
Hague Court in 1933 went no further than to describe its medieval

[1] GHM, III, 122. Nørlund, *Viking Settlers in Greenland*, 1936, p. 134.

[2] *Nýji Annáll*, sub. 1407. There appears to have been something other than morals
or theology behind this brutal, and in Iceland and Greenland rare, punishment. So
Jón Jóhannesson, 'Í Grænlandshrakningum', in *Íslendinga Saga*, II, 246-7. The
unhappy Steinunn went out of her mind and died soon after the burning.

[3] *The Flatey Book and Recently Discovered Vatican Manuscripts Concerning America as
early as the Tenth Century*, Norroena Society, 1906, pp. 167-9.

[4] In the summer of 1962 the remains of an extensive irrigation system were discovered at Brattahlid, designed to conduct lake water to pastures much nearer the
fjord—pastures which still tend to dry up after a warm summer. The dykes served
both the North and River Farms, and are probably of the fourteenth century. Similar
but lesser systems have been reported from the Western Settlement, and there is a
very long man-made channel serving one of the farms in Sermilik-Isafjord. Further
discoveries of a similar or related kind would invite a reconsideration of the efficiency
of farming methods in Greenland.

9. DORSET ESKIMO

10. KAVDLUNAK (NORSE GREENLANDER)

status as 'independent') have not been preserved, but we may assume that the compensating benefit expected by the Green-landers for the surrender of their independence in 1261 was a guarantee of regular communications with the adoptive parent country. The Norway-Iceland agreement of 1262 stipulated that six ships should sail from Norway to Iceland during each of the next two years, whereupon the situation should be fairly reviewed. In the long run, as we know, the Icelanders were much deceived. And so was Greenland. At the end of the century the Crown made the Greenland trade the monopoly of the Norwegian merchants of Bergen. We can trace the consequences for Iceland with fair exactitude: in the years 1326, 1350, 1355, 1374, and 1390 no ship reached Iceland from Norway, and in 1324, 1333, 1357, 1362, 1367, and 1392 one ship only. The consequences for Greenland would be even more severe, as trading developments in Norway erased so remote, perilous, and unprofitable a route from the merchant's portolan. Bergen had become glutted with cheaper furs and hides and walrus tusks raked from nearer hunting grounds; Martin IV in Rome and the Archbishop of Nidaros wag sad heads at each other over the resultant devaluation of the Greenland tithe, payable in such commodities. Oh, for gold and silver for one more Crusade! And this as early as 1282, before the bottom fell out of the market. Besides, Norway was distraught with political and economic troubles of her own. After 1261 too her maritime glory was fast passing away. The viking ship, so victory-fraught, so beautiful, was being run out of business by the commodious and economic German cog, and Norwegian designers and shipwrights were failing completely to meet their challenge. Concurrently the kingdom's strength was sapped; foreign-born or incompetent rulers sacrificed her interests to their own; and in 1349 the Black Death, ship-borne from England, slew one in three of her population, then crossed the seas to ravage the Hebrides, Orkney and Shetland, and the helpless Faeroes. At home Bergen was particularly hard hit. Savaged now by pestilence, the town would be sacked and burned in 1393 by the Victual Brethren, and in 1428–29 by Bartolomæus Voet, while the Bryggen three times suffered almost total destruction in the fires of 1322, 1413, and 1476. Worst of all was the rising power of the Hansa merchants of Germany, whose growth during the thirteenth and fourteenth centuries was sensational. They were a

6

harsh problem for Bergen well before 1300; in 1343 they established their kontor there, and as the century progressed secured a stranglehold on its carrying trade—and by 1400 on that of all Norway. Strangely enough, they appear never to have dispatched a ship to Greenland, and to have left Iceland to her own resources till the English started fishing the banks in 1408–09. Probably they felt no urge to exert themselves; till that date all exports from both countries fell into their hands at Bergen. Possibly in the case of Greenland the Crown-implemented monopoly was still

6. DE NAUFRAGIIS GRUNTLANDIÆ
Wreckage and driftwood off the Greenland coast (Olaus Magnus).

respected. In the light of Icelandic experience we can assume that after 1382 the Crown levied a tax of one-twentieth on all business done with Greenland too, that this sackgeld (*sekkjagjald*) was payable in advance, and that without the royal consent no one might sail there to buy or sell. The Crown had its commissioner in Greenland to enforce these regulations. And we know that the royal prerogative was so strongly enforced that a hapless mariner storm-driven to Greenland's western shore incurred the royal wrath by the mere process of supplying his necessities. Such blinkered cupidity brought profit to no one and cruelly harassed the contracting colony. The indifference of Danish or half-German monarchs to their more distant dependencies after the Union of Kalmar in 1397 could be expected.

Evidence for communication between Greenland and the outside world after the middle of the fourteenth century may be summarized thus. For the first few decades one ship, safeguarded by royal monopoly, made the Greenland run at frequent intervals, though apparently not every year. This was the *Grœnlands knörr*, the Greenland carrier; but she seems not to have been replaced after her loss in 1367 or '69. Thereafter communications were scanty. What records we have of visits to Greenland relate to a strange assortment of men: Bjorn Einarsson Jorsalafari or Jerusalem-farer was cast away there in 1385 for two years; a party of Icelanders was driven off course to arrive there in 1406 and remain for four years; a somewhat shadowy pair, Pining and Pothorst, made a shadowy voyage to Greenland and perhaps more widely about the western ocean, and even to Labrador, soon after 1470, thereby adding fresh shades of fantasy to Renaissance cartography and as much cloud as daylight to sixteenth-century adumbrations of the remoter North.[1] In addition we may conclude that an occasional ship was storm-driven to Greenland of whose

[1] Didrik Pining must have been a remarkable man, a Norwegian admiral in the Danish navy under Christian I and king Hans, a 'matchless freebooter' against the English and the Hansa, and sea-raider upon the Spanish, Portuguese, and Dutch. He was also governor of Iceland for a while, and later of Vardöhus, though it is not easy to distinguish parts of his career from that of his young kinsman of the same name. According to *Purchas his Pilgrimes*: 'Item, Punnus and Potharse, have inhabited Island certayne yeeres, and sometimes have gone to Sea, and have had their trade in Groneland.' (Glasgow edtn. 1906, xiii, p. 168). New light, though in part but darkness visible, was shed upon their activities by Bobé's discovery in 1909 at Copenhagen of a letter dated 3 March 1551 from Carsten Grip, Burgomaster of Kiel, to king Christian III (part of which has been quoted above, p. 59): 'The two admirals (*sceppere*) Pyningk and Poidthorsth, who were sent out by your majesty's royal grandfather, king Christian the First, at the request of his majesty of Portugal, with certain ships to explore new countries and islands in the north, have raised on the rock Wydthszerck [Hvitserk], lying off Greenland and towards Sniefeldsiekel [Snæfellsjokul] in Iceland on the sea, a great sea-mark [a recognizable cairn] on account of the Greenland pirates, who with many small ships without keels fall in large numbers upon other ships.'

Four comments: (i) Pining and Pothorst appear to have met with Eskimo, not Norse Greenlanders, and provoked them to a scuffle. This suggests that they did not reach the west coast. (ii) Probably the obscure John Scolvus was with them as pilot, and another of their company may well have been João Vaz Cortereal, both on fame's bede-roll worthy to be filed. (iii) By transposing Hvitserk to the open sea our *piratæ* continued a process which would end by cluttering the Atlantic with Hvitramannaland, Friesland, Estland, *et. al.* (iv) It is sad to learn that Pining and Pothorst, by land or water, tempest, rope, or the knife of a smiler, came after all to a bad end (Nansen, *In Northern Mists*, 1911, II, p. 129).

fate we hear nothing, and that resolute and high-handed English skippers in the fifteenth century sailed into Greenland waters for fish and sea-beasts, for honest trade where it offered, and for plunder where it lay to hand.[1] Of Bjorn Jorsalafari we hear specifically that it was the polar ice which prevented his getting away; and probably it was for the same reason that the visitors of 1406 had to spend four years in Eystribyggd. During their stay they witnessed two Christian ceremonies, the burning of Kolgrim, to which we have already referred, and a wedding in the church at Hvalseyjarfjord, at which Síra Eindridi Andresson, then acting as officialis pending the appointment of a new bishop of Greenland, and Síra Pal Hallvardsson officiated. This last was no maimed ceremony, but was marked by the calling of the banns on the three preceding Sundays, and the nuptial mass was read at the altar. Everything was done in form and with its proper dignity, and neither then nor at any other point of this astonishingly well-documented sojourn do we hear anything to imply a weakening of the Christian faith in the settlement. The circumstance is important, for when these Icelanders got safely away in the late summer of 1410, waved hands and called their last farewells, silence and the dark enfold the Greenland Settlements, and the last act of the

---

[1] There was a swarming of English ships in Icelandic waters in the fifteenth century, a hundred a year come from Bristol and other ports 'unto the costes colde'. Their skippers and crews were hard men plying a hard trade in a hard age; they included among their number adventurers and (some) rascals, and abduction, robbery, ill-treatment, and murder were among the islanders' occasional hazards. If anything, matters grew worse when the Scots and Germans came seeking their cut of northern profit. That a number of Icelanders, including children, found their way to England is certain, but whether they were purchased, stolen away, or simply transported, is not always clear. But taking the worst view of the English-Icelandic venture, we should not accept such partisan charges as Hannes Palsson's in 1425 or forget that the English were frequently blamed for the wrongdoing of others. Also, English trade with Iceland was indispensable to the Icelanders and helped them through a very bad time. For a general review see E. M. Carus-Wilson, 'The Iceland Venture', in *Medieval Merchant Venturers*, 1954, pp. 98–142, and Björn Thorsteinsson, 'Henry VII and Iceland', in *Saga-Book*, XV (1957–59), pp. 67–101. As for Greenland, direct evidence for English piracy is slight, but clauses in successive treaties between Denmark and England allow us to assume trespass in Greenland waters. For Bristol ventures north and north-west see J. A. Williamson, *The Cabot Voyages and Bristol Discovery under Henry VII*, Hakluyt Society, Second Series, No. CXXX, 1962, and with respect to Greenland, pp. 13–14 and 18. There is the papal letter of 1448 already referred to (see p. 66, above), which suffers from the double disability that it is probably a forgery and that its exhortatory style hides rather than reveals the identity of the barbarians who 'gathering together in a fleet on the neighbouring shores of the Pagans, attacked the entire people in a cruel invasion', and carried off the natives of both sexes into slavery. There is also the testimony of Niels Egede's *Beskrivelse over Grønland* (ed. H. Ostermann, *MGr.* 120, 1939, p. 268) but this is of the late eighteenth century, which is late indeed.

tragedy at Eystribyggd was to be played out without a spectator from the outside world.

Eighty years later the long memory of the Roman Church stirred with regard to Greenland. No action followed stronger than a letter from Pope Alexander VI favouring the proposal of Matthias bishop-elect of Gardar to sail to Greenland in person and lead the souls of the strayed and the apostate to the path of eternal salvation.

Since, as we have been informed, the church at Gardar is situated at the world's end in the country of Greenland, where the inhabitants for lack of bread, wine, and oil, are accustomed to feed on dried fish and milk, by reason of which and because of the very infrequent sailings which were wont to be made to the aforesaid country due to the severe freezing of the seas, no ship is believed to have put into land there for eighty years, or if such sailings happen to have been made they could not have been made, it is considered, save in the month of August when the ice had melted; and whereas it is likewise reported that for eighty years or thereabouts no bishop or priest whatsoever has in personal residence been in charge of that church; because of which and because too of the absence of orthodox priests it has come about that a great many of that diocese who were formerly believers have, alas, renounced their sacred baptismal vows; and in as much as the inhabitants of that country have no relic of the Christian faith save for a certain corporal [the small square linen cloth on which the chalice and the host are placed during Mass] which is displayed once a year, upon which a hundred years earlier the Body of Christ was consecrated by the priest last in residence there:—for these, then, and other considerations. . . .[1]

This is a grim picture, not correct in all its details (as to diet, it is certain that the settlers ate more meat than dried fish), and in its account of the spiritual life of Eystribyggd contradictory of the evidence of the Icelanders who sailed from there in 1410, and to whose eighty-year-old voyage it seems specifically to refer. One suspects that the letter is not based on fresh intelligence, but on oppressive rumour and garbled recollection, in which the black art of Kolgrim hung like a cloud over the bright ceremony in Hvalseyjarfjord church. After all, the cry of apostasy in Greenland had by now been sounded for a century and a half. And the

[1] The letter was printed in *Norsk Historisk Tidsskrift*, 1892, p. 407, and with an English translation (not used here) in *The Flatey Book and Recently Discovered Vatican Manuscripts Concerning America as Early as the Tenth Century*, Norroena Society, 1906, pp. 175–6 ff.

increase in polar ice off Greenland was a fact known to every
mariner who sailed the northern seas, and to every merchant
prince from the Tyskebryggen of Bergen to Canynges' wharves
in Bristol, and from Bristol to the counters of the Portingales.

Yet some sailing after 1410 there must have been, at least to
Herjolfsnes in the south of the Eastern Settlement, and for the in-
coming traveller his first port of call. Here for long centuries the
sea has been fingering the bones and coffin shards of the old
Norse burial ground on the point, pawing them into the light of
day, then scrabbling them off to their fresh oblivion. And here
in 1921 Poul Nørlund found dead Greenlanders buried in exactly
such costumes as were current in continental Europe throughout
the fourteenth century, and even a few examples of the latest
fashions of the second half of the fifteenth.[1] But to erect on this
a theory of regular visits and trade is to force the evidence. One
ship and a single voyage, planned or involuntary, could account
for it all. Though this, no doubt, is to force the evidence in the
opposite direction, and the truth will lie in between.

The wave-eroded graveyard of Herjolfsnes yielded not only
these shrouding garments to the raised eyebrows of Denmark's
archaeologists, but the skeletons inside them too, some of which
have been made to tell a story, and a gruesome one, of malnutri-
tion, deformity, disease, and early death. These descendants of the

[1] Most of the garments from Herjolfsnes, including the liripipe hoods, says
Nørlund, 'may without hesitation be placed in the latter half of the fourteenth
century and the period round about 1400' (*Viking Settlers*, p. 126). These present no
problem, in view of the recorded sailings of the Greenland knörr till 1367–69 and
the Annal entries concerning ships driven to Greenland in 1381, 1382, 1385, and
1406. The pieces from the second half of the fifteenth century are less numerous than
some commentators assume. Nørlund speaks of three children's caps. 'Two caps are
very simple, round with a flat crown, the sides fairly high. Any period might have
designed them, but we recognize them as a head covering that was very popular in
the fifteenth century, whereas caps from earlier times are different, mostly rounded or
conical in the crown. Now if any doubt should be entertained that these small caps
can be given a fairly exact dating, there remains one about which there cannot be
much discussion. It is 25 to 30 cm high, rather conical, standing steeply up from the
forehead but widening out at the back of the neck. It is one of the high caps shown
us on the paintings of Dirk Bout, Memling and other Flemish painters, worn in the
time of Louis XI and Charles the Bold, in the latter half of the fifteenth century. This
makes our cap a very important document in Greenland's medieval history, testimony that as late as towards the sixteenth century there must have been ships going
to Greenland from Europe. It is not a solitary witness either. There are fragments of
dresses with quite close folds sewn at the waist, one of them also with a V-shaped
neck opening, and these two are fashion details belonging to the later part of the
fifteenth century' (p. 125). 'Among the other objects found during the excavations
are some which presumably are imported fifteenth-century wares, a knife from the
episcopal kitchen, a fragment of a Rhenish stone jug, which lay at the foundation of
the banqueting hall at Herjolfsnes' (p. 126).

tall, strong, vigorous, and fertile Norse stock appeared to be short of stature and puny of build, victims of a crippling physiological morbidity, small of cranium, and the two most handsomely attired women of curved spine and constricted pelvis. Neither, we are told, could have brought a living child into the nightmare world in which they dragged out their own brief, maimed, painful existence. In the incongruously fashionable gowns which are also their cereclothes they seemed the pathetic symbols of a decayed culture and a doomed race.

But they died Christians and received Christian burial. True, the Herjolfsnes dead speak only for themselves, but theirs was an entirely uncontaminated Norse enclave in an Eskimo sub-continent. There is still not the slightest trace of assimilation to the Eskimo in any of the graves—those tell-tale graves which grew progressively shallower as more of the ground became permanently frozen. And there is a second respect in which they speak only for themselves, for the other skeletons of Eystribyggd and those of Vestribyggd are eloquent against them. These are the bones of normal men and women, well-nourished, bothered a good deal by rheumatism (who in the medieval world was not?), but untouched by chronic disease, and free of morbidity. These remains are admittedly earlier than those at Herjolfsnes, but it has of late become very much open to question whether we should accept too harrowing an interpretation of these last either. The Herjolfsnes skeletons are few in number and in an extremely poor state of preservation. Hansen's deductions after the excavations of 1921 have come under heavy fire at home and in Norway. What were regarded as small skulls compare closely with viking age skulls of Sogn and Jaeren, from which so many of the colonists' forebears came, and with Irish skulls; and whether the people were as short and shrunken as Hansen calculated is open to doubt. Finally, the pelvic material on which such gloomy prognostication had been based for the survival of the race is too fragmentary for such far-reaching conclusions as Hansen drew from it.[1]

[1] The argument may be followed in Fr. C. C. Hansen, *Anthropologia medico-historica Grœnlandiæ antiquæ*, MGr. 67, 1924; K. Fischer-Möller, *Skeletons from Ancient Greenland Graves*, MGr. 119, 1938; *The mediæval Norse settlements in Greenland*, MGr. 89, 1942; K. Bröste and K. Fischer-Möller, *The mediæval Norsemen at Gardar*, MGr. 89, 1944; J. Balslev-Jørgensen, *The Eskimo Skeleton*, MGr. 146, 1953; Jón Steffensen, *Stature as a criterion of the nutritional level of Viking Age Icelanders*, Þriðji Víkingafundur, 1958; Helge Ingstad, *Landet under Polarstjernen*, pp. 339–44 (summary with an opinion on the evidence from Professor dr. med. Johan Torgersen and Prosektor dr. med. Bernhard Getz), 1960.

When and how the Eastern Settlement was extinguished we may never know. Most probably it was soon after the year 1500. There must have been a prolonged weakening of the colony in readiness for the final act. Possibly at Herjolfsnes, more probably at Unartoq, there is evidence of mass burial which points to the ravages of an epidemic, maybe the Black Death, though this is without confirmation from historical sources. As had happened at Vestribyggd, we must imagine the colony contracting under Eskimo pressure, outlying families falling back upon the main areas of habitation, and some (and these not necessarily the weaker spirits) seizing their opportunity to get away to Iceland and Norway. Others were carried off forcibly by rough-dealing marauders from Europe, among whom it is to be feared that the English held a bad pre-eminence; and it is reasonable to believe that their deep-felt isolation, in addition to these other troubles, bred a moral and mental debility which affected their will to survive. On the whole, the old theory of the Greenland colony dying out in increasing isolation from an indifferent world must still hold the field.[1]

The archaeological evidence is not without its bizarreries. In 1950 the Danes excavated the remains of a remarkably long long-house in Vatnahverfi, consisting of a byre and the house proper, of six or seven rooms. It had a kitchen and a pantry, and in the pantry floor, which had been dug down a little to receive them, were the remains of three wooden barrels. These had been used to store milk, probably in the form of skýr. In one of the barrels were the tiny bones of almost a hundred mice—remarkable, since till that moment no one knew that mice had existed in the Greenland settlements. They must have climbed in when the farm went derelict, eaten the last food they could find, failed to get out, and so perished. Nearby, in another big farm of the Vatnahverfi, were found fragments of two small crucifixes carved in steatite, various artefacts of iron, including knives, and in a passage-way some human bones, including the badly decomposed pieces of a skull. Anthropology tells us that its owner in life was white and a

[1] Ingstad suggests that the people of the Eastern Settlement went off to join their compatriots of Vestribyggd on the North American mainland, or that they transferred wholesale to England (p. 371). But there is no weighable evidence for either alternative. From Vestribyggd the natural asylum was Eystribyggd; from Eystribyggd it was Iceland and Norway. But whether in their few and poor ships they reached it, whether they perished on the way, or whether they ever made the attempt, these are things we do not know.

Norseman. It would seem then that he was the last inhabitant of
the farm, and therefore unburied. It is even possible that he was
the last man left alive in the settlement.[1]

What trust we should place in the story of Jon Greenlander,
who claimed to have sailed into a deep fjord near Cape Farewell
somewhere about 1540, is hard to determine. He had been blown
off course when sailing from Hamburg to Iceland. On both mainland and islands they saw houses; and on one island there were
many sheds and booths and stone houses for drying fish. Here too
they discovered 'a dead man lying face downwards on the ground.
On his head he wore a well-made hood, and in addition clothes

7. GREENLAND ESKIMO

both of frieze and of sealskin. Near him was a sheath-knife, bent
and much worn and wasted away. This knife they took with them
as a keepsake'.[2] *Se non è vero, è ben trovato.* Whether in this wretched
place or another the last Norseman in Greenland lay dead, and
the Iron Age was all wasted away.

When in 1586 the Englishman John Davis escaped from the
loathsome desolation of Greenland's south-eastern coast and
beheld with relief the 'plain champaign country, with earth and

[1] C. L. Vebæk, 'Topographical and Archaeological Investigations in the Norse
Settlements in Greenland', pp. 116–19 (in *Þriðji Víkingafundur*).
[2] GHM, III, 513–14. Jon was called Greenlander because he had been blown off
course thither no less than three times.

grass' within the fjords of the west, he found no white men nor traces of them, 'nor saw anything, save only gripes, ravens, and small birds, as larks and linnets'. These were the fjords of the ancient Western Settlement, but it was the same in the Eastern Settlement too. Land and water and all they contained belonged to the cheerful, enduring Eskimo. The Norse story of Greenland was ended.

3

Vinland the Good

VENTURE AND WITHDRAWAL

ABOUT the Norse discovery of Iceland and Greenland, we have seen, blew the winds of accident and chance, which were the winds of destiny too. In the late summer of 986, a month or so after Eirik the Red stood out past Snæfellsnes with his Greenland-bound armada of twenty-five ships, they would blow again, triumphantly, to fill the sails of a young Icelander named Bjarni Herjolfsson, and after three days' sailing drive him south to an unknown fogbound region of ocean. It was some days before the fog lifted and he was able to determine the quarters of the heavens. One day's sailing more and his eyes beheld the shores and forests of the New World. In his own lifetime this young man was to win the reproaches of the Norwegians for not going ashore and spying out the land; and during ours he has taken rough handling from scholars disgruntled at his presumption in sighting America before Leif the Lucky. It is therefore worth recalling to mind the purpose of his epoch-making journey and the qualities of seaman-ship which brought it against all probability to its fortunate ending. Bjarni had spent the winter of 985–86 in Norway. In the summer he sailed to Iceland with a full cargo, intending to spend the winter with his father. But when he reached Eyrar (i.e., Eyrarbakki), near the mouth of Olfus river, it was to hear the startling news that Herjolf had sold his estates and departed for Greenland. We discern a certain stubbornness in Bjarni: he had set out for home, and home he meant to go. So with the consent of his crew he set off on what they all knew would be a risky journey, pilotless, chartless, compassless, for the south-western fjords of Greenland. Three days out, and the mountains and glaciers of Iceland whelmed under the horizon, they fell a prey to north winds and then to fog, and for many days had no notion which way they were going. Then the sun broke through, they took fresh bearings, hoisted sail, and journeyed for a whole day before sighting a land which was not mountainous, but well forested, with low hills. His crew, metaphorically speaking, were still all at sea, but Bjarni, if he did not know where he was, at least knew where he was not. This could not be Greenland—and it was for Greenland he was headed. Too single-minded, perhaps too prudent, to go ashore, he held north along the coast for two days' sailing. The land here, they saw, was still well-forested but flat. Again he refused to put in, and sailed with a south-west wind for three more days till they came to a land which was high, mountainous and glaciered. A land in Bjarni's opinion good for nothing. So yet again he turned his prow from the land, and after four days' sailing before a strong wind he reached Herjolfsnes in Greenland. Without imperilling his ship and crew he had done exactly what he set out to do, and *Grœnlendinga Saga* has preserved what to all intents and purposes is his log-book—the plain record of a practical man.[1]

Tenth- and twentieth-century criticism of Bjarni amounts to little more than that he was not another Gardar, Ottar or Eirik the Red. He was a trader and later a farmer, not an explorer. But the entire pattern of life and thought in the viking North made it certain that his discovery would not be forgotten or neglected by people as endlessly daring as they were incurably land-hungry. It was not even necessary to put to sea to know that Bjarni spoke truth about new lands to the west. Medieval geography favoured the notion of more land to be found beyond Greenland, and, more practically, when men climbed the high mountains behind the settlement areas of Greenland (as the *King's Mirror* informs us they did) they would see far in the distance either land itself or the cloud formations they associated with land. At the narrowest point of Davis Strait just two hundred miles separate Cumberland Peninsula from Greenland. It is unthinkable that during the great age of Norse exploration men would not have undertaken so short and challenging a passage.

In the light of the record speculation is unnecessary. There was considerable discussion of Bjarni's voyage down in the Eastern

[1] The problem of his four-day journey from Helluland to Herjolfsnes is touched on later, pp. 88–9.

Settlement, and the sons of Eirik the Red were quick to act upon it. There was a suggestion that Eirik himself should undertake a new voyage of glory into the west, but this was not in his destiny; he fell off his horse on his way to the ship, and various broken bones kept him at home. The ship was Bjarni's, purchased from him by Eirik's son Leif, a tremendous sailor, and the first skipper to make direct voyages between Greenland, Scotland, Norway, and back again. He would certainly get every scrap of information he could from Bjarni, and it is reasonable to assume that he enlisted some of his crew. He sought to follow Bjarni's course in reverse, and did so with precision. First they reached the land which Bjarni had reached last, mountainous and glaciered, grassless and barren. One look ashore was enough. Bjarni had been right: there was nothing here to tempt a husbandman, and having named it Helluland, Flatstone Land, they sailed on their way to the south.

When next they stood in to the land and put out their ship's boat they were in the flat and forested country where Bjarni's crew had vainly hoped to go ashore for wood and water. We learn rather more about it on this second visit. There were extensive white sands there, and the coast itself was level and cliffless. Here too Leif bestowed a name in accordance with the land's main feature: Markland, Wood or Forest Land. But he was still anxious to be on his way and probe these new lands further. After two days' sailing with a north-east wind they came to an island lying north of what appeared to be a mainland with a cape projecting northwards from it. This was that region of the New World which Leif was to name Vinland, the Promontorium Winlandiæ of the maps which would be prepared by Sigurður Stefánsson about 1590 and Hans Poulson Resen in 1605.[1] Leif wintered in Vinland, and his booths and big house at Leifsbudir mark the first area of European habitation of the American continent. The following spring they made ready to sail away, had a good wind, and came to Greenland safe and sound.

[1] Sigurður's map survives only in a copy made by Thórður Thorláksson in 1670 (Ny kgl. Saml. 2881 4to, f. 10 v., in the Royal Library, Copenhagen). The map is there wrongly dated 1570, roughly the date of Sigurður's birth. Whether Resen's map was based on Sigurður's, or whether both were copied from a common original, has been much debated. When allowance is made for the fact that Sigurður's lines of latitude are consistently rated too high over the whole western Atlantic (note the correspondence of northern Newfoundland and southern Ireland), both maps indicate northern Newfoundland with exactitude as the Promontorium Winlandiæ.

Characterum in hac mappa occurrentium explicatio ipsius Auctoris.

A *Hi sunt ad quos Angli per venerunt, ab ariditate nomen habent, tangram, vel solis vel frigoris adustione torridi et exsiccati*

B *His proxime est Vinlandia quam propter terrae facundi tatem et utilium rerum ubi rem proventum, Bonam dixere. Hanc a meridie oceanum finire voluere nostri, sed ego ex recentiorum historiis colligo, aut freto aut sinum hanc ab America distinguere.*

C *Regionem Gigantum vocant quod ibi Gigantes cornuti sint quos Skrickfinna dixere.*

D *Orientaliores sunt, quos klofina ab unguibus appella runt.*

E *Jotunheimar idem est ac regio Gigantum mon, strosorum, hic Regiam Geruthi et Gudmundi fuisse existimare licet.*

F *Sinum hic ingentem intelligimus in Russiam excurrentem.*

G *Regio petrosa, hujus in historia saepe fit mentio.*

H *Haec quae sit insula nescio nisi ea forte quam Venetus ille invenit Frislandiamq Germani vocant.*

Autor hujus tabellae Geographicae perhibetur esse Sigurdus Stephanius Islandus vir eruditus, Scholae Schalholtinae quondam Rector dignissimus, qui etiam alia nonnulla ingenii et eruditionis specimina edidit videlicet Descriptionem Islandiae quam apud Serenissi: Regia Maj: Antiquarium Thormodu Torfaeum vidisse me memini, nec non opusculum de Speleris, quod praeterita aestate ab amico quodam in Patria mecum comunicatum, penes me asservatur. Delineationem autem hanc suam, ex antiquitatibus Islandicis maxima ex parte desumptisse videtur. De Hellulandia Marelandia et Skrælingialandia, viden poterit Arngrimus Jonas, qui ad calcem opusculi de Gronlandia, Gronlandorum aliquot navigationes ad has terras annotavit, in terrarum etiam hyperborearum et ultra Gronlandiam delineatione, ubi Risaland et Jothunheima collocat, antiquitates quoq Islandicas secutum esse Autorem, sat scio, sed, an authentica illa sint dubito. Cum priore Gronlandiae mappa Dni Gulbrandi parum consentire hanc, constat. Islandia hic justo majorem habet latitudinem, Promontorium etiam Buriolfsnes, ingentis continentis potius quam Isthmus vel promontorii speciem praefert, ut catera omittam, quorum ca. curiositatis potius quam necessitatis ergo hanc mappam annotavi.

8. THE SKÁLHOLT MAP OF SIGURDUR STEFÁNSSON, 1590.

Back home in Greenland Leif's western voyage came in for the same close scrutiny as Bjarni's. He had done much, admittedly; yet there was a sense in which he merely whetted the curiosity of his fellow colonists. His brother Thorvald for one (we can almost hear his father speaking through him) wanted to know more, and so far as Leif was concerned he was welcome to learn the hard way and go to Vinland to know it. Which is what Thorvald did. By this time he was traversing a known route and reached Leifsbudir without incident, to spend a quiet winter there. In the spring he proceeded to act on his expressed notion that Vinland needed an altogether more extensive exploration. He sent his ship's boat to examine its western coast, and throughout the summer they explored a beautiful and well-wooded country without coming across any sign of human habitation other than a solitary wooden grain-holder. The following summer Thorvald took his ship first east and then north in the general direction of Markland. He gave the name Kjalarnes, Keelness, to a certain cape, repaired his ship there, and shortly afterwards headed into a beautiful, well-forested fjord. Here they encountered their first Skrælings, killed those they could lay their hands on, and in a retaliatory raid Thorvald was killed by an arrow which whipt into him from between gunwale and shield. His crew got back to Leifsbudir without more damage; they wintered there, and the following spring sailed away and reached Eiriksfjord with a freight of heavy but exciting news.

Thorvald's well-conducted though fatal expedition, with its considerable additions to Norse geographical knowledge, was to be followed by the abortive voyage of his brother Thorstein, who wanted to bring his body home to rest among his kinsmen, but who in fact spent a trying summer storm-tossed on the immense triangle of ocean between Iceland, Ireland, and Cape Farewell. This in its turn was followed by Thorfinn Karlsefni's attempt to establish a permanent colony in Vinland. It is time therefore to ask, and if possible establish, where this repository of so many Norse hopes and disappointments lay.

A useful approach to this complicated and long-debated problem is to view it in the general context of the Norse voyages westward across the North Atlantic. These show a steady progression through a belt of latitude whose extremities in Norway rest on Trondheim in the north and Jaeren or Lindesnes in the south. Within or in direct contact with this 360 miles wide stretch of ocean lie the Faeroes, Shetlands, Orkneys, and Hebrides, the first settlements in Iceland and Greenland, and the nearest regions of the North American continent. It is an area of strong winds, violent storms, and immense seas, and the sagas make frequent mention of ships driven south as far as Ireland. There is therefore a case for first seeking Helluland and Markland within latitudes 64° to 58° N, with a permissible extension south to latitude 52° when we hear of mariners driven off course by powerful northerly winds. Such mariners, that is, as Bjarni

Herjolfsson, who three days out from the south coast of Iceland was overtaken by north winds and fog and for many days was blown or drifted south. In Bjarni's case, fortunately, we have not only a general probability but various definite aids to identification of his three landfalls. The first was the south coast of Labrador, and the likeliest area for a close definition is that around Sandwich Bay, which conforms to his description of it. The second was not more than two hundred miles further north, still south of the late tenth-century forest-line, and hence south of present-day Nain. His third was the southern extremity of Baffin Island, in the general area of Resolution Island and Frobisher Bay. Leif's voyage in the reverse direction took him first to Baffin Island, then southwards to the afforested Markland, and thereafter by two days' sailing to the northern tip of Newfoundland. Here, if we accept the evidence of *Grænlendinga Saga*, in an area defined by Cape Bauld in the east, Pistolet Bay in the west, and the White Mountains in the south, lay the original Vinland.

For many scholars the 'if' has proved a big one, and Vinland has been sought and found at numerous points on the American continent between Hudson Bay and the state of Florida.[1] The difficulties are many: the literary evidence is often less than consistent and not rarely appears contradictory; the facts of geography, strung out as they are over thousands of miles of varied coastline, can all too easily be made to fit very different interpretations of this evidence; and every 'Norse' archaeological discovery made on the American continent (if for the moment we except those announced in 1961 and 1962, and as yet not fully displayed to the learned world) has failed to command a general confidence. The problem of Vinland is therefore like the *Arthurfrage*: it is easy

[1] To confine the illustration to Karlsefni's Straumfjord: this has been placed in Hudson Bay (Reman, *The Norse Discoveries and Explorations in America*, Berkeley and Los Angeles, 1949); Labrador (Fernald, 'The Plants of Wineland the Good', *Rhodora* XII, 1910); Labrador and Newfoundland (Straumfjord and Hop respectively: Hovgaard, *The Voyages of the Norsemen to America*, New York, 1914); the St. Lawrence Estuary (Steensby, *The Norsemen's Route from Greenland to Wineland*, *MGr.* 56, 1918); Baie de Chaleur (Hermannsson, *The Problem of Wineland*, Ithaca, New York, 1936); New Brunswick (Matthías Thórðarson, *The Vinland Voyages*, New York, 1930, and *Íslenzk Fornrit IV*, 1933); Nova Scotia (Storm, *Studier over Vinlandsreiserne*, Copenhagen, 1887); southern New England (Haugen, *Voyages to Vinland*, New York, 1942); Massachusetts (Fiske, *The Discovery of America*, Boston, 1892; Arbman, *The Vikings*, 1961); Rhode Island (Rafn, *Antiquitates Americanæ*, Boston, 1837); Long Island Sound (Gathorne-Hardy, *The Norse Discoverers of America*, 1921); Virginia (Mjelde, followed by Næss, *Hvor lå Vinland?*, Oslo, 1954). Reuter's theory of Georgia and Florida (*Germanische Himmelskunde*, München, 1934) need not be taken seriously.

to deny the notions of others, hard to establish a more durable case of one's own. Yet the attempt must be made.

Fortunately the discrepancies between our two literary sources, the Flateyjarbók version (*Grænlendinga Saga*), and the AM 557 and *Hauksbók* version (*Eiríks Saga Rauða*), whilst troublesome enough are not unmanageable. Both versions are the workings over of original material in accordance with the well-established facts of saga-making. Deviations, accretions, influences, reinterpretations, misunderstandings (especially as to the different places reached by the different explorers), changes of emphasis, and varying allocations of credit are to be expected; but the important thing to recognize is that these confirm rather than deny a sound underlying historical tradition. For a start *Grænlendinga Saga* is much less interested in Iceland and the Icelanders than is *Eiríks Saga Rauða*. *Grænlendinga Saga* is concerned with the family of Eirik the Red (which incidentally gives great weight to its account of Bjarni Herjolfsson); *Eiríks Saga Rauða* is more interested in the Icelanders Gudrid and Karlsefni, from whom Hauk Erlendsson, the owner and part-scribe of *Hauksbók*, was proud to claim descent. It follows that they sometimes handle quite different material, like Freydis's murderous expedition to Vinland in *Grænlendinga Saga*, Bjarni Grimolfsson's heroic death in *Eiríks Saga Rauða*; or sometimes, by following different strands of the same tradition, they produce differing and yet reconcilable versions of the same event, for example the death of Thorstein Eiriksson by plague and of Thorvald his brother by a flighted arrow. It is clear too that the author of *Grænlendinga Saga* was less well informed about the topography of Vinland than the author of *Eiríks Saga Rauða*. He makes all his voyagers, Leif, Thorvald, Karlsefni, and Freydis, reach the same place, Leifsbudir, and with the single exception of Thorvald there they stayed. In *Grænlendinga Saga* Leifsbudir and Vinland are more or less synonymous terms.[1] But in *Eiríks Saga Rauða* this is not so. There we have two encampments described in detail, Straumfjord and Hop, and it is curious to note how closely the description of Leifsbudir corresponds with that of Hop: the shoals, the river, and the lake. This cannot be coincidence. Even the climate was the same. At Leifsbudir 'the nature of the land was so choice it seemed to them that none of the cattle would require fodder for the winter. No frost came during

[1] G. M. Gathorne-Hardy, *The Norse Discoverers of America*, p. 222.

7

the winter, and the grass was hardly withered'. At Hop 'no snow fell, and their entire stock found its food grazing in the open'. Yet the identification of Leifsbudir with Hop is highly improbable, the more so because Leifsbudir and Straumfjord also have features in common, and appear from the sailing directions and geographical evidence to be one and the same place in northern Newfoundland. Presumably the author of *Grœnlendinga Saga* was conscious of his ignorance in these matters and worked up a description of Leifsbudir from tradition persistent in Snæfellsnes in Iceland, with the puzzling consequence for posterity that in his saga, to adopt Thórhallur Vilmundarson's equation, Straumfjord +Hop=Leifsbudir. But, to widen our terms of reference for a moment, the credibility of *Egils Saga* is not destroyed because we cannot accept as a headquarters communiqué its account of the battle of Brunanburh; the antiquarian and historical value of *Eyrbyggja Saga* is not cancelled out by its profusion of supernatural stories; and if Gudmund the Mighty cuts a different figure in *Njála* from the earlier versions of *Ljósvetninga Saga* no informed person doubts that he existed or questions the outlines of his career. So with *Grœnlendinga Saga* and *Eiríks Saga Rauða*. We can begin by shedding the more obvious fictions and apocrypha from all the Vinland voyages: Leif's sweet dew, Haki and Hekja, Thorhall the Hunter's unknown species of whale, the second Gudrid, the uniped who shot an arrow into Thorvald's guts.[1] This neither affects the voyages nor simplifies the real problems. But it rids them of some clutter.

There has been much argument during the last twenty years whether we should rid them of the grapes and the vines too. Vinland however we interpret it is a descriptive name, one of a long succession of such: Iceland, Greenland, Flatstone Land, Wood Land, as well as Sheep Isles, Bear Isles, Keelness, and Marvelstrands. We find the name first in the *Descriptio insularum aquilonis*

---

[1] There have been ingenious attempts to rationalize most of these. The sweet dew was 'den såkaldte honningdug', the secretion of the greenfly, GHM, I, 268; there is Mallery's plea in *Lost America*, 1951, p. 85, for the purgative qualities of the fat of the bottle-nosed whale of the genus Hyperodon; and the same author's explanation of the uniped as an Eskimo dancing on one foot, p. 95. Munn, *Wineland Voyages*, p. 28, quotes Professor Howley of the Newfoundland Geological Survey: 'this Uniped was undoubtedly an Eskimo woman of short stature, and dressed in the conventional Eskimo woman's attire with a long-tailed coat, she would undoubtedly look to the men who chased her as if she had only one leg.' Hermannsson, *The Problem of Wineland*, pp. 23–4, thinks the *einfœtingr* was either one-legged or made to appear so by reason of his dress or outfit.

or 'Description of the island countries of the North' which forms the fourth book of Adam of Bremen's *Gesta Hammaburgensis ecclesiæ pontificum*. Adam tells us that he derived his information about Vinland from Svein Estridsson, king of the Danes, who died in 1076.

He told me too of yet another island, discovered by many in that ocean, which is called Wineland from the circumstance that vines grow there of their own accord, and produce the most excellent wine. While that there is abundance of unsown corn there we have learned not from fabulous conjecture but from the trustworthy report of the Danes.

King Svein then, and Adam after him, had the same notion of Vinland as Thorhall the Hunter who in verses generally accepted as old and genuine lamented that all he had to drink for his undoubted pains was water from the well (see p. 181, below). In saga tradition Vinland was certainly *Vínland*, Wineland, or Wineland the Good, *Vínland hit góða*, because it was a place which produced grapes which in turn produced wine. Saga evidence as to this is overwhelming, which makes it difficult to accept recent theories that Vinland was not *Vínland* at all, but *Vinland* (*vin*, pl. *vinjar*, with a short vowel), Grass Land, Pasture Land, Land of Good Grazing.[1] Grass was as desirable, and essential, to the would-be colonizers of Vinland as to their fathers in the Faeroes, Iceland, and Greenland. Timber and pasture together would delight them. But grape-clusters

---

[1] This view was advanced by the Swedish philologist Sven Söderberg in 1888 and published in the *Sydsvenska Dagbladet Snällposten* of 30 October 1910. He thought that the saga-writers uncritically accepted the ideas of Adam of Bremen, who was given to wild and whirling accounts of distant places. To adopt it, as has been done by the recent equaters of Vinland with the northern tip of Newfoundland, i.e. the Finn V. Tanner, the Norwegian Helge Ingstad (who however does not reject the possibility of vines and wild wheat growing in Vinland), and the Dane Jørgen Meldgaard, disposes of many problems, among them the need to fit Vinland within the northern limits of the wine-producing grape at the end of the tenth century, or, if that cannot be done, to provide evidence that to the Greenlanders and Icelanders grapes were not grapes and vines not vines, but squash-berries, cow-berries, red, white, black and blue berries, or even birch trees (by no means a full list of the proffered substitutes). It also provides a rational and attractive sequence of lands proceeding south: stone, wood, grass. Perhaps, indeed, too rational. There is no doubt that *vin*, pasture, meadow, grazing, is a frequent element in early Norwegian local names, but it appears to have fallen into complete, or almost complete, disuse before the time of the Vinland voyages, and is not to be found in the placenames of the Faeroes, Iceland or Greenland. It is certainly not impossible that the bookish saga-men of Iceland, unacquainted with the element (almost always a suffix) *-vin*, and influenced by notions of the Insulæ Fortunatæ, too easily inclined to *vín-*. But on balance there seems no compulsive reason for setting aside the overwhelming saga tradition with respect to *Vínland*, Wineland, and with all doubts registered I retain it.

might supply the headier flavour that Leif needed to incite the Greenlanders to fresh land-takings. In land-naming as in other ways Leif was his father's son, and Wineland out-tops Greenland as Grassland could never do. Besides we can believe in the grapes. Their northern limit of growth today is about latitude 45° N, but in the 1530's Jacques Cartier, the discoverer of the St. Lawrence, found abundance of grapes on both sides of the river, and wild corn rather like rye or oats at the Baie de Chaleur and on various islands in the Gulf. Champlain, Leigh and Denys support him.[1] It may therefore be assumed that in far more favourable climatic conditions, such as obtained at the time of the Vinland voyages, the northern limit of the wild grape included Newfoundland's northern peninsula. Finally, it is not fatal to the credibility of the saga accounts of these voyages if we conclude that grapes were met with not in the northern tip of Newfoundland but when the Norsemen sailed further south, as we are explicitly told they did on at least two occasions. For we must at all times remember that there is no theory of the Vinland voyages of discovery reconcilable with *all* the evidence.

Probably the most difficult discard of all to make is the observation that at Leifsbudir, 'The sun had there *eyktarstaðr* and *dagmálastaðr* on the shortest day (*or* days).' This looks the kind of factual, unemotional statement which could determine the latitude of this particular part of Vinland beyond any argument. But there is no question on which the experts are more divided and the layman more helpless. That those making the observation were impressed by the more even balance of day and night in winter in Vinland than back home in Greenland and Iceland is stated; and that on a particular day or days in winter the sun was visible, though presumably then at point of rising and setting, at a certain time in the morning and a certain time in the afternoon. These could not be clock times, for the Norsemen had no clocks in the early eleventh century. Therefore *eyktarstaðr* and *dagmálastaðr* are points on the horizon, such as were used by the Icelanders to estimate the time of day by the position of the sun, or, more positively, they are bearings of the sun itself. From this, all other things being certain, for example, the exact significance of *eykt* in Iceland in Leif's time,

---

[1] The evidence has been many times presented, from Anspach, *A History of the Island of Newfoundland*, edition of 1827, to Gathorne-Hardy, *The Norse Discoverers of America*, 1921.

the exact significance of *um skammdegi*, and all such corrections of calculation as are needed for the effects of refraction, changes of sea level, the actual as well as the astronomical horizon, and a knowledge of what a Norse sailor meant by sunrise and sunset (i.e. the rise or descent of edge or centre)—all these things established for the early eleventh century if not beyond the possibility of error at least within a negligible margin of error, Vinland should stand revealed, at least in its northernmost possibility. But of the three most distinguished students or partnerships of students who have tried to determine the northernmost limit at which the observation could have been made, Storm and Geelmuyden, supported by Captain Phythian of the United States Naval Observatory, settled for latitude *c.* 49° 55′; Mr. Gathorne-Hardy first for latitude *c.* 49°, though 'in all probability the words indicate a much more southerly latitude', but later for south of latitude 37°; while Dr. Almar Næss, re-working and revising the calculations of M. M. Mjelde, thinks it 'very probable' that Vinland lay south of Chesapeake Bay (36° 54′ N).[1] In other words, while this famous sentence may help to convince us that someone made a significant observation somewhere in America, it helps not at all to determine the site of Leif's booths.

In short, until the archaeologists find and describe (as one day they will) houses, weapons, artefacts, and possibly Norse skeletons in North America which can be convincingly attributed to the first quarter of the eleventh century, our best means of identifying the early sites of Norse exploration is to read the sagas. Which brings us back to the explorations of Thorvald Eiriksson, as recorded in *Grœnlendinga Saga*, and to the attempt at colonization by Thorfinn Karlsefni, as recorded in both versions of *Eiríks Saga Rauða*. If it is objected that there is something uncritical in picking and choosing among the sagas, the answer is that it would be even less critical to swallow down any one saga, hook, line and fictional sinker.

[1] Dr. Næss's computations in *Hvor lå Vinland?*, Oslo, 1954, with a summary in English, pp. 241–6, are the most elaborate and thoroughgoing yet. Dr. Næss is emphatic that the latitude established by means of the *eykt* observation is not that of Leifsbudir. He believes, as many others have done, that the Vinland voyages were not all made to the same place, and that the Vinlands of Leif and Karlsefni were not the same. The *eykt* observation, he thinks, was made at Hop, not Leifsbudir. 'Hóp is the central Vineland, but it is quite impossible that Leiv reached 36° 54′ north. Leiv has not been in "Vinland". The actual explorer is Torfinn.' It is noticeable how many of Næss's admirers flinch at the last moment from latitude 37° N, adjust it to 41° N, and in no time at all are even further up the coast in Massachusetts.

Karlsefni then. His voyage was made in three ships with a hundred and sixty men, some of them accompanied by their wives, and taking 'all sorts of livestock' with them, including, one would guess, cows and a bull, mares and a stallion, ewes and a ram, and maybe goats and pigs. They began by moving up the coast with the warm north-setting coastal current as far as the Western Settlement, possibly because Karlsefni's wife had property there, but far more likely because this had already revealed itself to be the most promising route. From the Western Settlement they sailed still further north, to Bjarney(jar), Bear Isle(s), which we cannot identify with any certainty, but may be in the neighbourhood of the modern Holsteinsborg, or may be Disco. The arguments for the Holsteinsborg region is that here the current turns west towards the North American shore, and that the twentieth-century mariner would regard it as a waste of time and effort to sail north of there before heading for the south of Baffin Island. Both Holsteinsborg and Disco might lay claim to an argument that Karlsefni would seek to reduce his time on the open sea to a minimum for the sake of his animals. From Disco he might well stand to benefit by the frequent northerly winds of the Davis Strait, and in theory at least by sailing from there he would be conforming to a classic principle of Norse navigation, to make the shortest practicable ocean passage and to use the clearest landmarks. So mariners from Norway and the Western Isles looked for the Vatnajokul of Iceland, and mariners from Iceland sailed past Snæfellsjokul, and as that lovely white-mantled volcano sank under the sea behind them would be seeking the white and black giants of East Greenland.[1] However, Holsteinsborg or Disco, the author of *Eiríks Saga Rauða* knew of this northern route, which was the result of increasing knowledge and experiment. It may not have been the original route, but later knowledge of it may explain the major difficulty in our interpretation of the last stage of Bjarni Herjolfsson's pioneer voyage. He took four days to reach Herjolfsnes from the Frobisher Bay area with a south-west wind, which is impossible. But a south-west wind would have seemed just the thing to a saga-man in Iceland with information as to the best but later route, and with information (sound or unsound) as to the duration of Bjarni's sea-crossing. Bjarni, we

[1] Anyone unable to accept the evidence for a better climate in this area in the early eleventh century might further consider Karlsefni's route designed to escape the ice there.

assume, reached the west Greenland coast well north of Herjolfsnes and coasted south till he found his father's home. Prudent
man that he was, he had collected all the available information
about Greenland, that is, Eirik's knowledge of it, before leaving
Eyrar.

So, sped by a wind from the north, Karlsefni reached Helluland,
Baffin Island. But not necessarily the precise area of Baffin Island
reached and named by his predecessors. Like Markland and presumably Vinland, Helluland was the name of an extensive stretch
of coast and country. Which in its turn makes it enough for
present purposes to say that when Karlsefni sailed before the same
north wind for two days and reached Markland he was somewhere
off the forested part of Labrador.[1] From there after a long while of
coasting he came to a quite closely described area of what was
still Labrador. Two of its features were unusual. There was a cape
on which they found the keel of a ship and which they named
Kjalarnes, Keelness, and beaches and sands of such remarkable
length that they called them Furdustrandir, Marvelstrands, because 'it was such a long business sailing past them'. We are
instantly reminded of events and places in the voyages of Leif
and Thorvald. When Leif arrived in the land he named Markland
he found the country 'flat and covered with forest, with extensive
white sands wherever they went, and shelving gently to the sea'.
Two days south they sighted Vinland. In turn, Thorvald sailing
north along the land from Leifsbudir met heavy weather off a
certain cape, they were driven ashore, and so damaged their keel
that they had to fit a new. Studying the old and broken one—
'Said Thorvald to his shipmates: "I should like us to erect the
keel on the cape here, and call it Kjalarnes." ' Clearly Thorvald's
Kjalarnes and Karlsefni's are the same, and if we seek to identify
it, whether we accept the sagas' accounts as literally true, read
into them a common principle of place-naming in Iceland,

[1] AM 557 says that they sailed for two days before a north wind; *Hauksbók* that
they sailed onwards from Helluland for two days and changed course from south to
south-east. Thereafter the accounts deviate. AM 557 says that from their landfall in
Markland they came to Kjalarnes after two days' sailing; *Hauksbók* that they sailed
'for a long while' before arriving there. Either we must emend the time of sailing
from an unspecified place in Baffin Island to an unspecified place in Labrador (a
shaky undertaking at best, though Finnur Jónsson's suggestion of v for ii is not too
daunting), or accept *Hauksbók*'s *langa stund* for Karlsefni's coastal sailing from his
landfall in Markland on down to Kjalarnes. This latter is much to be preferred.
GS offers no details. Karlsefni left Greenland, and in an unspecified time and by an
unspecified route reached Leifsbudir in Vinland.

Norway, and Denmark, or find in them a well-known type of onomastic story, is not all that important. What is important is the verifiable existence of remarkably long white sandy beaches and a keel-shaped cape two days' sailing north of Leifsbudir. They are to be found immediately south of Hamilton Inlet, on the south-eastern coast of Labrador. These sandy beaches for sailors along the rocky and formidable coasts from Baffin Island south are indeed 'marvelstrands', over forty miles in length, with a low-lying background of grass and spruce and juniper. The sand, says Captain Munn, fine and hard, is 'fit for the old-fashioned hour-glass'. From the Strand, as these turf-backed fifty-yard-wide white beaches are called, Cape Porcupine extends two miles to sea, an impressive keel-shaped profile, still in our own day a main land-mark for all who fish these waters.

There are two other points of high importance for the identi-fication of this area. The first is that *Eiriks Saga Rauða*'s descrip-tion of Markland-Vinland topography fits south-eastern Labrador and northern Newfoundland better than anywhere else. South of Furdustrandir, says the saga, the coast becomes indented with bays (*vágskorit*), which is true of the coast of Labrador, with Sandwich Bay as its most impressive immediate example. Later it became indented with fjords (*fjarðskorit*), or possibly as in *Hauks-bók* by one particular fjord. If fjords, these are the entries from north of Battle Harbour to the Strait of Belle Isle; if fjord, the entrance to the Strait of Belle Isle itself. On this reading of the evidence Karlsefni's Straumfjord, Stream or Current Fjord, was the northern entrance of the Strait of Belle Isle, which he had no reason to know was a passage to the south rather than a penetra-tion of the land. These were sailors with experience of the im-mense fjords of Greenland, Iceland, and Norway, and their error, if it can with propriety be called such, was shared by a list of distinguished navigators till the 'discovery' by Jacques Cartier more than five centuries later. Straumey, Stream Island, may have been Belle Isle, or even Great Sacred Island, lying in an arm of sea between Cape Bauld, the northern tip of Promontorium Win-landiæ, and Cape Onion. A few miles south are the grassy shores of Sacred Bay and in particular Lance-aux-Meadows (i.e. L'Anse-au-Medee: *Midi* or a ship's name *Médée*) and Épaves Bay, where Black Duck Brook curves to the sea round a bluff whose environs have been the scene of human settlement over a long period of

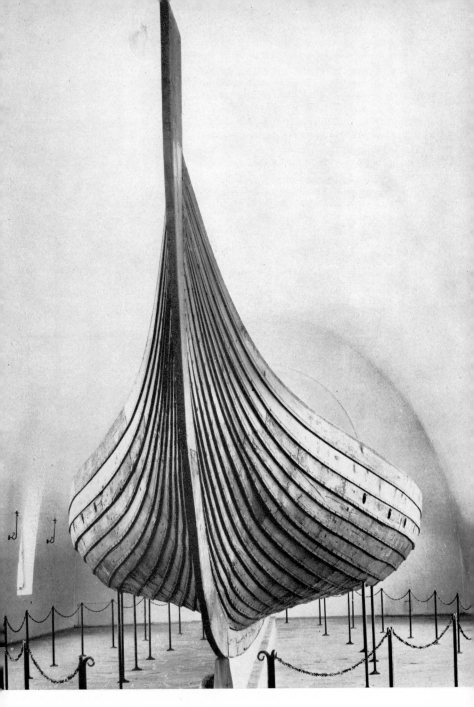

II. THE GOKSTAD SHIP

12. KJALARNES AND FURDUSTRANDIR

Cape Porcupine and the Strand on the coast of Labrador.

history.[1] Immediately west is Pistolet Bay. The outlook over Lance-aux-Meadows and the adjacent countryside, out over the island-dotted Strait of Belle Isle, with Cape Bauld to the right and the coast of Labrador to the left, is a splendid one. *Þar var fagrt landsleg.*[2] The prospect here would be one to charm a stock-farmer's eye: after long sailing off rock-bound barren coasts he could put his animals ashore amidst miles of fair grazing—the 'tall *or* abundant grass' of *Eiríks Saga Rauða*—with genial forest and wind-breaks. The soil was comparable with anything known in Iceland or Greenland, the rivers teemed with salmon and the ocean's harvest was inexhaustible. And there were sea-beasts and caribou to fill a hunter's dreams. There was a further advantage too. During the first two winters of Eirik's exploration of Greenland he made his home on islands outside the fjords, where the hunting was good and he was within sight of the open sea. Similarly the explorers of Vinland found a base which promised them the greatest possible freedom of movement as well as supplies. Indeed, their prospect was all too good—they banked on an easy winter and were hard hit when the cold came (like Floki Vilgerdarson in Iceland before them). But with the spring a good country once more. And empty. Or seeming so.

In Iceland the Norse settlers found a few papar, and the books and bells and croziers they left behind them. In Greenland they found the habitations of men, fragments of boats and stone arte-facts, but no people. So far in America they had come across a grain-holder when Thorvald's men explored the west coast of Newfoundland, and Thorvald had encountered and brutally handled some Skrælings on the voyage that led to his death. Who were these Skrælings? Indians or Eskimo? Recent investigations suggest that the Norsemen fell foul of both. About the year 1000 the Eskimo were to be found much further south than their present limit; they occupied the southern indented coastal area of Labrador from above Hamilton Inlet down to the Strait of Belle Isle and the Newfoundland-Vinland promontory north of a line from Port Saunders on the west coast to the mouth of White Bay on the east. South of them in Newfoundland, and south and west

[1] The most important recent stages in the argument that northern Newfoundland is the Promontorium Winlandiæ are set out in Appendix IV, 'Straumfjord in Vinland.'
[2] Curiously enough, since Karlsefni was a Skagafjord man, it strongly reminds Icelandic observers of Skagafjord itself.

of them in Labrador, were Indians, Algonquins. More important is the circumstance that there were Indians living *north* of the Dorset Eskimo of Newfoundland, thus supplying a proof from ethnology that Karlsefni's Straumfjord and therefore the Promontorium Winlandiæ was in northern Newfoundland, and impressive evidence that Thorvald Eiriksson was killed near Lake Melville and could not have been killed anywhere else. For no other region of the eastern coast of North America seems to show in the early eleventh century a similar racial distribution.[1] That the saga narratives under the general title of Skrælings speak of both Indians and Eskimo, sometimes leaving us in doubt as to which is which, is just what might be expected from saga-men in touch with remote but genuine tradition: there are parallels to this confusion in the journals of rediscovery from the end of the fifteenth century, and on maps of the sixteenth. The Strait of Belle Isle has been a cross-roads during the whole period of which we have record. Norse, Basque, French, English, all have been drawn here, Indian and Eskimo too. Meldgaard in 1954 and 1956 excavated ancient settlements of Dorset Culture Eskimo in Arctic Canada, Labrador, and Newfoundland, and in the latter year dwellings of their contemporary Indian neighbours in the Northwest River area of Lake Melville, with illuminating results for our assessment of Thorvald's and Karlsefni's northern expeditions from Leifsbudir-Straumfjord. According to *Grœnlendinga Saga* Thorvald set off eastward then north from Leifsbudir, reached Kjalarnes, and then turned into the mouth of the next fjord they came to, Hamilton Inlet, where he was killed by an arrow. According to *Eiríks Saga Rauða* Thorvald and Karlsefni set off northwards from Straumfjord, passed Kjalarnes, then bore away west (Hamilton Inlet offering the only possible entrance), with a forest wilderness to port. When they had been on their travels for a long time they lay at anchor by the mouth of a river flowing from east to west, exactly as English River flows into Lake Melville, where Thorvald was killed by an arrow. The use of the bow and arrow was unknown to the Eskimo of this culture and time, so Thorvald was killed by an Indian arrow, bearing the same kind of arrowhead as was found in 1930 by Aage Roussell at Sandnes in the Western Settlement of Greenland, where it had lain in the north-west corner of the churchyard, and the same kind

[1] J. Meldgaard, *Fra Brattalid til Vinland*, pp. 371–2.

of arrowhead as Meldgaard found in the ancient Indian settlement by Northwest River at the extremity of Lake Melville in
1956. The Sandnes arrow is pure Indian, made of quartzite identical with the quartzite of Labrador. It therefore may be regarded
as the one almost indisputable and clinching piece of archaeological evidence of Norse significance from the American continent
before the summer of 1962. Likewise the boats found by Thorvald on this expedition were Indian boats. Though they are called
'skin-boats', they could hardly be Eskimo kayaks.[1] It is the
Indians of whom we have plentiful evidence that they slept under
their upturned birch-bark canoes. Additional though not incon-
testable saga evidence of Indians living, as we suspect they did,
inland of the Eskimo-held coastal strip of East Labrador, will be
found in *Eiríks Saga Rauða*'s reference to the whiteclad inhabitants
of Hvitramannaland; for if this has any meaning at all it must
refer to the white chamois or buckskin dancing robes of the Naskaupi. Conversely, the five Skrælings butchered by Karlsefni as
they lay asleep in fur doublets by the sea between Hop and
Straumfjord, with their wooden containers in which was animal
marrow mixed with blood, were Eskimo.[2] So too, to a high
degree of probability, were the Skrælings with whom Karlsefni
first traded and later fought at Hop, south of Straumfjord (if,
indeed, this encounter did not take place at Straumfjord itself).[3]
In their skin-boats or canoes, brandishing their double paddles,
and on their second appearance so plentiful that it looked as
though the bay had been sown with coals, one feels they *must*
be Eskimo.[4] There was a shower of missiles (*skothríð*), but no
mention of arrows, and the Skrælings had 'warslings' too (*höfðu
ok valslöngur, Skrælingar*), whose nature has been much debated.
It may have been 'the formidable instrument to which the name
of "balista" may be applied', described by Schoolcraft as an

[1] There is no evidence that the Dorset Culture Eskimo had kayaks. Probably they
had not. In any case, it is not to be expected that saga tradition two hundred and
fifty years later would distinguish clearly, even scientifically, between what the
Norsemen over so long a period saw of the Dorset Culture Eskimo in Vinland and
the Thule Culture Eskimo in Greenland. Every Eskimo and every Indian was a
Skræling.
[2] For Vilhjálmur Stefánsson's letter to Mr. Gathorne-Hardy explaining how the
Eskimo of Canada fill sealskin containers with caribou marrow suffused with blood,
esteeming this a great delicacy, see Hermannsson, *The Vinland Sagas*, pp. 39–40. It
disposes of earlier notions of (Indian) pemmican or moose butter.
[3] See note 2, pp. 94–5.
[4] There is a photograph of Ferdinand Vogel's by way of frontispiece to
Stefánsson's *Greenland*, 1943, which might have been taken to illustrate this passage.

9. KAYAKS AND UMIAK

The nearer kayaker's dress is modern (nineteenth century). Both kayaks carry a bladder-float harpoon and double-bladed paddle. Large skin-boat (*umiak*) in the background.

Algonquin weapon in ancient times;[1] or it might be, as Meldgaard believes, the Eskimo bladder-float harpoon, or harpoon with a blown up bladder attached, unknown to the Indians but a main weapon among the distinctive Dorset Culture Eskimo folk of the year 1000.[2] The second appears on all counts the likelier.

[1] The following has been many times quoted: 'Algonquin tradition affirms that in ancient times, during the fierce wars which the Indians carried on, they constructed a very formidable instrument of attack, by sewing up a large boulder in a new skin. To this a long handle was tied. When the skin dried it became very tight round the stone, and after being painted with devices assumed the appearance and character of a solid globe upon a pole. This formidable instrument to which the name of "balista" may be applied, is figured (Plate 15, fig. 2) from the description of an Algonquin chief. It was borne by several warriors who acted as balisteers. Plunged upon a boat or canoe it was capable of sinking it. Brought down upon a group of men on a sudden it produced consternation and death.' H. R. Schoolcraft, *Indian Tribes of the United States*, 1851, I, 85 (For a conflicting view see De Costa, *The Pre-Columbian Discovery of America by the Northmen*, 1890, p. 130, n.3). The Montagnais and Naskaupi were of Algonquin origin and still speak dialects of the original Algonquin language (Tanner, *Newfoundland-Labrador*, p. 575).
[2] *Fra Brattalid til Vinland*, p. 372. It would help here if we could be reasonably sure where Karlsefni's lodgement at Hop took place. It was certainly south of Straumfjord. Thorhall the Hunter, according to both *Hauksbók* and AM 557, wished to proceed north from there by way of Furdustrandir and look for Vinland. Straumfjord had not come up to his expectations, with its cold, hungry winter and absence of wine. He was a skilled and resourceful explorer of empty places who seems to have been impressed by a land of promise just north of Kjalarnes—that very Hamilton Inlet which had attracted or was to attract Thorvald and Karlsefni in their turn. But for the present Karlsefni intended to explore in a southern direction, and more specifically (*Hauksbók*) down the eastern coast of Promontorium Winlandiæ (according to GS Thorvald had already sponsored a probe down its western coast). And so he did, and came after a good while (*lengi*) to a river mouth and landlocked bay so protected by sandbars or islands that it was only at full flood they could enter the river itself. Here they found wild wheat and vines, a hand-harvest of 'holy fish',

This pitched battle with the warlike Skrælings was decisive for the fate of Karlsefni's attempt to establish a permanent European colony in North America. His numbers were small, and their weapons inadequate. They were unwilling to woo and unable to conquer. So for a start they pulled back from Hop and returned to their base at Straumfjord. Karlsefni, a right-thinking man where any save Skrælings were concerned, considered it his duty to try and find Thorhall the Hunter and his eight or nine comrades, who had gone off dissatisfied in the hope of finding the winy Vinland in the Hamilton Inlet–Lake Melville area. So he undertook the voyage north and west which brought him into fresh collision with the Skrælings. Not wishing to imperil his comrades any further he withdrew to Straumfjord for a third, unhappy winter. The presence of women in the camp led to sour quarrels and deep division, and it must have been with the taste of failure in their mouths that they sailed from Vinland next spring. In their company sailed the infant Snorri, Karlsefni's son, the first known white man to be born in that vast continent—and Bjarni Grimolfsson and his crew, half of whom were to perish miserably on that vast sea.

and an abundance of many kinds of animals in the forest. And here they found Skrælings, aborigines, 'natives'. The information supplied by *Hauksbók* as to where this new encampment might be is not easy to understand, but probably is intended to tell us that Hop lay as far south of Straumfjord as Thorvald's death-scene (here embellished with rhetoric as derivative as it is pseudo-heroic—cf. Thormod Coal-brow's-poet's dying words after the battle of Stiklastadir, as reported in *Heims-kringla*) was north of it. In this case Hop lay in Indian country, which contradicts the ethnographical evidence. AM 557, which we must regard as closer to the original *ESR* than *Hauksbók* is, says nothing under this head; while for the author of *GS* there was no journey south, therefore no Hop, and Karlsefni's encounter with the Skrælings took place at Leifsbudir, which if we are to identify it with any place in *ESR* should be Straumfjord. Relevant here is the intriguing and possibly very important sentence in both versions of *ESR* that, 'It is some men's report that Bjarni and Freydis [H. Gudrid] had remained behind there (*i.e.* at Straumfjord), and a hundred men with them, and proceeded no farther, while Karlsefni and Snorri had travelled south with forty men, yet spent no longer at Hop than a bare two months, and got back again that same summer.' This could be taken as meaning that Karlsefni's expedition to Hop was a summer voyage of exploration (on the face of it sensible enough), that the Norsemen did not spend a winter there, and that, as in *GS*, the encounter with the Skrælings, including Freydis's folk-magical share in it, took place at Leifsbudir-Straumfjord. Another seeming witness to confusion in *ESR* is that Karlsefni decides twice to sail for the north, first for Straumfjord, and then for Greenland, and on each occasion finds five Skrælings near the coast.

From the many uncertainties two facts emerge, the first that by the time the two Greenland-Vinland sagas were written down in the form in which we have them, marked contradictions had developed in the topographical and geographical traditions associated with the areas of settlement, the second that we cannot place Hop on the map, and if we accept *ESR*'s account of Karlsefni's spending a winter there, it must be with misgiving.

There would be other voyages to Helluland, Markland, Vinland. The very next summer Eirik's virago of a daughter would undertake a bloodstained mission to Leifsbudir. A century later, in 1121, the Icelandic Annals record that 'Bishop Eirik of Greenland went in search of Vinland' (*Konungsannáll*); 'Eirik the Greenlanders' bishop went to look for Vinland' (*Gottskálksannáll*); to what end and with what success we do not know.[1] Nor do we know whether he ever returned. The next, and last, reference to the lands beyond Greenland is from the Annals for 1347. 'There came also a ship from Greenland, smaller in size than the small Icelandic boats; she came into the outer Straumfjord [near Budir, on Snæfellsnes], and had no anchor. There were seventeen men on board. They had made a voyage to Markland, but were afterwards storm-driven here' (*Skálholtsannáll hinn forni*); 'At this time came a ship from Greenland, which had made a voyage to Markland, and had eighteen men on board' (*Flateyjarannáll*). Presumably they had been to Markland to fetch timber, and possibly furs, and but for the accident of their being driven clean across the sea to Iceland the Annals of that country would not have mentioned them. Which leaves us to speculate how many successful voyages were made between Greenland and Markland during the preceding three centuries, and whether after the loss of the Western Settlement and the Nordseta towards the middle of the fourteenth century such voyages could ever be undertaken again.

It is tempting to assume that such skilled and intrepid seamen as the Norsemen were till their glory dimmed towards the end of the thirteenth century would have pressed on south of the Promontorium and maybe north of the original landfalls in Baffin Island. Yet nothing we hear of the unsettled parts of Helluland in the 'lying sagas' invites a full trust. Southwards it could well be different, especially if we interpret the phrase 'Promontorium Winlandiæ' as indicating the northern extremity of an undefined area extending south. Maybe after all it was as a result of far-ranging voyages to coasts below the Promontorium that tales of grape-clusters and warm winters enriched the Norse tradition of Vinland; maybe longer voyages and later travellers blurred the outlines of Leif's landing and Karlsefni's settlement. A single

---

[1] The Greenlanders had no bishop before the consecration of Arnald in 1124 (see *Einars Tháttr*, p. 192). Was Eirik a bishop *in partibus infidelium*, sent to convert the Skrælings?

archaeological discovery in Massachusetts or Rhode Island (or
Virginia) could yet convert the theory into fact. For what good
reason, one asks, must the area of Sacred Bay be '*hið eina sanna
Vínland*'—Vinland the one and only? Yet, at present, there is
little trustworthy evidence that the Norsemen reached New
England, much less sailed further south.[1] Karlsefni had shown
that there was nothing south but trouble, and so far as the record
goes (and it may not go far enough) his countrymen respected
the lesson. In any case, long journeys south would in course of
time become impracticable, indeed impossible, if only because the
Greenlanders had no ships good enough for the purpose. The
ship that came to the outer Straumfjord in 1347 was small by
even the degenerate Icelandic standard, and the heart had gone
out of Norse seamanship.[2]

[1] The argument from topography is not enough, whatever one's theory of the
location of Vinland. That the Eskimo would be found as far south as New England
by the year 1000 is most unlikely (his natural limit would be the limit of the iceberg,
the polar bear, and the marine mammals); the *eykt* observation has so far proved
unhelpful; the sagas' accounts of tides and currents are equally so; and the lump of
anthracite coal recovered in 1930 from a deep layer in one of the rooms of a Norse
house in Lysufjord in the Western Settlement of Greenland, once believed to have
come from New England, is now thought to be of European origin.

[2] The entries in the Icelandic Annals for 1285 concerning the discovery of New
Land (*nýja land*) by the priests and brothers Adalbrand and Thorvald, the sons of
Helgi; and for 1289, telling how King Eirik Magnusson of Norway sent Land-Rolf
(*Landa-Rólfr*) to Iceland to seek New Land, with the confirmation of 1290 that he
did indeed solicit men for the journey; these I have not pursued. They most pro-
bably relate to somewhere on the east coast of Greenland.

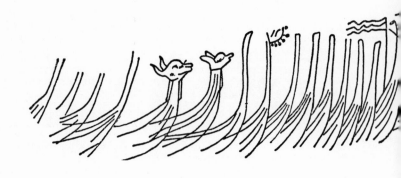

Part Two

THE SOURCES

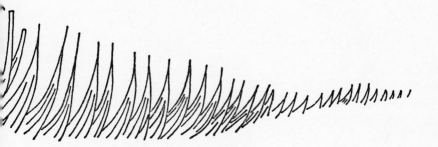

4

The Book of the Icelanders

Íslendingabók or Libellus Islandorum

Prologue

THE Book of the Icelanders I composed first for our bishops
Thorlak and Ketil, and showed it both to them and to Sæmund
the priest; and according as it pleased them to have it just as it was,
or augmented, I have written this too, covering the same ground
but omitting the Genealogies and the Lives of the Kings, while
adding to it what has since become better known to me, and is
now more fully related in this version than in that. But anything
that is set down wrongly in this history, it is our duty to give
preference to what is proved to be more correct.

In this book are contained chapters, 1, Of the Settlement of
Iceland; 2, Of the Settlers and Legislation; 3, Of the Establishment
of the Althing; 4, Of the Calendar; 5, Of the Division into
Quarters; 6, Of the Settlement of Greenland; 7, Of how Chris-
tianity came to Iceland; 8, Of Foreign Bishops; 9, Of Bishop
Isleif; 10, Of Bishop Gizur.

HERE BEGINS THE BOOK OF THE ICELANDERS

1. *Of the Settlement of Iceland*

Iceland was first settled from Norway in the days of Harald
Fairhair, son of Halfdan the Black, at the time (according to the
belief and count of Teit my tutor, son of bishop Isleif, and the
wisest man I have known; of Thorkel Gellisson, my father's
brother, whose recollection reached far back; and of Thurid
daughter of Snorri Godi, who was at once variously wise and a
trusty informant) when Ivar Ragnar Lodbrok's son had the
English king Saint Edmund put to death; and that was 870 years

after the birth of Christ, according to what is written in his, Edmund's, saga.

A Norwegian named Ingolf is the man of whom it is reliably reported that he was the first to leave there for Iceland, when Harald Fairhair was sixteen years old, and a second time a few years later. He settled south in Reykjavik. The place is called Ingolfshofdi, east of Minnthakseyr, where he made his first landing, and Ingolfsfell, west of Olfus river, where he afterwards took land into his possession. At that time Iceland was covered with forest between mountain and seashore.

There were Christian men here then whom the Norsemen call 'papar'. But later they went away because they were not prepared to live here in company with heathen men. They left behind Irish books, bells and croziers, from which it could be seen that they were Irishmen.

Then came a great movement of men out here from Norway, till king Harald set a ban on it, because he thought Norway would grow depopulated. They reached this agreement, that every man who was not exempted and should leave there for here must pay the king five ounces. It is said too that Harald was king for seventy years, and lived to be eighty years old. These were the origins of that tax which is now called land-ounces; at times more was paid, at times less, till Olaf Digri laid it down that everyone who made the journey between Norway and Iceland should pay the king half a mark, except for womenfolk and such men as he exempted. So Thorkel Gellisson informed us.

2. *Of the Settlers and Legislation*

Hrollaug, son of earl Rognvald of Mœr, settled east in Sida; whence are come the Men of Sida.

Ketilbjorn Ketilsson, a Norwegian, settled south at the Upper Mosfell; whence are come the Men of Mosfell.

Aud, daughter of Ketil Flatnose, a lord in Norway, settled west in Breidafjord; whence are come the Men of Breidafjord.

Helgi Magri, a Norwegian, son of Eyvind Eastman, settled north in Eyjafjord; whence are come the Men of Eyjafjord.

And when Iceland had become settled far and wide a Norwegian named Ulfljot first brought law out here from Norway (so Teit told us); this was called Ulfljot's Law. He was the father of that Gunnar from whom the Djupadalers are descended in Eyjafjord. For the most part these laws were modelled upon the then Gulathing Law, on the advice of Thorleif the Wise, Horda-Kari's son, as to what should be added, taken away, or be differently set out. Ulfljot lived east in Lon. It is said that Grim Geitskor was his foster-brother, he who at Ulfljot's direction explored the whole of Iceland before the Althing was established. For this, every man in the land gave him a penny, which he later donated to the temples.

3. *The Establishment of the Althing*

The Althing was established where it now is at the instance of Ulfljot and all the people of Iceland; but before this there had been a Thing at Kjalarnes, which Thorstein, son of Ingolf the Settler, and father of Thorkel Mani the Lawspeaker, held there together with those chieftains who allied themselves with it. But a man who owned the land at Blaskogar had been outlawed for the murder of a thrall or freedman. His name is given as Thorir Cropbeard, and his daughter's son was called Thorvald Crop-beard, the one who later went to the Eastfirths and there burned his own brother Gunnar to death in his house (so Hall Oraekjuson told us). The name of the murdered man was Kol, from whom that ravine gets its name which has ever since been called Kolsgja, where the corpse was discovered. The land thereafter became public domain, and the Icelandic people set it apart for the use of the Althing, for which reason wood can be cut free for the Althing in the forests there, and on the heath there is common pasture for the use of the horses. This Ulfhedin told us.

Wise men have said too that in the space of sixty years Iceland was fully occupied, so that after that there was no further taking of land. About then Hrafn, son of Hœng the Settler, took the lawspeakership next after Ulfljot and held it for twenty summers [930–49]. He was from Rangarhverfi. This was sixty years after the slaughter of king Edmund, and a winter or two before king Harald Fairhair died, according to the reckoning of well-informed men. Thorarin, brother of Ragi and son of Oleif Hjalti, took the lawspeakership next after Hrafn and held it a further twenty summers [950–69]. He was a Borgarfjord man.

4. *Of the Calendar*

It was at this same time, when the wisest men here in the land had

been counting 364 days in the two alternating seasons of the year
(which means 52 weeks, or twelve months of thirty days apiece,
plus four days over), that men noticed by the course of the sun
how the summer was moving backwards into the spring. But no
one could enlighten them how in a full year there is one day over
and beyond the full count of weeks—which was the cause of this.
There was, however, a man by the name of Thorstein Surt, a
Breidafjord man, son of Hallstein the son of Thorolf Mostrarskegg the Settler and of Osk, daughter of Thorstein the Red, who
had a dream, and imagined he found himself at the Law Rock
when there was a great congregation there, and he was awake,
whereas all the rest, he imagined, were asleep; but afterwards he
imagined himself asleep, and all the rest, as he thought, grew
awake. This dream Osvif Helgason, the maternal grandfather of
Gellir Thorkelsson, interpreted thus, that all men should be
silent while he spoke at the Law Rock, but once he himself fell
silent they would all applaud what he had said. These two were
both very shrewd men. So later on, when men came to the Thing,
he proposed this motion at the Law Rock, that every seventh
summer a week should be added on, and see how it worked. And
exactly as Osvif had interpreted the dream, everybody woke up to
the implications of this, and it was immediately made law by the
counsel of Thorkel Mani and other wise men.

By true reckoning there are 365 days in each and every year,
if it is not leap-year, when there is one day more; but by our
reckoning there are 364. So when by our reckoning there is an
addition made of one week to every seventh year, but nothing
added by the other reckoning, then seven years will prove of equal
length by either reckoning. But should two leap-years occur
between the years which must be added to, then it becomes
necessary to make the addition to the sixth year.

5. *Of the Division into Quarters*

A great lawsuit arose at the Thing between Thord Gellir, son of
Oleif Feilan from Breidafjord, and that Odd who was known as
Tungu-Odd, a Borgarfjord man. Odd's son Thorvald had taken
part with Hen-Thorir in the burning to death of Thorkel Blund-
Ketilsson in Ornolfsdal. But Thord Gellir came to lead in the
suit because Herstein, son of Thorkel Blund-Ketilsson, was
married to his niece Thorunn, the daughter of Helga and Gunnar

and sister to Jofrid, the wife of Thorstein Egilsson. They were prosecuted at the Thing which used to be in Borgarfjord, at the place since called Thingnes; for it was then the law that suits for manslaughter must be prosecuted at the Thing which was nearest to the spot where the manslaughter had taken place. But they came to blows there, and the Thing could not be carried on by law. Thorolf Fox, brother of Alf of Dalir, fell there from Thord Gellir's party. So later they carried their suits to the Althing, where once again they came to blows. This time men fell from Odd's party, and in addition Hen-Thorir was outlawed and later killed, together with others too who were at the burning.

Then Thord Gellir made a speech about this at the Law Rock, what a disadvantage it was for men to have to travel to strange Things to bring a case for manslaughter or for hurt to themselves; and he recounted what had happened to him before he could bring this case to law, arguing that many would run into trouble in their turn unless a remedy was found.

The land was then divided into Quarters, so that there were three Things in each Quarter, and men of the same Thing must hold their lawsuits together; save that in the Northerners' Quarter there were four, because they could not reach any other agreement (the men who lived north of Eyjafjord were not prepared to attend the Thing there, while those who lived to the west there would not attend at Skagafjord). Still, the nomination of judges and the constitution of the Logretta should be the same from this Quarter as from any other. But later the Quarter Things were established, as Ulfhedin Gunnarsson the Lawspeaker told us.

Thorkel Mani, son of Thorstein Ingolfsson, took the lawspeakership after Thorarin the brother of Ragi, and held it for fifteen summers [970–84]. Then Thorgeir Thorkelsson of Ljosavatn held it for seventeen summers [985–1001].

6. *Of the Settlement of Greenland*

The land which is called Greenland was discovered and settled from Iceland. Eirik the Red was the name of a Breidafjord man who went out there from here and took land in settlement at the place which has ever since been called Eiriksfjord. He gave the land a name, and called it Greenland, arguing that men would be drawn to go there if the land had a good name. Both east and west in the country [i.e. at both the Eastern and Western Settlements] they found the habitations of men, fragments of boats [? of skin, *keiplabrot*], and stone artefacts, from which it may be seen that the same kind of people had passed that way as those that inhabited Vinland, whom the Greenlanders call Skrælings. When he began to settle the land, that was fourteen or fifteen years before Christianity came to Iceland [i.e. 985 or 986], according to what a man who had himself gone out with Eirik the Red told Thorkel Gellisson in Greenland.

7. *Of how Christianity came to Iceland*

King Olaf Tryggvason (Tryggvi the son of Olaf, the son of Harald Fairhair) introduced Christianity into Norway and into Iceland. To this country he sent a priest whose name was Thangbrand, who taught men Christianity and baptized all who embraced the faith. For Hall Thorsteinsson of Sida had himself baptized early, and likewise Hjalti Skeggjason from Thjorsardal, and Gizur the White, the son of Teit, the son of Ketilbjorn of Mosfell, and many other chieftains. But they were the majority even so who opposed and rejected it. When he had been in Iceland a year or two he took himself off, having been the death of two or three men here who had lampooned him. And when he returned to Norway he informed king Olaf of all that had happened to him, declaring it a thing past hoping for that Christianity should be accepted here, at which the king grew very angry, and proposed as a consequence to have those of our countrymen who were over in Norway maimed or killed. But that same summer Gizur and Hjalti arrived there from Iceland and persuaded the king to let them off, promising him their help in a fresh attempt to get Christianity even yet adopted here, and affirming their conviction that it would be successful.

The following summer they left Norway, together with a priest by the name of Thormod, and arrived in the Vestmannaeyjar when ten weeks of summer were past, having had an excellent passage. Teit said he was told this by a man who was present there himself. It had been made law the summer before this that people should come to the Althing when ten weeks of summer were past, whereas until then they used to come a week earlier. Gizur and his men proceeded to the mainland without delay, and then to the Althing, but they persuaded Hjalti to stay behind in Laugardal with eleven men, because he had already been con-

victed a lesser outlaw the summer before at the Althing for
blasphemy. This came about because he spoke this little ditty at
the Law Rock:

> The gods I'd not blaspheme:
> Yet bitch I Freyja deem.

Gizur and his men went on their way till they reached a place
called Vellankatla, by Olfusvatn, and from there sent word to the
Althing that all their supporters should come and meet them, for
they had heard tell how their adversaries meant to bar them from
the Thingfield by force of arms. But before they moved off from
there, Hjalti came riding in along with those who had stayed
behind with him. They then rode on to the Thing, and their
kinsmen and friends had already come to join them, just as they
had requested. But the heathen men gathered together, armed to
the teeth, and it came so near to a fight that there was just no
saying how things would go.

The next day Gizur and Hjalti went to the Law Rock and made
known their message, and report has it it was remarkable how
well they spoke. And what followed from this was that one man
after another, Christian and heathen, called witnesses, each swear-
ing that he would not live under the same laws as the other, after
which they left the Law Rock.

Then the Christians requested Hall of Sida that he should proclaim that law which was right and proper for Christians; but he
got out of this, in that he made payment to Thorgeir the Lawspeaker that he should proclaim the law—even though he was
still a heathen. And later when men had returned to their booths,
Thorgeir lay down and spread his cloak over him, and lay quiet all
that day and the night following, and spoke never a word. But the
next morning he sat up and announced that men should proceed
to the Law Rock. And once men had made their way there he
began his speech. The affairs of the people, he said, would be in
sorry plight if men were not to have one law, all of them, in this
land; and he put this to men in many ways, how they must never
let such a state of affairs come about, maintaining that strife
would be the result, so that it could be taken as certain that such
contention would arise among men that the land would be laid
waste by reason of it. He related how the kings of Norway and
Denmark had carried on war and battles between them for a long

time, till the people of those countries made peace between them, even though they themselves did not want it. And that policy answered so well that in no time at all they were sending each other precious gifts, and peace was maintained for the rest of their lives. 'And now,' he added, 'I think it policy that we do not let those prevail who are most anxious to be at each other's throats, but reach such a compromise in these matters that each shall win part of his case, and let all have one law and one faith. It will prove true, if we break the law in pieces, that we break the peace in pieces too.' And he so concluded his speech that both sides agreed that all should have that one law which he would proclaim.

Then it was made law that all men should be Christians, and be baptized, those who so far were unbaptized here in Iceland.[1] But as for the exposure of infants the old laws should stand, and for the eating of horse-flesh too. Men might sacrifice in secret if they so wished, but it would be a case for lesser outlawry should witnesses come forward. But a few years later this heathendom was abolished like the rest. This was the way, Teit told us, that Christianity came to Iceland.

And this same summer, according to what Sæmund the priest relates, king Olaf Tryggvason fell. He was fighting then against Svein Haraldsson, king of the Danes, and Olaf the Swede, son of Eirik king of the Swedes at Uppsala, and Eirik Hakonarson who later was earl of Norway. That was 130 years after the slaughter of Edmund, and 1000 after the birth of Christ, according to the general count.

8. *Of Foreign Bishops*

These are the names of the foreign bishops that have been in Iceland, according to Teit's account. Fridrek came here in heathen times, while these were here later: Bjarnhard the Bookwise, five years; Kol, a few years; Hrodolf, nineteen years; Johan the Irish, a few years; Bjarnhard, nineteen years; Heinrek, two years. And yet another five came here who styled themselves bishops: Ornolf and Godiskalk, and three Armenians [*?ermskir*], Petrus, Abraham, and Stephanus.

Grim Svertingsson of Mosfell took the lawspeakership after

---

[1] *Kristni Saga* adds the pleasant detail that all the men of the North and South Quarters, and most of the West Quarter men, were baptized at the hot springs, 'because they had no wish to enter cold water'.

Thorgeir and held it two summers [1002–03], when he got per-
mission for his nephew Skapti Thoroddsson, his sister's son, to
have it, because he himself was hoarse of speech. Skapti held the
lawspeakership twenty-seven summers [1004–30]; it was he who
established the constitution of the Fifth Court, and this in addition, that no manslayer should make legal declaration of a slaying
against any person other than himself, whereas until then the same
law in respect of that applied here as in Norway. In his day many
chieftains and great men were outlawed or exiled for manslaying
or assault by virtue of his power and authority. He died the same
year Olaf Digri fell (the son of Harald, son of Gudrod, son of
Bjorn, son of Harald Fairhair), thirty years after Olaf Tryggvason
fell; whereupon Stein Thorgestsson took the lawspeakership
and held it for three summers [1031–33]. Then Thorkel Tjorvason
held it twenty summers [1034–53]; then Gellir Bolverksson for
nine summers [1054–62].

9. *Of Bishop Isleif*

Isleif, son of Gizur the White, was consecrated bishop in the time
of king Harald of Norway (the son of Sigurd, son of Halfdan, son
of Sigurd Hrisi, son of Harald Fairhair). And once the chieftains
and good men saw how Isleif was a man altogether more able than
those other clerics who were to be found here in the land, many
gave him their sons to teach, and had them ordained as priests; of
whom two were afterwards consecrated bishops: Kol, who lived
in Vik in Norway, and Jon of Holar.

Isleif had three sons, who were all able chieftains: bishop Gizur,
Teit the priest, father of Hall, and Thorvald. Teit was brought up
by Hall [Thorarinsson] in Haukadal, the man who by universal
report was the most generous and magnanimous of laymen here
in Iceland. And I too came to Hall, when seven years old, the
winter after Gellir Thorkelsson, my father's father and my
fosterer, died; and there I lived for fourteen years.

Gunnar the Wise had taken the lawspeakership when Gellir
[Bolverksson] relinquished it, and held it for three summers
[1063–65]; then Kolbein Flosason held it for six [1066–71]; the
summer he took the lawspeakership king Harald fell in England.
Then Gellir held it a second time, for three summers [1072–74];
then Gunnar held it a second time, for one summer [1075]; whereupon Kolbein's nephew Sighvat Surtsson held it for eight

[1076–83]. In those days Sæmund Sigfusson came to Iceland from down south, from France, and had himself ordained priest.

Isleif was consecrated bishop when he was fifty; Leo the Ninth was Pope at the time. The next winter he spent in Norway, and came out here thereafter. He died at Skalholt, after he had been bishop for twenty-four years (so Teit told us): this was on the Lord's Day, six nights after the Feast of Peter and Paul, and eighty years after the fall of Olaf Tryggvason [i.e. 6 July 1080]. I was there at the time with Teit my tutor, and was twelve years old.

But Hall, who was of good memory and truthful and remembered when he was baptized, told us this, that Thangbrand baptized him at the age of three—which was one year before Christianity was established here by law. He set up housekeeping at the age of thirty, lived at Haukadal for sixty-four years, and was ninety-four years old when he died—which was on the Feast of Bishop Martin, the tenth winter after the death of bishop Isleif [11 November 1089].

10. *Of Bishop Gizur*

Bishop Gizur, son of Isleif, was consecrated bishop at the prayer of his fellow-countrymen in the days of king Olaf Haraldsson, two years after the death of bishop Isleif. One of these years he spent here in Iceland, the other in Gautland. And his right name then was Gisrod, so he told us.

Markus Skeggjason held the lawspeakership next after Sighvat, taking it up that summer when bishop Gizur had been just one year here in the land, and holding office for twenty-four years [1084–1107]. From his relation are written in this book the periods of office of all the lawspeakers who lived too early for our own memory; but his brother Thorarin, and Skeggi their father, and other wise men informed him as to the periods of those who lived too early for his memory, in accordance with what their paternal grandfather Bjarni the Wise had told them, who remembered Thorarin the Lawspeaker together with six of his successors.

Bishop Gizur was better loved by the whole populace than any other man of whom we have knowledge here in Iceland. By reason of the affection he was held in, the persuasion of himself and Sæmund, and the counsel of Markus the Lawspeaker, it was made law that all men should count and evaluate their entire property, then swear that it was valued correctly, whether it was in land or chattels, and then give tithes thereof. It is a powerful token of how obedient the population was to this man that he could bring it about that all the property then existing in Iceland was valued under oath, tithes apportioned therefrom, and a law passed that this shall hold good as long as Iceland is inhabited.

Bishop Gizur also had it laid down as law that the see of the bishop that was in Iceland should be at Skalholt, whereas before it had been nowhere; and he endowed the see with the land at Skalholt and further riches of many kinds, both in land and chattels. And when he thought this establishment had prospered well in the matter of its wealth, he gave away more than one-fourth of his diocese to this end, that there might be two bishops' sees in the country, as the Northlanders requested of him, rather than one. But first he had a count made of all the franklins in Iceland. In the Eastfirthers' Quarter they were 840, and in the Rangriver Men's [Southern] Quarter 1200; in the Breidafirthers' [Western] Quarter 1080, and in the Eyjafirthers' [Northern] Quarter 1440. But there was no count made of men who were not subject to Thingfaring tax throughout the whole of Iceland.

Ulfhedin, son of Gunnar the Wise, took the lawspeakership after Markus and held it nine summers [1108–16]; then Bergthor Hrafnsson held it for six [1117–22]; and then Gudmund Thorgeirsson held it twelve summers [1123–34]. The first summer Bergthor recited the law there was this innovation made, that our law should be committed to writing at Haflidi Masson's house the following winter, at the dictation and under the surveillance of Haflidi and Bergthor and such other wise men as were appointed for the purpose. They were to make all such new provisions in the law as appeared to them to be improvements on the old, and these were to be announced the following summer in the Logretta, and all of them which were not then opposed by the majority should be adopted. So what happened was that the Manslaughter Section and many other portions of law were committed to writing and recited by clerics in the Logretta that following summer. And all were well pleased with it, and not a soul spoke against it.

It happened further, that first summer Bergthor recited the law, that bishop Gizur failed to attend the Thing because of an illness. He sent word to the Althing, to his friends and the chieftains, that they should pray Thorlak, son of Runolf, the son of Thorleik, the brother of Hall of Haukadal, to let himself be consecrated bishop. Without exception they acted upon his instruction, and the thing came about, because Gizur himself had pressed for it so strongly. Thorlak went abroad that summer, and returned the summer after, and was then consecrated bishop.

Gizur was consecrated bishop when he was forty. Gregory the Seventh was Pope at the time. He spent the winter after that in Denmark, and the following summer returned here to Iceland. When he had been bishop for twenty-four years, like his father before him, then Jon Ogmundarson was consecrated bishop, the first to the see of Holar. He was then fifty-four years old. Twelve years later, when Gizur had been a bishop for thirty-six years all told, Thorlak was consecrated bishop. Gizur had him consecrated to the see of Skalholt in his own lifetime. Thorlak was then twenty-eight years old. And bishop Gizur died thirty nights later at Skalholt, on the third day of the week, the fifth of the kalends of June [28 May 1118].

In that same year died Pope Paschalis the Second, earlier than bishop Gizur, and Baldwin king of Jerusalem, and Arnald patriarch of Jerusalem, and Philip king of the Swedes; and later that same summer Alexius king of the Greeks died, after he had occupied the throne of Constantinople for thirty-eight years. Two years later there was a change of lunar cycle. By then Eystein and Sigurd had been for seventeen years kings in Norway, in succession to their father Magnus, son of Olaf Haraldsson. This was 120 years after the fall of Olaf Tryggvason, 250 after the slaughter of Edmund king of the English, and 516 years after the death of Pope Gregory, who it is recorded introduced Christianity into England. He died in the second year of the reign of the emperor Phocas, 604 years after the birth of Christ, according to the general count. Which makes 1120 years in all.

Here this book ends.

Appendix

This is the kindred and genealogy of the bishops of the Icelanders:

Ketilbjorn the settler who settled south at the Upper Mosfell was father of Teit, father of Gizur the White, father of Isleif who was the first bishop of Skalholt, father of bishop Gizur.

Hrollaug the settler who settled east in Sida, at Breidabolstad, was father of Ozur, father of Thordis, mother of Hall of Sida, father of Egil, father of Thorgerd, mother of Jon, who was the first bishop of Holar.

Aud the settler who settled west in Breidafjord, at Hvamm, was mother of Thorstein the Red, father of Olaf Feilan, father of Thord Gellir, father of Thorhild Rjupa, mother of Thord Horsehead, father of Karlsefni, father of Snorri, father of Hallfrid, mother of Thorlak, who is now bishop of Skalholt in succession to Gizur.

Helgi Magri the settler who settled north in Eyjafjord, at Kristnes, was father of Helga, mother of Einar, father of Eyjolf Valgerdarson, father of Gudmund, father of Eyjolf, father of Thorstein, father of Ketil, who is now bishop of Holar in succession to Jon.

5

The Book of the Settlements

Landnámabók

1. *Iceland*

[S. 1–2] In the book *De Ratione Temporum* which the Venerable
Bede composed, there is mention of an island which is called
Thile, of which books record that it lies six days' sail north of
Britain. There, said he, there came no day in winter, and no night
in summer when the day is at its longest. The reason scholars
believe that Iceland is called Thile is because over much of the
country the sun shines all night when the day is at its longest, and
then again over much of it the sun is not seen by day when the
night is at its longest.

Now according to what is written, Bede the priest died 735
years after the Incarnation of our Lord, and more than a hundred
years before Iceland was settled by Norse men. But before Iceland
was settled from Norway, there were men there whom the Norse
men style 'papar'. These were Christians, and people consider that
they must have been from the British Isles, because there were
found left behind them Irish books, bells and croziers, and other
things besides, from which it might be deduced that they were
Vestmenn, Irishmen. [H. *adds* These things were found east in
Papey and in Papyli.] It is recorded in English books that at that
time there was trafficking to and fro between those countries.

When Iceland was discovered and settled from Norway, Adrian
was pope in Rome, and after him John, who was the fifth of that
name in the apostolic seat; Louis son of Louis was emperor north
of the Alps, and Leo and Alexander his son over Byzantium.
Harald Fairhair was king of Norway; Eirik Eymundarson king of
Sweden, and Bjorn his son; and Gorm the Old was king of
Denmark. Alfred the Great was king of England, and Edward his
son; Kjarval in Dublin, and earl Sigurd the Mighty in Orkney.

13. THINGVELLIR, ICELAND

14. THE HOLY MAN OF FLATATUNGA

A mid-eleventh century representation of an Icelandic scholar, priest, or saint.

Learned men state that from Stad in Norway it is seven days' sail west to Horn in the east of Iceland; and from Snæfellsnes, where the distance is shortest, it is four days' sea west to Greenland. And it is said if one sails from Bergen due west to Hvarf in Greenland that one's course will lie some seventy or more miles south of Iceland. [H. From Hernar in Norway one must sail a direct course west to Hvarf in Greenland, in which case one sails north of Shetland so that one sights land in clear weather only, then south of the Faeroes so that the sea looks half-way up the mountainsides, then south of Iceland so that one gets sight of birds and whales from there.] From Reykjanes in the south of Iceland there is five days' sea to Jolduhlaup in Ireland [H. *adds* in the south; and from Langanes in the north of Iceland] it is four days' sea north to Svalbard in the Polar Gulf. [H. *adds* And it is a day's sail to the unlived in parts of Greenland from Kolbeinsey (*i.e.* Mevenklint,) in the north.]

2. *The Discoverers*

[*Sturlubók* version, 3–5] It is reported that men had a voyage to make from Norway to the Faeroes: some make mention in this connexion of Naddod the Viking. But they were storm-driven into the western ocean and discovered a big country there. In the Eastfirths they walked up on to a high mountain and had a good look all round, whether they would be able to see smoke or some sign that the land was inhabited, but saw nothing. In the autumn they returned to the Faeroes. As they sailed away there was a heavy snowfall on the mountains, for which reason they called the land Snæland, Snowland. They praised the land highly. The place they had come to is now known as Reydarfjall in the Eastfirths. So said priest Sæmund the Learned.

There was a man named Gardar Svavarsson, a Swede by descent: he set off to find Snæland at the direction of his mother, a seeress. He reached land east of the Eastern Horn, where in those days there was a haven. Gardar sailed round the land and found that it was an island. He spent the winter north at Husavik in Skjalfandi, and built a house there. In the spring, when he was ready for sea, their boat was torn adrift with a man named Nattfari on board, together with a thrall and a bondwoman. He made a home at the place since called Nattfaravik, but Gardar returned to Norway and praised the land highly. He was the father of Uni,

9

father of Hroar Tungu-godi. After this the land was called Gardarsholm: there was forest growing then between mountain and seashore.

There was a man named Floki Vilgerdarson, a great viking. He set off to find Gardarsholm and sailed from the place now known as Flokavardi, at the junction of Hordaland and Rogaland. But first he made for Shetland, and lay at anchor there in Floka-vag: his daughter Geirhild lost her life there in Geirhildarvatn. On board ship with Floki was a franklin named Thorolf and another named Herjolf, while there was also a Hebridean on board by the name of Faxi. Floki had taken three ravens to sea with him. When he loosed the first, it flew aft astern; the second flew high into the air, then back to the ship; the third flew straight ahead in the direction in which they found land. They made Horn from the east and sailed along the south coast. As they sailed west round Reykjanes and the fjord opened out before them so that they could see Snæfellsnes, 'This must be a big country we have found,' said Faxi. 'There are big rivers here!' Ever since it has been called Faxaos, Faxi's Estuary. Floki and his crew sailed west across Breidafjord and made land at what is now called Vatnsfjord, by Bardarstrand. The fjord was full of fish and seals, and because of the fishing they overlooked the need to make hay, and all their livestock perished during the winter. The spring was very cold. Floki walked up on to a high mountain, and north beyond the mountain could see a fjord full of drift ice, so they called the country Ísland, Iceland, the name by which it has been known ever since. Floki and his followers were determined to get away that summer, but completed their preparations to leave only a short while before winter. They failed to make their way round Reykjanes, their boat was torn adrift with Herjolf on board, who got ashore at what is now called Herjolfshofn. Floki spent the winter in Borgarfjord, where they found Herjolf, and next summer they sailed for Norway. When men inquired about the country, Floki gave it a bad name, Herjolf had both good and bad to say of it, while Thorolf swore that butter dripped from every blade of grass in that land they had found, for which reason he was nicknamed Thorolf Butter.

[*Hauksbók* version, 3–5] There was a man named Gardar, son of Svavar the Swede; he owned estates in Seeland but had been born in Sweden. He made a journey to the Hebrides to claim his wife's inheritance from her father, but as he was sailing through the Pentland Firth a gale drove him off course, and he was carried into the western ocean. He reached land east of Horn. Gardar sailed round the land and found that it was an island. He came to a fjord which he called Skjalfandi, put out a boat there, and his thrall Nattfari went aboard. The mooring-line broke, and he came ashore at Nattfaravik, away beyond Skuggabjorg. Gardar, though, made land the other side of the fjord and spent the winter there, which was why he called it Husavik, House Bay. Nattfari stayed behind with his thrall and bondwoman, which is why the place is called Nattfaravik;[1] but Gardar sailed back east and praised the land highly and called it Gardarsholm.

There was a man named Naddod, the brother of Oxen-Thorir, and a relation by marriage of Olvir Barnakarl. He was a great viking, who went off to make a home for himself in the Faeroes for the good reason that he had nowhere else where he would be safe. He left Norway with the Isles in mind, but was sea-tossed to Gardarsholm, where he arrived at Reydarfjord in the Eastfirths. They walked up on to a very high mountain to find whether they could see any human habitation or smoke, but saw never a sign. As they sailed away, there was a heavy snowfall, for which reason he called it Snæland, Snowland. They praised the land highly.

There was a great viking by the name of Floki Vilgerdarson who set out from Rogaland to seek Snæland. They lay in Smjorsund. He offered up a big sacrifice and hallowed three ravens which were to guide him on his way, for in those days sailors in the Northlands had no loadstone. They built a cairn where the sacrifice had been made and called it Flokuvardi—it is at the junction of Hordaland and Rogaland. But first he made for Shetland, and lay at anchor there in Flokavag: his daughter Geirhild lost her life there in Geirhildarvatn. On board ship with Floki was a franklin named Thorolf, another named Herjolf, and Faxi, a Hebridean. From Shetland Floki sailed to the Faeroes, where he found a husband for that daughter of his from whom Thrond of Gata is descended. From there he sailed out to sea with the three ravens he had hallowed in Norway. When he loosed the first,

---

[1] But Landn. S. 247 says further: 'Nattfari, who had come out with Gardar, owned Reykjadal earlier and had marked the trees; but Eyvind Askelsson drove him away and let him have Nattfaravik.'

it flew aft astern; the second flew high into the air, then back to the ship; the third flew straight ahead in the direction in which they found land. They made Horn from the east and sailed along the south coast. As they sailed west round Reykjanes and the fjord opened out before them so that they could see Snæfellsnes, 'This must be a big country we have found,' said Faxi. 'There are big rivers here!' Ever since it has been called Faxaos. Floki and his crew sailed west across Breidafjord and made land at what is now called Vatnsfjord, by Bardarstrand. The entire fjord was full of fish and seals, and because of the fishing they overlooked the need to make hay, and their livestock perished during the winter. The spring was very cold. Floki walked north to a mountain and saw a fjord full of drift ice, so they called the country Iceland. They went away that summer, but were late with their preparations. The site of their hall is still to be seen east of Brjanslœk, likewise their boat-house and fire-pit. They failed to make their way round Reykjanes, their boat was torn adrift with Herjolf on board, who got ashore at Herjolfshofn. Floki got ashore in Borgarfjord; they found a whale on a bank west of the fjord, so called it Hvaleyr; and there they found Herjolf. Next summer they sailed for Norway. Floki gave the land a bad name, Herjolf had both good and bad to say of it, while Thorolf swore that butter dripped from every blade of grass in that land they had found, for which reason he was nicknamed Thorolf Butter.

3. *The Settlers*

INGOLF AND HJORLEIF

[S. 6–9] There was a man named Bjornolf, and another Hroald: they were the sons of Hromund Gripsson. They left Telemark because of some killings and made their home at Dalsfjord in Fjalir. The son of Bjornolf was Orn, the father of Ingolf and Helga, while the son of Hroald was Hrodmar, the father of Leif.

The foster-brothers Ingolf and Leif went on viking cruises with the sons of earl Atli the Slender of Gaular, Hastein, Herstein, and Holmstein. All their activities together turned out well, and when they returned home they arranged to make an expedition together the next summer. That winter the foster-brothers made a feast for the earl's sons, and at this feast Holmstein made a vow that he would marry Orn's daughter Helga or no woman at all. This vow of his got a poor reception; Leif turned red, and there was little love lost between him and Holmstein when they parted at the feast.

Next spring the foster-brothers made ready to go off warring: they planned a meeting with earl Atli's sons. Their meeting-place was at Hisargafl, and Holmstein and his brothers promptly attacked Leif and his party. When they had been fighting a while, up came Olmod the Old, Horda-Kari's son and a kinsman of Leif's, and lent him and Ingolf a hand. In this fight Holmstein fell and Herstein fled, whereupon Leif and his foster-brother went off warring. The following winter Herstein marched against them, meaning to kill them, but they got news of his movements and moved against him. Once again there was a big fight, and Herstein fell. Following this, their friends from Firthafylki came crowding in to join the foster-brothers; emissaries of theirs were sent to meet earl Atli and Hastein, to offer peace terms, and the terms they reached were that Ingolf and Leif should pay over their estates to that father and son.

Then the foster-brothers fitted out a big ship of theirs, and set off to find that land Raven-Floki had discovered—the one called Iceland. They found it, and made a stay in the Eastfirths, in the southern Alptafjord. The land looked to them more promising south than north. They spent one winter in the land and then returned to Norway.

After this Ingolf laid out their money for the Iceland voyage, while Leif went on a viking cruise to the British Isles. He went harrying in Ireland, where he found a big underground house, which he entered. All was dark till light shone from a sword which a man was holding. Leif killed this man, and took the sword from him and great riches too, and from there on was known as Hjorleif, Sword-Leif. Hjorleif harried far and wide in Ireland, winning great riches there, and taking captive ten thralls, whose names are as follows: Dufthak and Geirrod, Skjaldbjorn, Halldor and Drafdrit (the rest are not named). After this Hjorleif returned to Norway to meet Ingolf his foster-brother. He had before this married Ingolf's sister, Helga Arnardottir. That winter Ingolf offered up extensive sacrifice and sought auguries of his destiny, but Hjorleif would never sacrifice. The auguries directed Ingolf to Iceland, so each brother-in-law fitted out his ship for the

Iceland voyage, Hjorleif putting his booty on board, and Ingolf their common stock; and once they were ready they put to sea.

The summer Ingolf and Hjorleif went off to settle Iceland, Harald Fairhair had been twelve years king of Norway; there had passed since the beginning of the world six thousand and seventy-three winters, and from the Incarnation of Our Lord eight hundred and seventy-four years. They sailed in company till they sighted Iceland, when they were parted. As soon as Ingolf sighted Iceland he cast his high-seat pillars overboard for an omen, vowing he would settle where the pillars came ashore. He reached land at the point now known as Ingolfshofdi, Ingolf's Head, but Hjorleif was carried west along the coast. He grew short of drinking water, so the Irish thralls tried a scheme of kneading meal and butter together; this, they claimed, was not a thirst-maker. They called it *minnpak*, but just as it was ready heavy rain came on, so they were able to catch water in the awnings. When the *minnpak* began to turn mouldy they threw it overboard, and it drifted ashore at the point now known as Minnthakseyr. Hjorleif reached land at Hjorleifshofdi, Hjorleif's Head. There was a fjord there in those days, and the end of the fjord turned in towards the headland. There he had two halls built, the walls of one eighteen fathoms long, and of the other nineteen. Hjorleif stayed there that winter; then in the spring he wanted to sow. He had only the one ox, so made his thralls drag the plough. While Hjorleif was occupied about the house with his men, Dufthak evolved a scheme whereby they were to kill the ox and report that a forest-bear had killed him, and afterwards set upon Hjorleif and the rest, if they went hunting the bear. So now they reported this to Hjorleif, and when they set off to hunt the bear and were scattered about the wood, the thralls attacked each his appointed prey and murdered them to the last man. Then they ran off with the women, the movable goods, and the boat. The thralls made their way out to the islands they could see in the sea to the south-west, where they continued living for a while.

There were two thralls of Ingolf's, Vifil and Karli by name, whom he sent west along the sea's edge looking for his seat-pillars. When they got as far as Hjorleifshofdi they found Hjorleif lying dead, so back they went to tell Ingolf what had happened. He was deeply moved by these killings, and afterwards set off west to Hjorleifshofdi, and when he saw Hjorleif lying dead, this is what he said. 'This was a sorry end for a brave man,' said he, 'that thralls should be the death of him; but so it goes, I see, with such as are not prepared to offer up sacrifice.' Ingolf had Hjorleif and his men buried and took charge of their ship and their share of the property. Ingolf then walked up to the headland and could see islands lying out to sea, to the south-west. It struck him that they would have run off there, because the boat had disappeared, so away they went to look for the thralls, and found them in the islands at the place now known as Eid. They were eating a meal when Ingolf surprised them. Panic whelmed them, and they ran each his own way. Ingolf killed them all. The place where Dufthak died is called Dufthaksskor. Many of them jumped off the cliff which has since been known by their name. The islands where these thralls were killed have been known ever since as the Vestmannaeyjar, because they were Vestmenn, Irishmen. Ingolf and his men took the wives of their own men who had been murdered away with them; they returned to Hjorleifshofdi, and it was there they spent the second winter.

The following summer he travelled west along the sea's edge, and spent the third winter under Ingolfsfell, west of Olfus river. This same season Vifil and Karli found his high-seat pillars by Arnarhval, west of the heath. In the spring Ingolf came down over the heath, to site his home where his pillars had come ashore, and lived at Reykjavik, and the pillars are there to this day in the living-room. Ingolf took land in settlement between Olfus river and Hvalfjord west of Brynjudalsa, and between there and Oxara, and the whole of the land projecting west. Said Karli: 'We travelled past good country to bad purpose, if we must live on this stuck-out limb of land!' So he cleared out, taking a bond-woman with him; but Ingolf gave Vifil his freedom, he made his home at Vifilstoftir, and Vifilsfell is named after him. He lived many a long day, and was a trusty man. Ingolf had a house built at Skalafell, and from it observed smoke over at Olfusvatn, where he found Karli.

Ingolf was the most celebrated of all settlers, for he came here to an unlived-in country and was the first to settle down in it: the other settlers did so by his example.

He married Hallveig Frodadottir, the sister of Lopt the Old. Their son was Thorstein, who had the Thing instituted at Kjalarnes before the Althing was established. Thorstein's son was Thorkel Mani the Lawspeaker, whose way of life was best of all those heathen men in Iceland of whom there is record. In his last illness he had himself carried out into the rays of the sun and committed himself into the hands of that God who had created the sun. Moreover he had lived as purely as those Christian men whose way of life is best. His son was Thormod, who was godi over the whole congregation when Christianity came to Iceland.

THOROLF MOSTRARSKEGG

[S. 85] Thorolf the son of Ornolf Fishdriver lived in Most—the reason why he was called Mostrarskegg. He was a great sacrificer who believed in Thor. He departed for Iceland because of the tyranny of king Harald Fairhair, sailing by way of the south coast; but when he arrived west off Breidafjord he cast overboard the pillars of his high-seat, on which the image of Thor was carved, supplicating Thor to come ashore wherever he would have Thorolf settle, with this undertaking, that he would dedicate his entire settlement to Thor and name it with his name. Thorolf sailed into the fjord and gave it a name, calling it Breidafjord, Broadfjord. He took land in settlement on its south shore, near the middle of the fjord, where he found Thor drifted on to a cape which is now known as Thorsnes. They landed further up in the bay which Thorolf named Hofsvag, where he built himself a home and raised a great temple, which he dedicated to Thor. The place is now known as Hofstadir. In those days there had been little or no settlement in Breidafjord.

Thorolf took possession of the land from Stafa in as far as Thorsa, and called the whole promontory Thorsnes. He had so great a reverence for the mountain which stood on that promontory, and which he called Helgafell, Holy Mountain, that no man should turn his unwashed face to it, and there was so inviolate a sanctuary there that nothing, neither man nor beast, should suffer harm there unless they left it of their own accord. It was the belief of Thorolf and his kindred that they would all die into this mountain.

There on the cape where Thor came ashore Thorolf had all courts held, and it was there that the district Thing was established with the approval of all who lived in that countryside. When men were in attendance at the Thing it was strictly forbidden for them to ease themselves on land, but a skerry known as Dritsker was earmarked for the purpose, for they would not defile so sacred a site as was there. But when Thorolf was dead, and Thorstein his son still young, Thorgrim Kjallaksson and Asgeir his brother-in-law were not prepared to walk to the skerry to ease themselves. But the Thorsnes men would not put up with this, the way they intended to defile so sacred a site, so they came to blows, Thorstein Thorskabit and Thorgeir Keng against Thorgrim and Asgeir; certain men fell and many were wounded before they could be parted. Thord Gellir made peace between them, and in as much as neither side would give way the field was then unhallowed by reason of the blood shed there. So now it was decided to remove the Thing from where it used to stand and up into the ness where it stands today, which consequently became a famous holy place. Thor's stone still stands there, on which they broke those men whom they sacrificed; and close by is the ring of judgement where men were sentenced to be sacrificed. There too Thord Gellir established the Quarter Thing with the approval of all who lived in the Quarter. . . .

[S. 123] Thorolf Mostrarskegg's son Hallstein took Thorskafjord in settlement and lived at Hallsteinsnes. He offered up a sacrifice that Thor should send him pillars for a high-seat, whereupon a tree drifted ashore on his land which was sixty-three ells long and two fathoms thick. This was used for high-seat pillars, and from it are made the high-seat pillars of practically every homestead throughout that network of fjords. The place is now called Grenitrenes, Pinetree Ness, where the tree came ashore. Hallstein had been out harrying in Scotland, where he captured those thralls he brought home with him. These he sent to the saltworkings on Svefneyjar.[1]

HELGI MAGRI

[H. 184] There was a nobleman in Gautland by the name of Bjorn, the son of Hrolf of the River; he was married to Hlif daughter of Hrolf the son of Ingjald, son of king Frodi (Starkad the Old was court-poet to both these kings), and their son's name was Eyvind.

---

[1] According to tradition he found his thralls asleep upon Svefneyjar, Sleep Isles, when they should be making salt, and hanged them by the cliffs called Galgi, Gallows.

Bjorn had a quarrel over land with Sigfast the father-in-law of Solvar king of the Gauts. Sigfast had married his daughter to earl Solvar, and the earl backed Sigfast so strongly that he laid forceful hands on all Bjorn's estates. So Bjorn made over all his goods in Gautland to Hlif his wife and Eyvind his son, and departed from the east with twelve horses laden with silver. But the night before he departed the country he burned Sigfast to death in his house together with thirty men, then made for Norway.

He came west to Agdir, to Grim the Hersir at Hvinir . . . who made him most welcome. Bjorn and his comrades spent the winter with Grim, but one night in late spring Bjorn woke to find a man standing over him with a drawn sword and shaping to cut at him. He grabbed at his arm—he had been hired by Grim to cut off Bjorn's head. Bjorn did not kill him. Grim had intended to betray him for the sake of his money. So away went Bjorn to Ondott Kraka who had his home in Hvinisfjord . . . Bjorn went on viking cruises to the British Isles in the summers, but his winters he spent with Ondott. It was now that Hlif died back in Gautland, so Bjorn married Ondott's sister Helga; their son was Thrond the Far-sailer. Next, Hlif's son Eyvind came from the east to Bjorn his father, and when Bjorn grew tired of campaigning he took over his father's warships together with that profession he had followed. Later, in Ireland, Eyvind married Raforta daughter of king Kjarval. She gave birth to a boy in the Hebrides, and he was put out to foster there. Eyvind was called Eastman because he had come west across the sea from the kingdom of the Swedes back east. Two years later they returned to the islands to see how the boy was doing, and saw a boy there with fine eyes but no flesh on his bones, for he was starved, which was why they nicknamed him Helgi Magri, Helgi the Lean. After this he was fostered in Ireland.

Bjorn died at Ondott his brother-in-law's. Grim argued that it was for the king to take over his entire inheritance, because he was a foreigner and his sons were west across the sea; but Ondott held on to that wealth on behalf of his nephew Thrond.

Helgi was brought up in Ireland; he married Thorunn Hyrna, the daughter of Ketil Flatnose of the Hebrides . . . they had a lot of children. In course of time Helgi went to Iceland with his wife and children, Hrolf and Ingjald and that Ingunn whom Hamund Heljarskin married (he too came out with Helgi). When Helgi sighted land he consulted Thor as to where he should go ashore; the oracle directed him to Eyjafjord, strongly enjoining him to hold neither east nor west of it. Before the fjord opened up ahead of them his son Hrolf asked whether, if Thor had directed them into the Arctic Ocean for winter quarters, he would have obeyed or not. [S. His son Hrolf asked whether Helgi would have held for the Arctic Ocean if Thor had directed him there, for it seemed to the crew high time to leave the sea now that summer was so far advanced.] Helgi made land beyond Hrisey and inwards of Svarfadardal, to spend his first winter at Hamundarstadir. They had so severe a winter that it was touch and go whether the livestock they brought with them would perish; but in the spring Helgi walked up on to Solarfjall and could see how the land looked much darker [i.e. freer from snow] up in the fjord [S. *adds* which they called Eyjafjord, Island Fjord, from the islands which lay off its mouth]. He carried everything he had back on board ship, and landed by Galtarhamar, where he put a couple of pigs ashore, a boar by the name of Solvi and a sow, and when they were found three years later in Solvadal, all told there were seventy of them.

That winter Helgi lived at Bildsa, then in the summer explored the entire countryside, taking in settlement the whole of Eyjafjord between Siglunes and Reynisnes, and building a big fire at every river mouth down by the sea, thus hallowing to himself the entire fjord between those nesses. One winter later Helgi moved his household to Kristnes, where he lived to the end of his days. He was very mixed in his beliefs: he believed in Christ, and yet made vows to Thor for sea-voyages and in tight corners, and for everything which struck him as of real importance.

While Helgi was moving house Thorunn Hyrna was delivered of a child on Thorunnarey in Eyjafjardararkvisl. This was when Thorbjorg Holmasol, Island-sun, was born.

And afterwards Helgi distributed land among his sons and sons-in-law.

KETILBJORN THE OLD

[S. 385] There was a nobleman in Naumudal by the name of Ketilbjorn, the son of Ketil and Æsa daughter of earl Hakon Grjotgardsson; he was married to Helga, Thord Skeggi's daughter.

Ketilbjorn went out to Iceland at a time when the land alongside
the sea was already extensively settled. He had a ship which bore
the name Ellidi, and brought her into Ellidaaros [the mouth of
Ellidi river] below the heath, and spent his first winter with his
father-in-law Thord Skeggi. In the spring he went up over the
heath to look for some good land. They had a place to sleep there
and built themselves a hall: the place is now known as Skala-
brekka, Hall-slope. When they left there they came to a river
which they called Oxara, Axe river, because they lost their axe
there. They spent some time under the mountain peak which they
named Reydarmuli, Trout-peak, because there they left behind
the river-trout which they had caught in the river. Ketilbjorn
took all Grimsnes in settlement north of Hoskuldslœk, the whole
of Laugardal, and all Byskupstunga up to Stakksa, and made his
home at Mosfell . . .

Ketilbjorn was so rich in money that he ordered his sons to
forge a cross-beam of silver for the temple they were building.
This they refused to do. So with Haki his thrall and Bot his
bondwoman he hauled the silver up on to the mountain with two
oxen, and they buried the treasure so that it has never been found
from that day to this. Whereupon he did away with Haki at
Hakaskard and with Bot at Botarskard.

[His son] Teit married Alof the daughter of Bodvar of Vors,
the son of Vikinga-Kari: their son was Gizur the White, the
father of bishop Isleif, father of bishop Gizur. Another son of
Teit was Ketilbjorn, the father of Kol, father of Thorkel, father
of Kol the Vik Men's bishop. Many great men are descended from
Ketilbjorn.

GEIRRID AND THOROLF

[S. 86] Geirrod was the name of a man who left Halogaland for
Iceland, and with him . . . Ulfar Kappi. Geirrod took land in
settlement inwards from Thorsa to Langadalsa, and lived at Eyr.
To Ulfar his shipmate he gave land on both sides of Ulfarsfell
and inland from the mountain.

Geirrod had a sister by the name of Geirrid, whom Bjorn son
of Bolverk Blindingatrjona, Gadfly Snout, married: their son's
name was Thorolf. After Bjorn's death Geirrid went out to
Iceland with her son, and they spent their first winter at Eyr.

In the spring Geirrod gave his sister a homestead in Borgardal, while Thorolf went abroad and applied himself to viking cruises. Geirrid was not grudging of her food to men: she had her hall built straddling the highway, and would sit on a stool outside and invite guests in, and there was always a table standing indoors with food on it.

Thorolf returned to Iceland after Geirrod's death. He challenged Ulfar for his land and offered him holmgang [*i.e.* island-going, wager of battle]. Ulfar was old by this time and childless; he fell on the island, while Thorolf was wounded in the leg; he walked lame ever after, for which reason he was nicknamed Bægifot. Thorolf took some of Ulfar's land in succession to him, and some Thorfinn of Alptafjord took.

4. *Strife and Feud*

MURDER ON GUNNBJORN'S SKERRIES

[S. 151–52] Snæbjorn, the son of Eyvind Eastman and brother of Helgi Magri, took land in settlement between Mjovafjord and Langadalsa, and made a home in Vatnsfjord. His son was Holmstein, the father of Snæbjorn Galti. Snæbjorn Galti's mother was Kjalvor, so he and Tungu-Odd were first cousins. Snæbjorn was fostered at Thingnes with Thorodd, but at times would be staying with Tungu-Odd or his mother.

Hallbjorn the son of Odd of Kidjaberg (the son of Hallkel the brother of Ketilbjorn the Old) married Tungu-Odd's daughter Hallgerd. They spent their first winter at Odd's, and Snæbjorn Galti was living there at the time. There was little love between husband and wife.

In the spring Hallbjorn made preparations for changing house at the moving-days in late May, and as he got ready Odd left home for the hot spring at Reykjaholt, where his sheep-houses stood. He had no wish to be present when Hallbjorn moved out, for he had a notion Hallgerd would be unwilling to go with him. Odd had always been a peace-maker between them.

When Hallbjorn had saddled their horses he walked into the women's bower, and there was Hallgerd, seated on the dais combing her hair. Her hair fell all about her and down to the floor, for she and Hallgerd Snuinbrok have had the loveliest hair

of all the women of Iceland. Hallbjorn told her to stand up and
be moving. She sat still and said nothing. Then he laid hands on
her, but she did not stir. This happened three times. Then
Hallbjorn stood in front of her and spoke this verse:

> 'My lady clad in linen
> Lets me stand and stare before her;
> Fair Goddess of the ale-cup,
> She turns her back and scorns me;
> Cold grows my love, and colder
> All hope such hate can alter;
> Pale on my cheek grief's pallor,
> And sorrow gnaws my heart-roots.'

After this he twisted her hair round his hand, intending to drag
her off the dais, but she sat firm and unstirring. So at that he drew
his sword and cut off her head, walked out and rode away, and
they were three men together, with a couple of pack-horses.

There were only a few people at home, but they sent instantly
to tell Odd. Snæbjorn was staying at Kjalvararstadir, and Odd
dispatched a messenger to him, asking him to see to the pursuit,
for he himself, he said, would be making no move. Snæbjorn
gave chase with eleven men, and when Hallbjorn and his companions saw that they were pursued they begged him to ride off,
but he refused. Snæbjorn and his men caught up with them at the
hillocks which are now known as Hallbjarnarvordur, Hallbjorn's
Cairns. Hallbjorn got up on to the hillocks with his men, and it
was from there that they made their defence. Three men from
Snæbjorn's party fell there and both Hallbjorn's companions.
Next Snæbjorn sheared off Hallbjorn's foot at the ankle-joint;
he hobbled off to the southernmost hillock, where he killed two
more of Snæbjorn's men, and where he himself fell. That is why
there are three cairns on that hillock, and five on the other. After
this Snæbjorn returned home.

Snæbjorn owned a ship in Grimsaros, and Hrolf of Raudasand
bought a half share in her. They were twelve in either party. With
Snæbjorn were Thorkel and Sumarlid, the sons of Thorgeir the
Red, son of Einar of Stafholt; and he further added to his company Thorodd of Thingnes, his foster-father, together with his
wife; while Hrolf took Styrbjorn, who after a dream he had spoke
this verse:

'I see the bane
Of both us twain:
Grim weird to dree
North-west o'er sea.
Frost there and cold,
Horrors untold;
By such revealed,
Know Snæbjorn killed.'

They set off in search of Gunnbjarnarsker and found land.
Snæbjorn was unwilling for them to go exploring by night.
Styrbjorn left the ship and found a purse of money in a burial
mound and hid it. Snæbjorn struck him with his axe, and the purse
fell down. They built a hall which became buried under snow.
Thorkel the son of Red discovered that there was water on a pole
which protruded from the house window (this was in Goi
[February and early March]), so they dug themselves out. Snæbjorn was mending the ship, while Thorodd and his wife stayed at
the house on his behalf, along with Styrbjorn and his men on
behalf of Hrolf. The others were fishing and hunting. Styrbjorn
killed Thorodd, and he and Hrolf together killed Snæbjorn. The
sons of Red and all the rest of them gave pledges, in order to save
their lives.

They made Halogaland, and from there voyaged to Iceland, to
Vadil. Thorkel Trefil had a shrewd idea how matters had gone
with the sons of Red. Hrolf built a fortress on Strandarheid, and
Trefil sent Sveinung for his head. First he came to Myr to
Hermund, then to Olaf at Drangar, then to Gest at Hagi, who
sent him on to Hrolf his friend. Sveinung killed both Hrolf and
Styrbjorn, then went back to Hagi. Gest exchanged sword and
axe with him, and supplied him with two black-maned horses;
then had a man ride round Vadil right to Kollafjord, and got
Thorbjorn the Strong to go and claim the horses; and Thorbjorn
killed him at Sveinungseyr because Sveinung's sword snapped off
below the hilt. Because of this Trefil would boast against Gest,
when their wits were matched together, that he had so out-witted
Gest that he himself sent a man to cut off the head of his own
friend.

LOVE THE DESTROYER

[S. 284] Uni the son of Gardar, who first discovered Iceland, went

out to Iceland at the bidding of king Harald Fairhair, proposing
to subjugate the land, after which the king had promised to make
him his earl. Uni reached land at the point now known as Unaos
and set up house there; he took land in settlement south of
Lagarfljot, the entire countryside as far as Unalœk. But once the
Icelanders got wind of his purpose they treated him very coolly,
would sell him neither livestock nor provisions, and he could not
keep his footing there. Uni went off to the southern Alptafjord,
failed to make a lodgement, so left the east with twelve men, and
came in the winter to Leidolf Kappi in Skogahverfi, who took
them in. He became the lover of Thorunn, Leidolf's daughter,
and by spring she was carrying his child. Uni now wanted to clear
out with his men, but Leidolf rode after him, they met by Flanga-
stadir and fought there, because Uni was not prepared to go back
with Leidolf. Certain of Uni's men fell there, and willy-nilly
back he went, for Leidolf wanted him to marry his daughter and
settle down, then take the inheritance after his day. Somewhat
later Uni ran away when Leidolf was absent from home; but
once Leidolf knew of it he rode after him and they met by Kalfagrafir. This time he was so angry that he killed Uni and all his
comrades.

[*Þórðarbók*. Uni the Dane the son of Gardar wished to make
Iceland subject to himself or to king Harald Fairhair. He lived at
Os, but knew no rest there, so set off to explore the land more
widely and found winter quarters with Leidolf. Uni became the
lover of Thorunn his daughter and wanted to take her away with
him, but Leidolf rode after him, they fought by Kalfagrafir, and
men fell on either side. Then they parted, but Uni got only a
short way before Leidolf came up in pursuit, they fought a second
time, and Uni and his comrades fell.]

The son of Uni and Thorunn was Hroar Tungu-Godi; he took
Leidolf's entire inheritance: he was an overpowering sort of man.
He married a daughter of Hamund (a sister of Gunnar of Hlidar-
endi); their son was Hamund the Halt, a notable manslayer.
Tjorvi the Mocker and Gunnar were Hroar's nephews.

Tjorvi asked for Astrid Manvitsbrekka, the daughter of
Modolf, but her brothers Ketil and Hrolf refused him the lady,
and gave her to Thorir Ketilsson. So Tjorvi drew their likenesses
on the privy wall, and every evening when he and Hroar went to
the privy he would spit in the face of Thorir's likeness and kiss

5. THOR

16. HEATHEN GRAVE AT SÍLASTADIR, ICELAND

A man's bones with axe, sword, shield boss (the shield had been placed to cover his head), knife, weights, and (out of the picture) a spear and the skeletons of two horses.

hers, until Hroar scraped them off. After that he carved them on the handle of his knife, and spoke this verse:

> 'First, Wealth-Thrud and her Thorir
> Well-drawn I set on wall,
> Young bride as well as bridegroom,
> So insolence matched insult!
> Now hold I carved on knife-hilt
> Her homage-laden image;
> Many's the word I've whispered
> In ear of that bright lady!'

From which arose the killing of Hroar and his sister's sons

THE SONS OF BAUG

[S. 348] There was a man named Baug, the foster-brother of Ketil Hœng, who went out to Iceland, to spend his first winter at Baugsstadir and his second with Hœng [at Hof in Rangarvellir]. At Hœng's direction he took in settlement the whole of Fljotshlid down from Breidabolstad to meet with Hœng's own land, and made a home at Hlidarendi. His sons were Gunnar of Gunnarsholt, Eyvind of Eyvindarmuli, and, third, Stein the Swift; while his daughter was that Hild whom Orn of Vælugerdi married.

Stein the Swift and Sigmund, Sighvat the Red's son, had a journey to make back home from Eyrar and they arrived all together at the Sandholar ferry (Sigmund, that is, and Stein's companions). Each party wanted to cross the river first. Sigmund and his men shoved Stein's housecarles out of their way, and sent them packing from the boat, but just then up came Stein and promptly struck Sigmund his deathblow. For this killing all Baug's sons were banished from Fljotshlid. Gunnar went off to Gunnarsholt, Eyvind east under Eyjafjall to Eyvindarhol, and Snjallstein [*i.e.* Stein the Swift] to Snjallsteinshofdi. Sigmund's daughter Thorgerd was far from pleased when her father's slayer came out there, and goaded Onund her husband into taking revenge for Sigmund. Onund made for Snjallshofdi with thirty men and set fire to the house there. Snjallstein came out and gave himself up; they led him up to the Head, where they killed him. Gunnar took up the bloodsuit for this killing. He was married to Hrafnhild Storolfsdottir, sister of Orm the Strong; their son was

Hamund, and the pair of them, both father and son, were out-standing men for strength and fine appearance.

Onund was outlawed for killing Snjallstein; for two years he sat tight with a strong body of men about him, while Gunnar's brother-in-law Orn of Vælugerdi watched his every move. The third winter, after Yule, in the light of Orn's information, Gunnar fell upon Onund with thirty men as he was going from the games with eleven men to fetch his horses. They clashed in Orrustudal, Battle Dale; Onund fell with three of his men, and one man of Gunnar's. Gunnar was wearing a blue cloak. He rode up along Holt to Thjorsa, then just short of the river fell off his horse, dead of his wounds.

Once Onund's sons Sigmund Kleykir and Eilif the Rich grew up they pressed their kinsman Mord Fiddle to take up the blood-suit. This was no easy matter, said Mord, in respect of an out-lawed man. They stressed that they felt strongest of all about Orn, who lived closest to them, so Mord's advice was this, that they should contrive a suit for full outlawry against Orn and so run him out of the district. So Onund's sons prosecuted Orn for un-lawful grazing, and he was outlawed to this extent, that he should fall unhallowed [*i.e.* without need for atonement] at the hands of the sons of Onund everywhere except at Vælugerdi and within arrow-shot range of his own land. Onund's sons lay in wait for him endlessly, but he took good care of himself; even so they got their chance at him one day when he was chasing cattle off his land; they killed him, and everyone thought he would have fallen unhallowed.

But Thorleif Gneisti, Orn's brother, paid Thormod Thjostar-son (he had just put in to Eyrar from abroad) to hallow Orn. He flighted so long a shot from his long-bow that Orn's death was found to have taken place inside his arrow-shot-range sanctuary. So now Hamund Gunnarsson and Thorleif took up the blood-suit for Orn, while Mord backed those brothers, who paid no fine but were banished out of Floi. Then, on behalf of Eilif, Mord asked for Thorkatla Ketilbjarnardottir, and Hordaland came with her from home by way of dowry, and it was there Eilif made his home; and on behalf of Sigmund he asked for Arngunn, Thorstein Drangakarl's daughter, so he left for the east. Finally Mord gave his sister Rannveig to Hamund Gunnarsson, who then returned to the Hlid, and their son was Gunnar of Hlidarendi.

5. *Thralls*

KETIL GUFA'S IRISHMEN

[S. 125] There was a man called Ketil Gufa Orlygsson ... [who] came out to Iceland when the period of settlement was well advanced. He had been on viking cruises in the west, on which he had captured Irish thralls, one called Thormod, a second Floki, a third Kori, a fourth Svart, and two by the name of Skorri. Ketil came to Rosmhvalanes, to spend the first winter at Gufuskalar, then in the spring went on to Nes and spent his second winter at Gufunes. It was now that Skorri the elder and Floki ran off with two women and a lot of goods; they went into hiding in Skorra-holt, but were killed in Flokadal and Skorradal.

Ketil found no place to live in the Nesses, so went into Borgar-fjord, to spend his third winter at Gufuskalar on Gufa river. Early in the spring he made a journey west to Breidafjord looking for a place for himself. Here he stayed at Geirmundarstadir; he asked for Geirmund's daughter Yr and got her, whereupon Geirmund [Heljarskin] directed Ketil to territories west in the fjord. But while Ketil was out west his thralls ran off and came by night to Lambastadir. At this time Thord was living there, the son of Thorgeir Lambi and Thordis Yngvarsdottir, the aunt of Egil Skallagrimsson. The thralls set the house on fire, and burned Thord to death with all his household; they broke into a store-house and seized a lot of goods and chattels, next drove in horses and loaded them, then headed off on the road to Alptanes. The morning they moved out Thord's son Lambi the Strong came home from the Thing; he set off in pursuit of them, and men flocked to him from the homesteads round about. When the thralls saw this they went running off, every one his own road. They caught Kori on Koranes, but some took to swimming. Svart they caught up with on Svartsker, Skorri on Skorrey off the Myrar, and Thormod out on Thormodssker, a mile from land.

And when Ketil Gufa came back he set off westward past the Myrar and spent his fourth winter on Snæfellsnes at Gufuskalar. Later he took in settlement Gufufjord and Skalanes out as far as Kollafjord.

ATLI OF FLJOT

[S. 149] There was a nobleman in Sogn named Geir, who was

known as Vegeir, Temple-Geir or Holy-Geir, he was such a great
man for sacrifices. He had many children. Vebjorn Sygnakappi,
the Sognmen's Champion, was his eldest son, and in addition
Vestein, Vethorm, Vemund, Vegest and Vethorn, while Vedis
was his daughter. After the death of Vegeir, Vebjorn fell foul of
earl Hakon, as was related earlier, so the brothers and their sister
set off for Iceland. They had a hard passage and a long, but reached
Hloduvik west of Horn in the autumn. Thereupon Vebjorn set
about a mighty sacrifice: earl Hakon, he said, was that very day
sacrificing in order that disaster might overtake them. But while
he was about his sacrifice his brothers pressed him to get moving,
he neglected his business, and they put to sea. That same day, in
foul weather, they were shipwrecked under huge cliffs; with great
difficulty they got themselves up, Vebjorn leading the way. That
is now called Sygnakleif, the Sognmen's Cliff. Atli of Fljot, a thrall
of Geirmund Heljarskin, took them all into shelter for the winter.
And when Geirmund heard tell of this resourceful act of Atli's he
gave him his freedom together with the farm he had charge of.
[H. Atli . . . took them all into shelter for the winter, telling them
there was nothing to pay for their keep. Geirmund, he assured
them, was not skimped for provisions. When Atli met Geirmund,
Geirmund asked him how he could be so bold as to entertain such
men at his, Geirmund's, expense. 'Because', replied Atli, 'it will
be remembered as long as Iceland is lived in how splendid was
that man's way of life when a thrall of his dared do such a thing
without asking his leave.' 'For this conduct of yours', announced
Geirmund, 'you shall receive your freedom, along with the farm
which was in your charge.'] In the days to come Atli became a
man of mark and substance.

The following spring Vebjorn took land in settlement between
Skotufjord and Hestfjord, Horsefjord, as far as he could walk
round in a day, and that piece over and beyond which he called
Folafot, Foalfoot. Vebjorn was a great man for fighting, and there
is a big saga relating to him. He gave Vedis in marriage to Grimolf
of Unadsdal; they quarrelled and Vebjorn killed him alongside
Grimolfsvatn, in return for which Vebjorn was killed at the
Quarter Thing at Thorsnes, and three others with him.

RODREK AND RONGUD

[S. 194] Hrosskel was the name of a man who took in settlement the whole of Svartardal and all Yrarfellsland at the direction of Eirik [of Goddalir]; he took land into his possession down as far as Gilhagi and lived at Yrarfell. He had a thrall whose name was Rodrek, whom he sent up along Mælifellsdal looking for settleable land on the high ground to the south. He came upon that ghyll leading south from Mælifell which is now known as Rodreksgil, where he set up a new-peeled staff which they called Landkonnud, Land-prober, and after that made his way back . . .

[S. 196] There was a man named Vekel the Shape-changer who took land in settlement down from Gila to Mælifellsa and lived at Mælifell. He heard about Rodrek's journey, and a little later went south himself to that high ground looking for settleable land. He came upon the mounds which are now known as Vekelshaugar, shot an arrow [*or* spear] between them, and at that point turned back. And when Eirik of Goddalir heard of this, he sent a thrall of his, Rongud by name, south to the high ground; he too went looking for settleable land. He came south to Blondukvisl, then went up along the river which flows down from west of Vinverjadal, and west to the lava between Reykjavellir and the mountain Kjol, Keel, where he came across the tracks of a man. As he saw it, these must have come from the south. It was there he erected the cairn which is now known as Rangadarvarda, Rongud's Cairn. At that point he turned back, and Eirik gave him his freedom for this journey of his; and from then on a route was established over the high ground between the Southlanders' Quarter and the Northlanders'.

6. *Animals*

SEAL-THORIR AND MARE SKALM

[S. 68] There was a man named Grim, the son of Ingjald, son of Hroald of Haddingjadal, the brother of Asi the hersir. He went to Iceland to look for land, sailing the northern route, and spent the winter on Grimsey in Steingrimsfjord. His wife's name was Bergdis, and his son's Thorir.

In the autumn Grim rowed out fishing with his housecarles, and the lad Thorir lay in the prow in a sealskin bag which was drawn in at the neck. Grim pulled up a merman, and when he came up asked him: 'What do you prophesy of our fortune? And where shall we settle in Iceland?' 'No point in prophesying of you and your men,' the merman answered him, 'but for the lad who lies in the sealskin bag, why, yes. He shall settle and take land where Skalm your mare lies down under her load.' Not another word could they get from him, but later that winter Grim and his men rowed out fishing, whilst the lad was left ashore, and were drowned to the last man. [H. In the winter Grim rowed out fishing with his thralls, and his son was with him. And when the lad began to grow chilly they wrapped him in a sealskin bag which they drew in at the neck. Grim pulled up a merman. 'Tell us our lives and how long we shall live,' said Grim, 'or you shall never see your home again.' 'There is no point in your knowing, save for the lad in the sealskin bag, for before spring comes you will be dead, but your son shall settle and take land where Skalm your mare lies down under her load.' Not another word could they get from him, but later that winter Grim died and is buried in a mound there.]

In the spring Bergdis and Thorir left Grimsey and went west over the heath to Breidafjord. Skalm kept moving ahead and never once lay down, and they spent their second winter at Skalmarnes in Breidafjord. The following summer they turned off south, and still Skalm kept going till they came off the heath south into Borgarfjord, at a point where two red sandhills stood before them, and there she lay down under her load under the westernmost hill. And it was there that Thorir took land in settlement from south of Gnupa to Kalda, below Knappadal, between mountain and seashore. He lived at the outer Raudamel, and was a great chieftain.

When Thorir was old and blind he came out of doors late one evening and saw how a man was rowing from the sea into the mouth of Kalda river in an iron boat, a big, evil-looking creature who walked ashore and up to the farm called Hripi, where he started digging at the entrance to the milking-shed. During the night fire erupted out of the earth, and it was then that Borgarhraun was blasted and consumed. The farm stood where Eldborg, the Fire-Fortress, stands now . . . Skalm, Thorir's mare, came to her death in Skalmarkelda, Skalmsquag.

DOVE-BEAK AND MARE FLY

[S. 202] Thorir Dufunef, Dove-beak, was a freedman of Oxen-Thorir's. He brought his ship into Gonguskardsaros at a time when the whole country west had already been settled, so off he went north over Jokulsa river to Landbrot and took land in settlement between Glodafeykisa and Djupa, and made a home at Flugumyr.

At that time a ship came here to Iceland into Kolbeinsaros with a cargo of livestock. They lost a young mare in the woods at Brimnesskogar, and Thorir Dufunef bought the reversion of her, and later found her: she was the fleetest of all horses, and was called Fluga, Fly.

There was a man named Orn who travelled the countryside and was a wizard. He waylaid Thorir in Vinverjadal, as he was making his way south past Kjol, and made a bet with him as to whose horse was the fleeter, for he had a fine stallion of his own. They bet a hundred in silver apiece. They rode south, the two of them, past Kjol, till they arrived at the course which has been known ever since as Dufunefsskeid, Dufunef's Course. The difference in their horses' speed was so marked that Thorir turned back to meet Orn half-way along the course. Orn took the loss of his wager so much to heart that he had no desire to live; he went up under the mountain now called Arnarfell and did away with himself. Fluga was left behind there, she was so exhausted, but when Thorir returned from the Thing he found a grey, black-maned stallion keeping her company, and she was in foal by him. From them sprang Eidfaxi, who was shipped abroad and caused the death of seven men at lake Mjor in one day, and perished there himself. Fluga was lost in a bog at Flugumyr, Fly-mire.

BUCK-BJORN

[S. 328–29] Living in Nordmœr in Norway at a place called Moldatun was a man known as Hrolf the Hewer. His sons were Vemund and Molda-Gnup, great manslayers and ironsmiths. Vemund recited this ditty while he was in the smithy working:

> 'I bore alone
> From eleven men
> A killer's name.
> Blow harder, man!'

Gnup departed for Iceland because of his own killings and his brother's, and took land in settlement between Kudafljot and Eyjara and all Alptaver. There was a big mere there in those days,

and wild swans for the catching. Molda-Gnup sold part of his
settlement to numerous men, and the district grew thick with
people before fire and lava over-ran it, and they fled away west
to Hofdabrekka to build booths and tent them over at a place
called Tjaldavoll. But Vemund the son of Sigmund Kleykir
would not allow them quarters there, so now they went to
Hrossagard where they built a long-house and spent the winter.
Quarrels arose because of them, and killings, so next spring
Molda-Gnup and the rest of them went west to Grindavik, where
they settled down. They had hardly any livestock. By now Molda-
Gnup's sons, Bjorn and Gnup, Thorstein Hrungnir and Thord
Leggjaldi, were grown to man's estate.

One night Bjorn dreamed that a rock-dweller appeared before
him, offering to go partners with him, and it seemed to him he
said yes to it. After which a buck came to his she-goats, and his
flocks multiplied so fast that soon he was rolling in money. Ever
after he was known as Hafr-Bjorn, Buck-Bjorn. Men with second-
sight saw how all the guardian spirits of the countryside accompanied Hafr-Bjorn to the Thing, and Thorstein and Thord when
hunting and fishing.

COALBITER AND BEAR

[S. 259] There was a man by the name of Arngeir who took in
settlement the whole of Sletta between Havararlon and Svein-
ungsvik. His children were Thorgils, Odd, and that Thurid who
married Steinolf of Thjorsardal. [H. *adds* Odd was for ever hanging about the fire when a lad; he was a sluggard and branded a
'coalbiter'.] Arngeir and Thorgils left home in a snowstorm
looking for sheep and never came back. Odd set off to look for
them and found them both dead. A white bear had killed them:
he was devouring his prey when Odd arrived on the scene. He
killed the bear, then hauled it back home, and men report that he
ate the whole of it, claiming that he avenged his father when he
killed the bear, and his brother when he ate it. From there on
Odd proved a very awkward one indeed. He was such a shape-
changer that he walked from home, from Hraunhofn, one evening
and next morning arrived in Thjorsardal to give help to his sister
when the Thjorsardalers were about to stone her to death [H. to
stone her for witchcraft and trolldom].[1]

[1] A walk of about 220 miles over some of Iceland's worst country.

7. *Hungry Years*

[*Skarðsárbók*, Viðauki, 1–2] There was a great famine-winter in Iceland in heathen days at the time when king Harald Graycloak fell and earl Hakon seized power in Norway [975–76], the severest there has been in Iceland. Men ate ravens then and foxes, and many abominable things were eaten which ought not to be eaten, and some had the old and helpless killed and thrown over the cliffs. Many starved to death, while others took to theft and for that were convicted and slain. Even the outlaws killed each other, for at the instance of Eyjolf Valgerdarson it was made law that anyone who killed three outlaws should himself go free.

Eighty years later came another year of dearth. It started that winter Isleif was consecrated as bishop by bishop Albertus of Bremen, in the days of king Harald Sigurdarson. And the first winter Isleif was in Iceland [1057–58] there was severe mortality here because of hunger. Everything was eaten then that tooth could fasten on.

During the summer the bishop had a vow taken at the Thing that men should fast on the twelfth day of Yule for three years, for that was the custom at Herford in Germany where he had been at school. There was such deep snow everywhere at this time that most men had to walk to the Thing [in June]. But as soon as this vow was taken the weather cleared immediately, it developed into a splendid summer, and the following winter was so clement that the earth was quite unfrozen, and men walked barefoot to service at Yule, and built houses and walls during January and February.

[*Kristni Saga*, c. 14] In the year bishop Gizur died [1118] there was a great famine in Iceland. During Holy Week there came so great a snowstorm that in some districts in the north men could not hold services in the churches. On Good Friday itself a merchant ship was driven ashore under Eyjafjall, spun into the air, fifty-four-oared vessel as she was, and dashed down bottom up. The first day of Easter few men could get to service to take the sacrament, and some perished out of doors.

A second storm came after his death, the day men rode to the Thing [19 or 20 June]. It was then that the church at Thingvellir for which king Harald Sigurdarson had had the timber cut was broken to pieces.

That summer thirty-five ships came out to Iceland; many were wrecked on the coast, some broke up at sea under their crews' feet, and only eight got away again, including those which had spent the previous winter here, while none of them got off the sea before Michaelmas. By reason of this host of men there was a great famine here . . .

One year after the death of bishop Gizur a notable person, Thorstein Hallvardsson, was killed. The year after that the Thing was very well attended. During those seasons the mortality had been so high that priest Sæmund the Learned made an announcement at the Thing that the men who had died of sickness could not be fewer in number than those who were then attending the Thing.

8. *Of the Settlement in General*

I

[H. 294] The Eastfirths were settled first in Iceland; but between Hornafjord and Reykjanes was the area last to be fully settled: there wind and surf stopped men getting ashore, what with the lack of harbours and the exposed nature of the coast.

Some of those who came out earliest lived close up to the mountains, remarking the quality of the land there, and how the livestock was keen to get away from the sea up to the high ground. Those who came out later thought that these first-comers had made over-extensive settlements; but king Harald Fairhair made peace between them on these terms, that no one should settle land more widely than he and his crew could carry fire round in one day.

They must light a fire when the sun showed in the east. They must light further smoke-fires, so that each might be observed from the other, and those fires which were lighted when the sun showed in the east must burn till nightfall. Afterwards they must walk until the sun was in the west, and at that point light other fires.

II

[*Skarðsárbók* 313] It was the law that a woman should not take land in settlement more widely than a two-year-old heifer, a half stalled beast in good condition, might be led round on a spring day between the rising and setting of the sun.

III

[H. 268] This was the beginning of the heathen laws, that men should not have a ship with a figure-head at sea, but if they had, they must remove the head before coming in sight of land, and not sail to land with gaping heads and yawning jaws, so that the spirits of the land grow frightened of them.

IV

[S. 398] Learned men say that the land was fully settled in a space of sixty years, so that the settlements have not been more numerous ever since. At that time many of the original settlers and their sons were still alive.

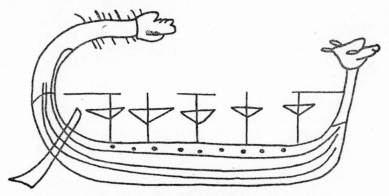

10. A Norse Ship
From Bergen, first half of the thirteenth century.

V

[S. 399] Learned men say that some of the settlers who occupied Iceland were baptized men, mostly those who came from west across the sea. Under this head are named Helgi Magri and Orlyg the Old, Helgi Bjola, Jorund the Christian, Aud the Deep-minded, Ketil the Fool, and still more men who came from west across the sea. Some of them remained faithful to Christianity to the day of their death, but this rarely held good for their families, for the sons of some of them raised temples and sacrificed, and the land was altogether heathen for about a hundred years.

VI

[H. 354] Now the settlements which were made in Iceland have been rehearsed according to what learned men have written, first priest Ari the Learned, Thorgils' son, and Kolskegg the Learned. But I, Hauk Erlendsson, wrote this book after the book written by Herra Sturla Thordarson the Lawman, a most learned man, and after another book written by Styrmir the Learned. I took from each book whatever it contained over and above the other, though for the most part they had the same matter to relate; it is not surprising therefore that this *Landnámabók* is longer than any other.

6

The Greenlanders' Saga

Grœnlendinga Saga

I

THERE was a man by the name of Thorvald, the son of Asvald, son of Ulf Oxen-Thorir's son. Thorvald and his son Eirik the Red left the Jaeder [in Norway] for Iceland because of some killings. Iceland was by this time extensively settled. They made their first home at Drangar, High Rocks, in the Hornstrandir, where Thorvald died. Eirik married Thjodhild, the daughter of Jorund and Thorbjorg Ship-bosom, who was by this time married to Thorbjorn the Haukadaler. Eirik now left the north and made his home at Eiriksstadir alongside Vatnshorn. Eirik and Thjodhild's son bore the name Leif.

After killing Eyjolf Saur and Holmgang-Hrafn, Eirik was driven out of Haukadal, moved west to Breidafjord, and made a home on Oxney at Eiriksstadir. He lent Thorgest his dais-beams, but failed to get them back when he asked for them, out of which arose the quarrels and strife with Thorgest and his people of which there is an account in Eirik's saga. Styr Thorgrimsson backed Eirik's case, as did Eyjolf from Sviney, the sons of Thorbrand from Alptafjord, and Thorbjorn Vifilsson; while backing Thorgest and his side were the sons of Thord Gellir together with Thorgeir from Hitardal.

Eirik was outlawed at the Thorsnes Thing. He fitted out his ship for sea in Eiriksvag, and when he was ready to leave, Styr and the others escorted him out past the islands. He told them he meant to look for that land Gunnbjorn Ulf-Krakason sighted the time he was storm-driven west across the ocean, when he discovered Gunnbjarnarsker, Gunnbjorn's Skerries. He would be coming back, he said, to get in touch with his friends should he discover that land.

Eirik sailed by way of Snæfellsjokul. He found that country, making his landfall at the place he called Midjokul, which is nowadays known as Blaserk, Blacksark. From there he headed south along the coast, to discover whether the land was habitable in that direction. He spent his first winter at Eiriksey, near the middle of the Eastern Settlement, and the following spring went on to Eiriksfjord where he sited his house. In the summer he made his way into the western wilderness, bestowing place-names far and wide. He spent his second winter at Holmar by Hvarfs-gnipa, but during the third summer pressed on north the whole way to Snæfell and into Hrafnsfjord. He now reckoned he had got as far as the head of Eiriksfjord, so turned back and spent the third winter at Eiriksey off the mouth of Eiriksfjord.

The following summer he returned to Iceland and brought his ship to Breidafjord. He called the country he had discovered Greenland [AM 53 fol. Green Land], for he argued that men would be drawn to go there if the land had an attractive name. He spent the winter in Iceland, but the following summer went off to colonize the land. He made his home at Brattahlid, Steep Slope, in Eiriksfjord.

Learned men tell us that this same summer Eirik the Red went off to colonize Greenland, thirty-five [AM 53 fol., 54 fol., 61 fol., and Bergsbók: twenty-five] ships set sail from Breidafjord and Borgarfjord, but only fourteen of them succeeded in getting there. Some were forced back and some perished. This was fifteen years before the Christian faith became law in Iceland. It was this same summer bishop Fridrek and Thorvald Kodransson returned to Norway from Iceland.

These men who went out with Eirik at this time took land in settlement in Greenland: Herjolf took Herjolfsfjord (he lived at Herjolfsnes); Ketil, Ketilsfjord; Hrafn, Hrafnsfjord; Solvi, Solvadal; Helgi Thorbrandsson, Alptafjord; Thorbjorn Glora, Siglufjord; Einar, Einarsfjord; Hafgrim, Hafgrimsfjord and Vatnahverfi; Arnlaug, Arnlaugsfjord. While some went on to the Western Settlement.

IA

When sixteen [AM 53 fol., 54 fol., 61 fol., and Bergsbók: four-teen] years had elapsed from the time Eirik the Red went off to settle Greenland, his son Leif made a voyage from Greenland to Norway. He reached Thrandheim that same autumn king Olaf Tryggvason had departed from the north, out of Halogaland. Leif brought his ship to Nidaros and went immediately to see king Olaf, who preached the Faith to him as to those other heathen men who came to see him. The king found Leif no problem; he was baptized with all his shipmates, and spent the winter with the king, and was well entertained by him. [*Flateyjarbók*, col. 222.]

That same summer [*i.e.* the year 1000] king Olaf sent Gizur and Hjalti to Iceland, as was recorded earlier. And now he sent Leif to Greenland, to preach Christianity there. The king provided him with a priest and various other holy men to baptize folk there and instruct them in the true faith. Leif set sail for Greenland that summer, and while at sea picked up a ship's crew of men who lay helpless there on a wreck. He reached Greenland at the end of summer and went to lodge at Brattahlid with Eirik his father. From this time forward men called him Leif the Lucky, but his father contended that one thing cancelled out the other, in that Leif had rescued a ship's company and saved the men's lives, but had also introduced a shyster (for such he styled the priest) into Greenland. Even so by the advice and persuasion of Leif Eirik was baptized, and all the people of Greenland.[1] [*Flateyjarbók*, col. 233.]

II

Herjolf was the son of Bard Herjolfsson; he was a kinsman of Ingolf the Settler. Ingolf gave [the elder] Herjolf and his people land between Vag and Reykjanes. At first Herjolf [the younger] lived at Drepstokk. His wife's name was Thorgerd, and their son's Bjarni, a most promising young man. From his early days onwards he was a keen traveller abroad, and had prospered both

---

[1] The statement of the saga, p. 153, that Eirik died in heathendom is to be preferred. His odour in tradition was certainly that of a heathen. One remembers his rumoured attachment to the white bear killed by Thorgils in *Flóamanna Saga* (see p. 50, above), and his shapestrong kinsman Farserk in *Landnámabók*. Yet when the news of the Conversion of Iceland blew over the intervening ocean, as it must have done soon after the year 1000, he may well have had himself primesigned in viking fashion (*i.e.* signed with the cross, but not baptized, so that he might live in fellowship with Christian men and even be buried in the outer verges of a Christian churchyard, and all this without formally renouncing his heathen beliefs). *Prima signatio* would have had the important result of reconciling Eirik with his strong-willed wife Thjodhild and securing him domestic peace (see p. 173, below).

in purse and general reputation. He spent his winters overseas or with his father alternately, and very soon had a ship of his own for voyaging. The last winter Bjarni spent in Norway, Herjolf went off to Greenland with Eirik and got rid of his farm. On board ship with Herjolf was a Christian from the Hebrides, he who composed the *Hafgerðingadrápa* or Lay of the Towering Waves,[1] which contains this verse:

> I pray the blameless monk-prover,
> Our Father, my journey to further;
> Heaven's lord, may he bless and let hover
> His hawk-perching hand my head over.

Herjolf made a home at Herjolfsnes, and a most admirable man he was. Eirik the Red lived at Brattahlid; his state was one of high distinction, and all recognized his authority. These were Eirik's children: Leif, Thorvald, and Thorstein, and a daughter whose name was Freydis, who was married to a man named Thorvard. They lived at Gardar, where the bishop's seat is nowadays. She was very much the virago, while Thorvard was just a nobody. She had been married to him mainly for his money. The people in Greenland were heathen at this time.

Bjarni brought his ship to Eyrar that same summer his father had sailed away in the spring. He was taken heavily aback by the news, and had no mind to discharge his ship's cargo. His shipmates asked him what he proposed to do, and he replied that he meant to carry on as usual and enjoy winter quarters at his father's home. 'I shall steer my ship for Greenland, if you are prepared to go along with me.' They all said they would stand by his decision. 'Our voyage will appear foolhardy,' said Bjarni, 'since no one of us has entered the Greenland Sea.' Even so they put out the moment they were ready, and sailed for three days before losing

---

[1] The author of the *King's Mirror* in his account of the marvels of the Greenland seas has this to say of the Sea-Hedges or Towering Waves: 'Now there is still another marvel in the seas of Greenland, the facts of which I do not know precisely. It is called "sea hedges", *hafgerðingar*, and it has the appearance as if all the waves and tempests of the ocean have been collected into three heaps, out of which three billows have formed. These hedge in the entire sea, so that no opening can be seen anywhere; they are higher than lofty mountains and resemble steep, overhanging cliffs. In a few cases only have the men been known to escape who were upon the seas when such a thing occurred' (Trans. Larson). Steenstrup's explanation is the one usually accepted: that these waves were the result of sea quakes (*Aarbøger for nordisk Oldkyndighed og Historie*, 1871).

sight of land. Then their following wind died down, and north winds and fogs overtook them, so that they had no idea which way they were going. This continued over many days, but eventually they saw the sun and could then get their bearings [*or* determine the quarters of the heavens]. They now hoisted sail, and sailed that day before sighting land, and debated among themselves what land this could be. To his way of thinking, said Bjarni, it could not be Greenland. They asked him whether he proposed to sail to this land or not. 'My intention', he replied, 'is to sail close in to the land.' Which they did, and could soon see that the land was not mountainous and was covered with forest, with low hills there, so they left the land to port of them and let their sheet turn towards the land.

After this they sailed for two days before sighting another land. They asked whether Bjarni thought this in its turn was Greenland. In his opinion, he said, this was no more Greenland than the first place—'For there are very big glaciers reported to be in Greenland.' They soon drew near to this land, and could see that it was flat country and covered with woods. Then their following wind died on them. The crew talked things over and said they thought it common sense to put ashore there; but this Bjarni would not allow. They reckoned they were in need of both wood and water. 'You lack for neither,' said Bjarni, and got some hard words for this from his crew.

He gave orders to hoist sail, which was done; they turned their prow from the land and sailed out to sea three days with a south-west wind, and then they saw the third land, and this land was high, mountainous, and glaciered. They asked whether Bjarni would put ashore there, but no, he said, he had no wish to. 'For to me this land looks good for nothing.' So without so much as lowering their sail they held on along the land, and came to see that it was an island.

Once more they turned their prow from the land and held out to sea with the same following wind. Soon the wind freshened, so Bjarni ordered them to reef, and not crowd more sail than was safe for their ship and tackle. This time they sailed for four days, and then saw the fourth land. They asked Bjarni whether he thought this was Greenland or not. 'This is very like what I am told about Greenland,' replied Bjarni, 'and here we will make for the land.'

So that is what they did, and came to land under a certain cape
in the evening of the day. There was a boat on the cape, and there
too on the cape lived Herjolf, Bjarni's father. It was for this
reason the ness got its name, and has been known ever since as
Herjolfsnes. Bjarni now went to his father's, gave over his sailing
and stayed with him for the rest of Herjolf's life, and later lived
there as his father's successor.

III

The next thing that happened[1] was that Bjarni Herjolfsson came
over from Greenland to see earl Eirik, and the earl made him
welcome. Bjarni gave an account of those travels of his on which
he had seen these lands, and people thought how lacking in enterprise and curiosity he had been in that he had nothing to report
of them, and he won some reproach for this. Bjarni became a
retainer of the earl's, and next summer returned to Greenland.

There was now much talk about voyages of discovery. Leif,
son of Eirik the Red of Brattahlid, went to see Bjarni Herjolfsson,
bought his ship from him, and found her a crew, so that they were
thirty-five all told. Leif invited Eirik his father to lead this
expedition too, but Eirik begged off rather, reckoning he was now
getting on in years, and was less able to stand the rigours of bad
times at sea than he used to be. Leif argued that of all their family
he would still command the best luck, so Eirik gave way to him,
and once they were ready for their voyage came riding from home.
When he had only a short way to cover to the ship, the horse he
was riding on stumbled, Eirik fell off, and damaged his foot. 'It
is not in my destiny', said Eirik then, 'to discover more lands than
this we are now living in. Nor may we continue further this time
all together.' Eirik returned home to Brattahlid, but Leif rode on
to the ship and his comrades with him, thirty-five of them all told.
There was a German on the expedition named Tyrkir.

They now prepared their ship and sailed out to sea once they
were ready, and they lighted on that land first which Bjarni and
his people had lighted on last. They sailed to land there, cast
anchor and put off a boat, then went ashore, and could see no

---

[1] The narrator means after the death of Olaf Tryggvason at the sea-fight at Svold,
in the year 1000. Earl Eirik Hakonarson, one of his adversaries there, then became
earl of Norway. See *Íslendingabók*, p. 108, above.

grass there. The background was all great glaciers, and right up to the glaciers from the sea as it were a single slab of rock. The land impressed them as barren and useless. 'At least,' said Leif, 'it has not happened to us as to Bjarni over this land, that we failed to get ourselves ashore. I shall now give the land a name, and call it Helluland, Flatstone Land.' After which they returned to the ship.

After that they sailed out to sea and lighted on another land. This time too they sailed to land, cast anchor, then put off a boat and went ashore. The country was flat and covered with forest, with extensive white sands wherever they went, and shelving gently to the sea. 'This land,' said Leif, 'shall be given a name in accordance with its nature, and be called Markland, Wood Land.' After which they got back down to the ship as fast as they could.

From there they now sailed out to sea with a north-east wind and were at sea two days before catching sight of land. They sailed to land, reaching an island which lay north of it, where they went ashore and looked about them in fine weather, and found that there was dew on the grass, whereupon it happened to them that they set their hands to the dew, then carried it to their mouths, and thought they had never known anything so sweet as that was. After which they returned to their ship and sailed into the sound which lay between the island and the cape projecting north from the land itself. They made headway west round the cape. There were big shallows there at low water; their ship went aground, and it was a long way to look to get sight of the sea from the ship. But they were so curious to get ashore they had no mind to wait for the tide to rise under their ship, but went hurrying off to land where a river flowed out of a lake. Then, as soon as the tide rose under their ship, they took their boat, rowed back to her, and brought her up into the river, and so to the lake, where they cast anchor, carried their skin sleeping-bags off board, and built themselves booths. Later they decided to winter there and built a big house.

There was no lack of salmon there in river or lake, and salmon bigger than they had ever seen before. The nature of the land was so choice, it seemed to them that none of the cattle would require fodder for the winter. No frost came during the winter, and the grass was hardly withered. Day and night were of a more equal

length there than in Greenland or Iceland. On the shortest day
of winter the sun was visible in the middle of the afternoon as
well as at breakfast time.[1]

Once they had finished their house-building Leif made an
announcement to his comrades. 'I intend to have our company
divided now in two, and get the land explored. Half our band
shall remain here at the hall, and the other half reconnoitre the
countryside—yet go no further than they can get back home in
the evening, and not get separated.' So for a while that is what
they did, Leif going off with them or remaining in camp by turns.
Leif was big and strong, of striking appearance, shrewd, and in
every respect a temperate, fair-dealing man.

One evening it turned out that a man of their company was
missing. This was Tyrkir the German. Leif was greatly put out
by this, for Tyrkir had lived a long while with him and his father,
and had shown great affection for Leif as a child. He gave his
shipmates the rough edge of his tongue, then turned out to go and
look for him, taking a dozen men with him. But when they had
got only a short way from the hall there was Tyrkir coming to
meet them. His welcome was a joyous one. Leif could see at
once that his foster-father was in fine fettle. He was a man with a
bulging forehead, rolling eyes, and an insignificant little face,
short and not much to look at, but handy at all sorts of crafts.

'Why are you so late, foster-father,' Leif asked him, 'and parted
this way from your companions?'

By way of a start Tyrkir held forth a long while in German,
rolling his eyes all ways, and pulling faces. They had no notion
what he was talking about. Then after a while he spoke in Norse.
'I went no great way further than you, yet I have a real novelty to
report. I have found vines and grapes.'

'Is that the truth, foster-father?' Leif asked.

'Of course it's the truth,' he replied. 'I was born where wine
and grapes are no rarity.'

They slept overnight, then in the morning Leif made this
announcement to his crew. 'We now have two jobs to get on
with, and on alternate days must gather grapes or cut vines and
fell timber, so as to provide a cargo of such things for my ship.'

---

[1] Literally: The sun had there *eyktarstaðr* and *dagmálastaðr* on the shortest day (*or*
days). The Norsemen had no clock time in the early eleventh century, but the period
indicated was more or less that extending three hours each side of noon.

They acted upon these orders, and report has it that their tow-boat was filled with grapes [?raisins]. A full ship's cargo was cut, and in the spring they made ready and sailed away. Leif gave the land a name in accordance with the good things they found in it, calling it Vinland, Wineland; after which they sailed out to sea and had a good wind till they sighted Greenland and the mountains under the glaciers.

Then a man broke silence and said to Leif: 'Why do you steer the ship so near the wind?'

'My mind is on my steering,' Leif replied, 'but on other things as well. Do you notice anything out of the way?'

No, they said, they saw nothing unusual.

'I am not clear,' said Leif, 'whether I see a ship there or a reef.'

Now they could see it too and reckoned it was a reef. But Leif's sight was so much ahead of theirs that he could pick out men on the reef.

'What I am thinking is for us to beat up into the wind,' said Leif, 'so that we can close them if they need a call from us, and we find ourselves obliged to go and help them. But if they are not peaceful men, we and not they will have command of the situation.'

So now they worked up to the reef, lowered their sail and dropped anchor, and put off the second small boat they had with them. Tyrkir asked who was in charge of their party.

His name was Thorir, their leader replied. He was a Norse man by descent. 'And what is your name?'

Leif told him.

'Are you a son of Eirik the Red of Brattahlid?' he asked him.

Leif said yes, he was. 'And what I want now is to invite you all aboard my ship with as much of your goods as she can take.'

They accepted the offer and afterwards sailed for Eiriksfjord with this load, till they reached Brattahlid, where they discharged their cargo. Then Leif invited Thorir to stay with him together with Gudrid his wife and three men besides, and found lodgings for the rest of the crews, Thorir's mates as well as his own. Leif lifted fifteen men off the reef. He was afterwards known as Leif the Lucky, and had prospered now in both purse and reputation.

That winter a severe sickness afflicted Thorir's company, and Thorir died, together with a great part of his crew. Eirik the Red died too that winter.

IV

There was now much discussion of Leif's expedition to Vinland. His brother Thorvald considered that the land had been explored in too restricted a fashion. So Leif said to Thorvald, 'If you want to, go you to Vinland, brother, in my ship; but first I want her to go for the timber which Thorir had on the reef.'

That was done, and now Thorvald made preparations for this voyage along with thirty men, under the guidance of Leif his brother. Later they put their ship ready and sailed out to sea, and nothing is recorded of their voyage till they came to Vinland, to Leifsbudir, where they saw to their ship and stayed quiet over the winter, catching fish for their food. But in the spring Thorvald ordered them to make their ship ready, and for the ship's boat and certain of the men to proceed along the west coast and explore there during the summer. It looked to them a beautiful and well-wooded land, the woods scarcely any distance from the sea, with white sands, and a great many islands and shallows. Nowhere did they come across habitation of man or beast, but on an island in the west found a wooden grain-holder. They found no other work of man, so returned and reached Leifsbudir that autumn.

Next summer Thorvald set off eastwards with the merchant-ship and further north along the land. Off a certain cape they met with heavy weather, were driven ashore, and broke the keel from under the ship. They made a long stay there, mending their ship. Said Thorvald to his shipmates: 'I should like us to erect the keel on the cape here, and call it Kjalarnes, Keelness.' This they did, and afterwards sailed away and east along the land, and into the mouth of the next fjord they came to, and to a headland jutting out there which was entirely covered with forest. They brought the ship to where they could moor her, thrust out a gangway to the shore, and Thorvald walked ashore with his full ship's company. 'This is a lovely place,' he said, 'and here I should like to make my home.' Then they made for the ship, and saw three mounds on the sands up inside the headland. They walked up to them and could see three skin-boats there, and three men under each. So they divided forces and laid hands on them all, except for one who got away with his canoe. The other eight they killed, and afterwards walked back to the headland, where they had a good look round and could see various mounds on up the fjord which they judged to be human habitations. Then after this so great a drowsiness overtook them that they could not keep awake, and all fell asleep. Then a cry carried to them, so that they were all roused up, and the words of the cry were these: 'Rouse ye, Thorvald, and all your company, if you would stay alive. Back to your ship with all your men, and leave this land as fast as you can!' With that there came from inside the fjord a countless fleet of skin-boats and attacked them. 'We must rig up our war-roof,' ordered Thorvald, 'each side of the ship, and defend ourselves to the utmost, yet offer little by way of attack.' Which they did. The Skrælings kept shooting at them for a while, but then fled away, each one as fast as he could.

Thorvald now inquired among his men whether anyone was wounded. Not a wound among them, they assured him. 'I have got a wound under my arm,' he told them. 'An arrow flew in between gunwale and shield, under my arm. Here is the arrow, and it will be the death of me. I command you, make the fastest preparations you can for your return. As for me, you shall carry me to that headland where I thought I should so like to make my home. Maybe it was truth that came into my mouth, that I should dwell there awhile. For there you shall bury me, and set crosses at my head and feet, and call it Krossanes for ever more.'

Greenland was at that time Christian, though Eirik the Red had died before the coming of Christianity.

Now Thorvald died. They did everything he had asked of them, and afterwards set off and rejoined their comrades, and they told each other such tidings as they had to tell. They stayed there that winter and gathered grapes and vines for the ship. The following spring they prepared to leave for Greenland, and brought their ship into Eiriksfjord, and the news they had to tell Leif was great news indeed.

v

Meanwhile, what had happened in Greenland was that Thorstein of Eiriksfjord had taken a wife, and married Gudrid Thorbjarn-ardottir, who, as was recorded earlier, had been the wife of Thorir Eastman. But now Thorstein Eiriksson felt impelled to go to Vinland to fetch the body of his brother Thorvald; he put the same ship in readiness, choosing her crew for their size and strength, and taking with him twenty-five men and Gudrid his wife. As soon as they were ready they sailed to sea and out of sight of land. They were storm-tossed the whole summer, had no notion where they were going, but after one week of winter reached land at Lysufjord in Greenland in the Western Settlement. Thorstein looked round for lodgings for them, and found such for all his shipmates, but he and his wife were left stranded and had to remain a couple of nights on board ship.

Christianity was still in its infancy in Greenland at this time.

It happened early one morning that some men came to their tent on board ship, and their leader asked what people they might be in the tent.

'There are two of us,' replied Thorstein. 'Who is asking?'

'My name is Thorstein, but I am known as Thorstein the Black. My purpose in coming here is that I would like to ask both you and your wife to come and stay with me.'

Thorstein said he would have to consult his wife, who however left it to him, so he accepted.

'Then I will come for you tomorrow with a carthorse, for I lack nothing in the way of provision for you both. But it is very lonely staying with me, for there are just the two of us, my wife and myself, at home. I am a very self-willed sort of man. Also I hold a different faith from yours, though I suspect you hold the better.'

He came for them next day with the carthorse, and they went to stay with Thorstein the Black, who looked after them well. Gudrid was a woman of handsome appearance, clever, and very good at getting on with strangers.

Early in the winter a sickness attacked Thorstein Eiriksson's company, and many of his shipmates died. He ordered coffins to be made for the bodies of those who perished, had them conveyed to the ship, and suitable arrangements made for them. 'For I mean to have all the bodies transferred to Eiriksfjord in the summer.' There was only a brief respite till the sickness attacked Thorstein the Black's household too. The first to fall ill was his wife, whose name was Grimhild. She was a great strapping woman, strong as a man, yet her illness brought her low, even so. Shortly afterwards Thorstein Eiriksson fell ill; they were both laid up at the same time; then Grimhild, Thorstein the Black's wife, died. Once she was dead Thorstein the Black went out of the room for a board to lay the corpse on. Said Gudrid: 'Don't be away long, my Thorstein!' So be it, he said. Then Thorstein Eiriksson spoke: 'Marvellous are the ways of our hostess now, for she is heaving herself up on her elbows, and swinging her feet over the bedstock, and feeling for her shoes.' At that same moment in came franklin Thorstein, and instantly Grimhild lay down, and every beam in the room gave out a groan. And now Thorstein made a coffin for Grimhild's body, and carried it out and made suitable arrangements for it. And though he was a man both big and strong, he needed all his powers before he succeeded in getting her out of the house.

Now Thorstein Eiriksson's illness grew worse, and he died. Gudrid his wife was quite distraught. They were all there in the living-room at the time. Gudrid had seated herself on a stool in front of the bench on which her husband Thorstein was lying, and now franklin Thorstein lifted her in his arms off the stool, and sat down with her on another bench opposite Thorstein's body, and spoke to her helpfully in many ways, comforting her, and promising that he would keep her company to Eiriksfjord with the bodies of Thorstein her husband and his shipmates. 'Also,' he told her, 'I will take on more people here, for your comfort and solace.'

She thanked him. But then Thorstein Eiriksson sat up, and— 'Where is Gudrid?' he asked.

Three times he asked this, but she stayed silent.

Then she asked franklin Thorstein: 'Shall I answer his question, or not?'

He told her not to answer. Then franklin Thorstein walked across the floor and sat on the stool, with Gudrid seated on his knees. 'What do you want,' he asked, 'namesake mine?'

There was a pause, then he answered: 'I am anxious to tell Gudrid what lies ahead of her, that she may bear my death more resignedly, for I have come to a good resting-place. What I have to tell you, Gudrid, is this, that you will be given in marriage to an Icelander, and long shall be your life together. Many descendants shall spring from you and him, vigorous, bright and noble, sweet and of good savour. You shall leave Greenland for Norway, and Norway for Iceland, and in Iceland make a home. There you will live, the two of you, for a long time, and you shall live longer than he. You shall go abroad, and make a pilgrimage south to Rome, and return home to Iceland to your own place, where-upon a church shall be raised there, where you will live and take the vows of a nun, and where you will die.'

Then Thorstein sank back, and his body was laid out and carried to the ship.

Franklin Thorstein made good all his promises to Gudrid. He disposed of his holdings and livestock in the spring, saw Gudrid to the ship together with everything he possessed, got the ship all ready and found her a crew, and afterwards made the journey to Eiriksfjord, where the bodies were laid to rest at the church. Gudrid went to Leif's at Brattahlid, while Thorstein the Black built himself a home in Eiriksfjord and lived there for the rest of his life, and was held to be a very fine man.

VI

That same summer a ship arrived in Greenland from Norway. Her captain was a man named Thorfinn Karlsefni, a son of Thord Horsehead, the son of Snorri Thordarson of Hofdi. Thorfinn Karlsefni was a very well-to-do man, and spent the winter at Brattahlid with Leif Eiriksson. It did not take him long to set his heart on Gudrid; he asked for her hand, and she left it to Leif to answer for her. So now she was betrothed to him and their wedding took place that winter.

There was the same talk and to-do over the Vinland voyages as before, and the people there, Gudrid as well as the rest, put strong pressure on Karlsefni to undertake an expedition. So his voyage was decided on, and he secured himself a ship's company of sixty men and five women. Karlsefni entered into this agreement with his shipmates, that they should receive equal shares of everything they made by way of profit. They took with them all sorts of livestock, for it was their intention to colonize the country if they could manage it. Karlsefni asked Leif for his house in Vinland. He would lend the house, he said, but not give it.

Next, then, they sailed their ship to sea and reached Leifsbudir all safe and sound, and carried their sleeping-bags ashore. They soon enjoyed a big and splendid catch, for a fine big whale was stranded there. They went and cut it up, and had no problem with regard to food. The livestock went on up ashore there, but it was soon found that the males grew unmanageable and played havoc all round. They had brought the one bull with them. Karlsefni had timber felled and dressed for his ship, laying the wood out on the rock to dry. They took every advantage of the resources the country had to offer, both in the way of grapes and all kinds of hunting and fishing and good things.

After that first winter came summer. It was now they made acquaintance with the Skrælings, when a big body of men appeared out of the forest there. Their cattle were close by; the bull began to bellow and bawl his head off, which so frightened the Skrælings that they ran off with their packs, which were of grey furs and sables and skins of all kinds, and headed for Karlsefni's house, hoping to get inside there, but Karlsefni had the doors guarded. Neither party could understand the other's language. Then the Skrælings unslung their bales, untied them, and proffered their wares, and above all wanted weapons in exchange. Karlsefni, though, forbade them the sale of weapons. And now he hit on this idea; he told the women to carry out milk to them, and the moment they saw the milk that was the one thing they wanted to buy, nothing else. So that was what came of the Skrælings' trading: they carried away what they bought in their bellies, while Karlsefni and his comrades kept their bales and their furs. And with that they went away.

The next thing to report is how Karlsefni had a formidable stockade built around his house and they made their preparations. At this time too his wife Gudrid gave birth to a boy whom they named Snorri. Early in the second winter the Skrælings came to visit them; they were much more numerous than last time, but had the same wares as before. 'And now,' Karlsefni ordered the women, 'you must fetch out food similar to what made such a hit before, and not a thing besides.' And once the Skrælings saw that they tossed their packs in over the palisade.

Gudrid was sitting inside in the doorway by the cradle of Snorri her son when a shadow fell across the door, and a woman walked indoors in a dark close-fitting kirtle [?*námkyrtill*]—rather short she was, and wearing a band round her head, her hair a light chestnut, pale of face, and with such big eyes that no one ever saw their equal in a human skull. She walked to where Gudrid was sitting.

'What is your name?' she asked.

'My name is Gudrid. And what is your name?'

'My name is Gudrid,' she replied.

At that Gudrid the housewife held out her hand to her, that she should sit down beside her, when all of a sudden Gudrid heard a loud crash and the woman disappeared. That very same moment one of the Skrælings was killed by a housecarle of Karlsefni's because he had tried to steal their weapons; and away they ran as fast as they could, leaving their clothes and their goods behind them. No one had noticed that woman except Gudrid.

'We had best lay our heads together now,' said Karlsefni, 'for I fancy they will be paying us a third and hostile visit in full force. So let us follow this plan, that ten men move forward on to the ness here, letting themselves be seen, while the rest of our company go into the forest to clear a passage there for our cattle, in readiness for when their host advances from the wood. Also we must take our bull and let him march at our head.'

The ground where their clash was to take place was set out after this fashion, that there was lake on one side and forest on the other, so they followed Karlsefni's plan. The Skrælings advanced to the spot Karlsefni had fixed on for battle, battle was joined, and many fell from among the Skrælings' host. There was one big, fine-looking man in the Skræling host who Karlsefni imagined must be their chief. One of the Skrælings had picked up an axe, he stared at it for a while, then swung at a comrade of his and cut at him. He fell dead on the instant, whereupon the big man caught hold of the axe, stared at it for a while, then flung it as far out over the water as he could. After which they fled to the forest, each as best he might, and that was the end of their encounter.

Karlsefni and his troop spent the entire winter there; but in the spring Karlsefni announced that he would be staying there no longer. He wanted to go to Greenland. They made ready for their journey, and fetched away with them many valuable commodities in the shape of vines, grapes, and furs. And now they sailed to sea, and reached Eiriksfjord safe with their ship, and it was there they spent the winter.

VII

There was now fresh talk of a Vinland voyage, for this appeared an enterprise at once profitable and honourable. The same

summer that Karlsefni returned from Vinland a ship arrived in
Greenland from Norway, commanded by two brothers, Helgi and
Finnbogi, who stayed there in Greenland over the winter. These
brothers were Icelanders by descent and from the Eastfirths. The
next thing to report is that Freydis Eiriksdottir made a journey
from her home at Gardar; she called to see the brothers Helgi and
Finnbogi, and invited them to take their vessel on an expedition
to Vinland, and have equal shares with her in all such profit as
they might obtain there. They said they would, so from them she
went on to see her brother Leif and asked him to give her the
house he had had built in Vinland. He made his usual answer: he
would lend the house, he said, but not give it. The arrangement
between Freydis and the brothers was this, that they should each
take thirty able-bodied men on their ship, in addition to any
womenfolk; but Freydis immediately showed her disregard for
this, taking an extra five men and so concealing them that the
brothers had no suspicion of it till they reached Vinland.

Now they put to sea, having arranged beforehand that so far
as possible they would sail in company. There was, indeed, little
between them, but even so the brothers arrived a shade ahead
and carried their gear up to Leif's house. But once Freydis arrived,
they too unloaded ship and carried their gear up to the house.

'Why have you carried your stuff in here?' Freydis demanded.

'Because we assumed,' they said, 'the whole arrangement between us would be kept to.'

'Leif lent the house to me,' she retorted, 'not to you.'

'We are no match for you in wickedness, we brothers,' said
Helgi. They moved their gear out and built their own hall, siting
it further away from the sea by the lakeside, and making the
necessary preparations, while Freydis had timber felled for her
ship.

Now winter set in, and the brothers suggested starting games
and holding entertainments to pass the time. That was the way
of it for a while, till there was a turn for the worse between them,
and deep division made, and the games ended, and no coming and
going between the houses. This went on for much of the winter.
Then early one morning Freydis got out of bed and put on her
clothes (but not her shoes and stockings), and such was the
weather that a heavy dew had fallen. She took her husband's
cloak, wrapped it about her, then walked over to the brothers'

house, to the door. A man had gone outside a little earlier and left the door ajar: she pushed it open, and stood in the entrance a while without saying a word.

Finnbogi was lying at the innermost end of the hall. He was awake. 'What do you want here, Freydis?'

'For you to get up and come outside with me. I want to talk to you.'

So that is what he did. They walked to a tree-trunk which lay under the wall of the house, and sat down on it.

'How are you liking things?' she asked him.

'I think the country a good and fruitful one,' he replied, 'but this cold wind blowing between us, I think that bad, for I swear there is no reason for it.'

'As you say,' said she. 'I think the same. But my business in coming to see you is that I should like to trade ships with you brothers, for you have a bigger one than mine, and I want to get away from here.'

'I can meet you on that,' he said, 'if it will please you.'

With that they parted, she went home, and Finnbogi back to bed. She climbed into bed with her cold feet, and at this Thorvard woke, and asked why she was so cold and wet. She answered in a passion. 'I have been to those brothers,' she said, 'asking to buy their ship—I wanted to buy a bigger one. But they took it so badly that they beat me, maltreated me—and you, wretch that you are, will avenge neither my shame nor your own! I can see now that I am not back home in Greenland, but I shall separate from you unless you take vengeance for this.'

He could not endure this baiting of hers. He ordered his men to turn out immediately and take their weapons, which they did, and crossed straightway to the brothers' house and marched in on the sleeping men, seized them and bound them, then led them outside, each man as he was bound. And Freydis had each man killed as he came out.

Now all the men were killed, but the women were left, and no one would kill them.

'Hand me an axe,' said Freydis.

Which was done, and she turned upon the five women they had there, and left them dead.

After this wicked deed they returned to their own quarters, and it was only too clear that Freydis felt she had handled the situation very well. She had this to say to her companions. 'If it is our fate to return to Greenland, I shall be the death of any man who so much as mentions what has taken place. What we must say is that they stayed behind here when we sailed away.'

So early in the spring they made ready the ship the brothers had owned, with every valuable commodity they could lay their hands on and the ship carry. Then they sailed to sea, had a good passage, and brought their ship to Eiriksfjord early in the summer. Karlsefni was still there and had his ship ready and waiting to put to sea. He was waiting for a wind, and men maintain that a more richly freighted ship never left Greenland than this one he was captain of.

Freydis now went to her house, for it had taken no harm all this while. She made lavish gifts to all the members of her crew, because she wanted to keep her misdeeds hidden. She now settled down at home. But they were not all so secretive by nature as to keep their mouths shut about their crimes and misdeeds, so that they did not come to light in the end; and eventually it came to the ears of Leif her brother, who thought it a sorry story indeed. He seized three of Freydis's crew and tortured them till they confessed to the whole thing together, and their stories tallied. 'I have not the heart,' said Leif, 'to treat my sister Freydis as she deserves, but I predict this of her and her husband: no offspring of theirs will come to much good.' And such proved the case, that from there on no one thought anything but ill of them.

But what must now be recounted is how Karlsefni made his ship ready and sailed to sea. He had a good crossing, reached Norway safe and sound, stayed there over the winter and disposed of his wares. They were made much of, both he and his wife, by the most notable people in Norway; but the following spring he made his ship ready for Iceland. When all was in readiness, his ship lying off the jetty and waiting for a wind, a southerner came up to him, a man from Bremen in Germany, and asked him to sell him his figurehead.[1]

'I don't want to sell,' said Karlsefni.

'I will give you half a mark of gold for it,' said the southerner.

[1] *húsasnotra*: the ornament of a ship's prow or stern, which could also serve as the weather-vane or gable-decoration of a house. See plate 18.

This struck Karlsefni as a handsome offer, so they closed the deal, and off went the German with the figurehead. Karlsefni had no idea what wood it was; but it was maple [birds-eye maple? paper birch? *mösurr*] fetched from Vinland.

Karlsefni now sailed to sea and brought his ship to the north of Iceland, to Skagafjord, where she was drawn ashore for the winter. In the spring he bought Glaumbæjarland, and built a house there in which he lived for the rest of his life. He was a man of great distinction and nobility, and from him and his wife Gudrid has sprung a numerous and splendid progeny.

And when Karlsefni was dead, Gudrid and her son Snorri (he who had been born in Vinland) took charge of the estate. But when Snorri got married Gudrid went abroad and made a pilgrimage south to Rome, and afterwards returned to the home of her son Snorri, who had by now had a church built at Glaumbær. In course of time Gudrid became a nun and recluse, and it was there she spent the rest of her days. Snorri had a son named Thorgeir, who was the father of Yngvild, the mother of bishop Brand. The daughter of Snorri Karlsefni's son was named Hallfrid, who was the wife of Runolf, father of bishop Thorlak. Another son of Karlsefni and Gudrid was named Bjorn, who was the father of Thorunn, mother of bishop Bjorn. A great many men are descended from Karlsefni, who has proved a man blest in his kin. And it is Karlsefni who of all men reported most succinctly what happened on all these voyages of which some account has now been given.

Part of Col. 283. The passage begins with Leif's 'Is that the truth, foster-father . . . ?' concerning Tyrkir's claim to have discovered vines and grapes, and ends with Thorvald's decision to go to Vinland.

18. THE HEGGEN VANE

Before serving as a church weather-
vane, this arrow-scarred bronze-
gilt standard had adorned a
fighting-ship at sea. Karlsefni's
snekkja bísærustæ was probably so

7

Eirik the Red's Saga

Eiríks Saga Rauða
also called
Þorfinns Saga Karlsefnis (Þórðarsonar)

I

THERE was a king named Olaf who was known as Olaf the
White: he was a son of king Ingjald, son of Helgi, son of Olaf,
son of Gudrod, son of Halfdan Whiteleg the Upplanders' king.
Olaf went raiding in the west and conquered Dublin in Ireland
along with the Dublin territory, and made himself its king. He
married Aud the Deep-minded, the daughter of Ketil Flatnose,
son of Bjorn Buna, a man of rank from Norway; and the name of
their son was Thorstein the Red. Olaf fell in battle there in Ireland,
after which Aud and Thorstein made their way to the Hebrides,
where Thorstein married Thurid the daughter of Eyvind Eastman
and sister of Helgi Magri. They had many children.

Thorstein became a warrior-king and allied himself with earl
Sigurd the Mighty, the son of Eystein Glumra, and they conquered Caithness and Sutherland, Ross and Moray, and more than
half Scotland. Thorstein made himself king there, till the Scots
betrayed him and he fell there in battle. Aud was in Caithness
when she heard tell of Thorstein's death. She had a merchant
ship built secretly in the forest, and once she was ready hoisted
sail for the Orkneys and found a husband there for Thorstein
the Red's daughter Groa, the mother of that Grelod whom earl
Thorfinn Skull-splitter married. After that she set off to seek
Iceland and had twenty freemen on board her ship. She reached
Iceland and spent the first winter in Bjarnarhofn with her brother

Bjorn. Later Aud took in settlement all Dalelands between Dogurdara and Skraumuhlaupsa. She made her home at Hvamm and had a place for her devotions at Krossholar, where she had crosses erected, for she had been baptized and held strongly to the Christian faith.

Many notable men accompanied her to Iceland who had been taken prisoner during the raiding west and were, in a manner of speaking, slaves. One of these was called Vifil. He was a man of good family who had been taken prisoner over the western sea and was, nominally at least, a slave till Aud set him free. When Aud gave homes to her ship's crew, Vifil asked why she didn't give him one like the rest of them, but Aud said it would signify little. He would be counted a fine man, she said, whatever his position Still, she gave him Vifilsdal and he made his home there. He married a wife, and their sons were Thorgeir and Thorbjorn. These were promising men and grew up with their father.

II

There was a man by the name of Thorvald who was the son of Asvald, son of Ulf Oxen-Thorir's son. Thorvald's son was called Eirik the Red, and both father and son left the Jaeder [in Norway] for Iceland because of some killings. They settled in the Hornstrandir and made a home at Drangar, where Thorvald died. Eirik then married Thjodhild, the daughter of Jorund Ulfsson and Thorbjorg Ship-bosom, who was by this time married to Thorbjorn the Haukadaler. Eirik now left the north and cleared land in Haukadal and made his home at Eiriksstadir alongside Vatnshorn. In time Eirik's thralls caused a landslide to crash down upon the farm of Valthjof at Valthjofsstadir, whereupon Valthjof's kinsman Eyjolf Saur killed the thralls by Skeidsbrekkur above Vatnshorn. For this offence Eirik killed Eyjolf Saur. He killed Holmgang-Hrafn too at Leikskalar. Gerstein and Odd of Jorvi, both kinsmen of Eyjolf's, took up his case, and Eirik was thrown out of Haukadal. He then took possession of Brokey, and lived at Tradir in Sudrey. But that first winter he went on to Oxney, and it was now that he lent Thorgest his dais-beams. Eirik made his home at Eiriksstadir. He asked for his beams, but failed to get them. Eirik went to Breidabolstad to fetch the beams away, but Thorgest gave chase, and they came to blows a short way from the house at Drangar. Two of Thorgest's sons fell there as well as certain other men.

From now on both sides kept a large body of men under arms. Styr and Eyjolf from Sviney, Thorbjorn Vifilsson and the sons of Thorbrand from Alptafjord backed Eirik, while backing Thorgest were the sons of Thord Gellir together with Thorgeir from Hitardal, Aslak from Langadal, and Illugi his son.

Eirik and his following were outlawed at the Thorsnes Thing. He put his ship all ready in Eiriksvag, while Eyjolf kept him in hiding in Dimunarvag for as long as Thorgest and his men were combing the islands for him. Thorbjorn, Eyjolf, and Styr escorted Eirik out past the islands, and they parted on warm terms of friendship, Eirik promising that they should receive just such help themselves, should it lie in his power to provide it and the occasion arise that they had need of him. He told them he meant to look for that land Gunnbjorn Ulf-Krakuson sighted the time he was storm-driven west across the ocean, when he discovered Gunnbjarnarsker, Gunnbjorn's Skerries. He would be coming back, he said, to get in touch with his friends should he discover that land.

Eirik sailed to the open sea by way of Snæfellsjokul and made his landfall at the glacier which is called Blaserk, Blacksark [557. Hvitserk, Whitesark]. From there he headed south, to discover whether the land was habitable in that direction. He spent his first winter at Eiriksey, near the middle of the Eastern [H. and 557. *wrongly* Western] Settlement and the following spring went on to Eiriksfjord where he sited his house. In the summer he made his way into the western wilderness [H. *adds* spending a good deal of time there], and bestowing place-names far and wide. He spent his second winter at Eiriksholmar off Hvarfsgnipa, but during the third summer pressed on north the whole way to Snæfell and into Hrafnsfjord. He now considered he had got as far as the head of Eiriksfjord, so turned back and spent the third winter at Eiriksey off the mouth of Eiriksfjord.

The following summer he returned to Iceland and reached Breidafjord. He spent the winter with Ingolf at Holmlat. In the spring he came to blows with Thorgest, and Eirik got the worst of it, but later they reached peace terms between them. This same summer Eirik went off to colonize the land he had discovered, calling it Greenland, for he argued that men would be all the more drawn to go there if the land had an attractive name.

Thorgeir Vifilsson found himself a wife, marrying Arnora the daughter of Einar of Laugarbrekka, the son of Sigmund, the son of Ketil Thistle who had settled Thistilfjord. The second of Einar's daughters was called Hallveig, whom Thorbjorn Vifilsson married, getting land at Laugarbrekka, at Hellisvellir, along with her. Thorbjorn moved house there and became a man of great note. He was a good farmer [557. a godord-man] and had a fine estate. His daughter, Gudrid by name, was a most beautiful woman and distinguished in everything she did and was.

Living at Arnarstapi was a man by the name of Orm, who had a wife named Halldis. Orm was a good farmer and a close friend of Thorbjorn's, and Gudrid was there a good long time with him as his foster-child.

Living at Thorgeirsfell was a man by the name of Thorgeir. He was prosperous and in his day had been freed from bondage. He had a son named Einar, a handsome, accomplished sort of person, and a great dandy too. He made his living by trading overseas, and had done well at it. He spent his winters in Iceland and Norway alternately. It must now be told how one autumn when Einar was here in Iceland he set off with his wares out along Snæfellsnes, with the intention of selling them there. He came to Arnarstapi, where Orm offered him hospitality which he accepted, for they were on very friendly terms together. Einar's goods were carried into a certain storehouse there, after which he unpacked them, showed them to Orm and his household, and invited him to help himself to anything he liked. Orm accepted, vowing that Einar was a good trader and one of fortune's favourites.

As they were busying themselves with the wares a woman walked past the storehouse door. Who could she be, Einar asked Orm, that lovely woman who walked past the doorway there? 'I have not seen her here before.'

'That is my foster-child Gudrid,' replied Orm, 'franklin Thorbjorn's daughter from Laugarbrekka.'

'She must be a fine match,' said Einar. 'Have not quite a lot of men come asking for her?'

'Why yes, she has been asked for, friend, naturally,' Orm told him, 'but she is not just for the picking up. It is the general opinion that she will be rather particular in her choice of a husband, and her father too.'

'All the same,' said Einar, 'she is the woman I mean to try for, so I should like you to put a case for me to her father, and make an effort to see that it succeeds, for I shall repay you with the full weight of my friendship. Master Thorbjorn must surely see that such family ties would suit us both admirably. He is a man of high reputation and great estate, yet his means I am told are diminishing fast; whereas I and my father with me are short of neither land nor money, and it would do Thorbjorn a world of good if this marriage could be arranged.'

'Certainly I regard myself as your friend,' said Orm, 'but I am not at all eager to put forward this proposal, even so, for Thorbjorn is a proud man, and ambitious too.'

Einar was emphatic that nothing would satisfy him but for his proposal to be put to Thorbjorn, so Orm agreed he should have his way. Einar then travelled back east [MSS. south] until he reached home again.

Some time later Thorbjorn held a harvest feast as was his custom, for he was a princely sort of man. Orm attended from Arnarstapi, together with a good many other friends of Thorbjorn's. Orm found an opportunity to talk to Thorbjorn. He told him how Einar from Thorgeirsfell had visited him recently, and what a promising sort of man he was turning out to be, then went on to raise the question of marriage on Einar's behalf, claiming it would prove a good thing for more persons and reasons than one. 'It could well prove of great assistance to you, franklin, from the money point of view.'

'I did not expect such words from you', replied Thorbjorn, 'as that I should marry daughter of mine to the son of a slave. You must be convinced my money is running out, and she shall not go back home with you, since you consider her worth so poor a marriage.'

After this Orm returned home, and all the other guests to their respective households. But Gudrid stayed behind with her father and spent the winter in her own home.

Then in the spring Thorbjorn sent out invitations to his friends, and a fine feast was prepared. A lot of people attended.

In the course of the feast Thorbjorn called for silence, then spoke as follows: 'I have lived here a long while and had strong proof of men's goodwill and affection for me. And I believe we have got on well together, you and I. But now my affairs are taking a turn for the worse, though so far my estate has been held a not dishonourable one. Now I prefer to uproot my home rather than destroy my good name, and will sooner depart the country than bring shame on my family. I plan to fall back on the promise of my friend Eirik the Red, which he made when we parted from each other in Breidafjord, and if things go as I would have them, I mean to go to Greenland this summer.'

[H. This change of plan of his dumbfounded his hearers, for Thorbjorn was a man with many friends; yet they felt sure that Thorbjorn had committed himself so deeply in speaking of this that there could be no question of dissuading him.] Thorbjorn gave presents to his guests, the feast came to an end, and with that everyone returned home. Thorbjorn sold his lands and bought himself a ship which had been laid up in Hraunhafnaros. Thirty men decided to undertake this voyage with him, among whom were Orm from Arnarstapi, together with his wife, and those of Thorbjorn's friends who could not bring themselves to part from him. In due course they put to sea. As they set off the weather was fine, but once they were out at sea the good wind dropped; they were caught in a great storm, and made slow progress the whole summer through. Next sickness broke out in their company, and Orm died, as did Halldis his wife, and half their ship's company. A big sea got up, and they suffered great hardship and misery of all kinds, yet with it all reached Herjolfsnes in Greenland right at the start of winter. Living there at Herjolfsnes was a man by the name of Thorkel, a man of many skills and an excellent farmer. He took Thorbjorn into his house for the winter with his entire crew, and right royally he entertained them. Thorbjorn and all his shipmates had a very good time there.

At this same time there was a great famine in Greenland; men who had gone out fishing and hunting made poor catches, and some never came back. There was a woman there in the Settlement whose name was Thorbjorg; she was a seeress and was called the Little Sibyl. She had had nine sisters [H. *adds* all of them were seeresses], but now only she was left alive. It was Thorbjorg's practice of a winter to attend feasts, and those men in particular invited her to their homes who were curious to know their future or the season's prospects. Because Thorkel was the leading householder there it was considered his responsibility to find out when these hard times which now troubled them would come to an end, so he invited her to his home, and a good reception was prepared for her, as was the custom when a woman of this kind should be received. A high-seat was prepared for her, and a cushion laid down, in which there must be hen's feathers.

When she arrived in the evening, along with the man who had been sent to escort her, this is how she was attired: she was wearing a blue cloak with straps which was set with stones right down to the hem; she had glass beads about her neck, and on her head a black lambskin hood lined inside with white catskin. She had a staff in her hand, with a knob on it; it was ornamented with brass and set around with stones just below the knob. Round her middle she wore a belt made of touchwood, and on this was a big skin pouch in which she kept those charms she needed for her magic. On her feet she had hairy calf-skin shoes with lengthy, strong-looking thongs to them, and on the thong-ends big knobs of lateen. She had on her hands catskin gloves which were white inside and furry.

Now when she came inside everyone felt bound to offer her fit and proper greetings, which she received according as their donors found favour with her. Master Thorkel took the prophetess by the hand and led her to the seat which had been made ready for her. Thorkel then asked her to run her eyes over household and herd and likewise the home. She had little comment to make about anything. During the evening tables were brought in, and what food was prepared for the seeress must now be told of. There was porridge made for her of goat's beestings, and for her meat the hearts of all living creatures that were available there. She had a brass spoon and a walrus-ivory-handled knife mounted with a double ring of copper, with its point broken off. Then when the tables were cleared away farmer Thorkel walked up to Thorbjorg and asked what she thought of the household there and men's state and condition, and how soon he [H. she] would be informed as to the things he had asked her and which men wanted to know. She replied that she would have nothing to announce till the following morning, when she had slept there the night through.

But on the morrow, in the latter part of the day, she was fitted out with the apparatus she needed to perform her spells. She asked too to procure her such women as knew the lore which was necessary for performing the spell, and bore the name Varðlokur [H. Varðlokkur], Spirit-locks. But no such women were to be found, so there was a search made right through the house to find whether anyone was versed in these matters.

'I am unversed in magic,' was Gudrid's reply, 'neither am I a prophetess, yet Halldis my foster-mother taught me in Iceland the lore [H. chant] which she called Varðlokur.'

'Then you are wiser than I dared hope,' said Thorbjorg.

'But this is a kind of lore and proceeding I feel I cannot assist in,' said Gudrid, 'for I am a Christian woman.'

'Yet it might happen,' said Thorbjorg, 'that you could prove helpful to people in this affair, and still be no worse a woman than before. Still, I leave it to Thorkel to procure me the things I need here.'

Thorkel now pressed Gudrid hard, till she said she would do as he wished. The women now formed a circle all round, while Thorbjorg took her seat up on the spell-platform. Gudrid recited the chant so beautifully and well that no one present could say he had ever heard the chant recited by a lovelier voice. The seeress thanked her for the chant, saying that she had attracted many spirits there who thought it lovely to lend ear to the chant—spirits 'who before wished to hold aloof from us, and pay us no heed. And now many things stand revealed to me which earlier were hidden from me as from others. And I can tell you that this famine will not last longer [H. *adds* than this winter], and that the season will mend when spring comes. The sickness which has long afflicted us, that too will mend sooner than was expected. As for you, Gudrid, I shall repay you here and now for the help we have derived from you, for your future is now an open book to me. You will make a match here in Greenland, the most distinguished there is, yet it will not prove of long duration; for your ways lie out to Iceland, where there will spring from you a great and goodly progeny, and over this progeny of yours shall a bright ray shine. And so, my daughter, farewell now, and happiness go with you.'

After this men approached the prophetess and inquired one by one about what they were most concerned to know. She was free with her information, and small part indeed of what she said failed to come true. Next she was sent for from another house, and off she went, and then Thorbjorn was sent for, because he was not prepared to stay in the house while such heathendom was practised. The weather quickly improved with the advent of spring, just as Thorbjorg had announced. Thorbjorn put his ship in readiness and journeyed on till he reached Brattahlid. Eirik welcomed him with open arms, expressing warm satisfaction that he had come there. Thorbjorn spent the winter with him together with his family [H. *adds* but they found lodgings for the crew among the farmers]. Later in the spring Eirik gave Thorbjorn land at Stokkaness, a fine house was built there, and there he lived from that time forward.

IV

Eirik had a wife whose name was Thjodhild, and two sons, one called Thorstein and the other Leif, both of them promising men. Thorstein was living at home with his father, and no man then in Greenland was held as promising as he. Leif had sailed to Norway, where he was resident with king Olaf Tryggvason.

But when Leif sailed from Greenland in the summer, they were driven off course to the Hebrides. They were a long time getting a good wind thence, and had to remain there for much of the summer. Leif took a fancy to a woman by the name of Thorgunna. She was a lady of good birth, and Leif had an idea she saw farther into things than most. As he made ready to sail away Thorgunna asked to come with him. Leif wanted to know whether her people were likely to approve of this, to which she answered that that was of no importance. Leif replied that he thought it imprudent to carry off so high-born a lady in a strange country. 'We are too few for it.'

'Don't assume,' said Thorgunna, 'you will necessarily find you have chosen the wiser course.'

'That is a risk I must take,' said Leif.

'Then let me tell you,' said Thorgunna, 'that it is not just a question of me alone. I am carrying a child, and that, let me tell you, is your doing. I believe too that when this child is born it will be a boy, and for all your indifference now, I shall still raise the boy and send him to you in Greenland once he can take his place among other men. I believe too that having this son will prove just such an asset to you as your present abandonment of me deserves. And I am thinking I may come to Greenland myself before the game is played out.'

Leif gave her a gold ring for her finger, a cloak of Greenland woollen, and a walrus-ivory belt. This boy came to Greenland, declaring that his name was Thorgils, and Leif admitted his paternity. It is some men's tale that this same Thorgils came to Iceland the summer before the Froda-marvels.[1] He certainly came to Greenland thereafter, and there was thought to be something rather queer about him before the finish.

Leif and his men set sail from the Hebrides and reached Norway in the autumn, where he proceeded into the court of king Olaf Tryggvason. The king paid him many honours, feeling sure he was a man of great ability.

Then came the day when the king found occasion to speak with Leif. 'Are you proposing to sail to Greenland this summer?' he asked him.

'I am,' said Leif, 'if such is your will.'

'I think it will be a good thing,' replied the king. 'You shall carry out a mission for me there and preach Christianity in Greenland.'

Leif said it was for the king to command, but added that he thought this mission would be a hard one to carry out in Greenland.

The king said he had never seen a man better fitted for it than he. 'You will bring it luck.'

'That will be the case,' said Leif, 'only if I enjoy your luck too.'

Leif put to sea as soon as he was ready, was storm-tossed a long time, and lighted on those lands whose existence he had not so much as dreamt of before. There were wheatfields growing wild [*lit.* self-sown] there and vines too. There were also those trees which are called maple [*mösurr*, see page 162], and they fetched away with them samples of all these things [H. *adds* some trees so big that they were used in housebuilding. Leif found men on a wreck and] carried them home with him, and provided them all with lodgings for the winter, showing great magnanimity and gallantry in this as in so much else, since it was he who

---

[1] The hauntings at Froda are recorded in *Eyrbyggja Saga*, chapters 50–55.

introduced Christianity into the country, besides rescuing these
men; and ever afterwards he was called Leif the Lucky.

Leif landed in Eiriksfjord and went home to Brattahlid, where
everybody welcomed him with open arms. He soon preached
Christianity and the Catholic Faith throughout the country, un-
folding to men the message of king Olaf Tryggvason, and telling
how much excellence and what great glory went with this
religion. Eirik took coldly to the notion of abandoning his faith,
but Thjodhild embraced it at once and had a church built, though
not over near the farm. This church was called Thjodhild's

11. THJODHILD'S CHURCH, BRATTAHLID, GREENLAND

A pictorial reconstruction by Jens Rosing. Eirik's North Farm is seen
to the left. Thorbjorn Vifilsson's farm at Stokkanes stood a little to
the north on the far side of the fjord.

Church, and it was there that she offered up her prayers, along
with those men who adopted Christianity, who were many.
Thjodhild would not live with Eirik as man and wife once she
had taken the faith, a circumstance which vexed him very much.

There was now a lot of talk to this end that men [557. he]
should go and find this land which Leif had discovered. Thorstein
Eiriksson was the leader in this, a good man, and shrewd and
popular too. Eirik likewise was invited along, for men felt that
his luck and good management would prove their best asset. He
took his time over it, but did not refuse when his friends pressed
him. So now they fitted out that ship Thorbjorn had brought to

Greenland, and twenty men were chosen as her crew. They had few goods with them, weapons for the most part, and provisions. The morning Eirik rode from home he took with him a little box which had gold and silver in it. He hid this treasure, then went on his way, but when he was still hardly any distance from home he fell off his horse, broke some ribs, damaged his shoulder joint, and cried aloud 'A iai!' Because of this mishap he sent word to his wife Thjodhild that she must remove the money he had hidden, for he reckoned he had paid this price for concealing it. Later they sailed out of Eiriksfjord as merry as can be, for they had high hopes of their venture. But for a long time they were storm-tossed on the ocean and could not hold to the course they intended. They came in sight of Iceland and encountered birds from Ireland likewise. Then their ship was driven away out and about the ocean, and in the autumn they turned back very battered and worn, and made Eiriksfjord at the beginning of winter.

'You were merrier in the summer sailing out of the fjord than you are now,' said Eirik. 'And yet you have much to be thankful for.'

'Be that as it may,' replied Thorstein, 'a leader's business just now is to hit on some plan for these men who are on their beam ends here, and make provision for them.'

Eirik agreed. 'It is true enough what they say, no one is wise till he knows the answer, and such will be the case here. You shall have your way in this.'

So all those who had nowhere else to go went along with that father and son. Later [H. they went home to Brattahlid and spent the winter there].

The story now goes on to tell how Thorstein Eiriksson asked for Gudrid Thorbjarnardottir in marriage, and his proposal found favour with both her and her father. So that was what they settled on, that Thorstein should marry Gudrid, and the wedding took place at Brattahlid in the autumn. The festivities went off well and there was a big gathering present. Thorstein owned an estate in the Western Settlement on a holding known as Lysufjord. Another man, also named Thorstein, owned a half share in this estate. His wife's name was Sigrid. Thorstein and Gudrid with him went to Lysufjord in the autumn, to his namesake's, where they got a warm welcome and stayed on over the winter. What happened now was that sickness attacked the homestead quite early in the winter. The foreman there was called Gardar, and very unpopular he was too. He was the first to fall ill and die, and after that it was not long till they were falling ill and dying one after the other. Next Thorstein Eiriksson fell ill, and Sigrid too, the wife of his namesake. One evening Sigrid wanted to go to the privy which stood opposite the outer door. Gudrid went with her, and they were seated there facing this door when 'Oh,' cried Sigrid, 'oh!'

'We have acted rashly,' said Gudrid, 'and you are in no fit state to be about in the cold, so let us get back in as quickly as we can.'

'I cannot go as things are now,' replied Sigrid. 'Here is the entire host of the dead before the door, and in their company I recognize Thorstein your husband, and I recognize myself there too. How dreadful it is to see such a thing!' And when this passed off, [H. *adds* 'Let us go now, Gudrid,'] she said, 'I do not see the host any longer. ' The foreman too had disappeared, who she thought earlier had had a whip in his hand and was trying to scourge the company.

After this they went back indoors, and before morning came she was dead, and a coffin was made for her body.

This same day men were planning to row out fishing, and Thorstein saw them down to the waterside. At twilight he went down to see what they had caught. Then Thorstein Eiriksson sent word to his namesake that he should come and see him, saying that things looked far from healthy there, and that the lady of the house was trying to get on her feet and under the clothes with him. And by the time he arrived back indoors she had worked her way up on to the edge of the bed alongside him. He caught her by the hands and laid a pole-axe to her breast.

Thorstein Eiriksson died towards nightfall. The other Thorstein told Gudrid to lie down and sleep, promising that he would himself keep watch over the bodies throughout the night. She did so, and soon fell asleep, but when only a little of the night was past Thorstein Eiriksson raised himself up and said it was his wish that Gudrid should be summoned to him, for he desired to speak to her. 'God wills that this hour is granted me by way of remission and for the amendment of my state.' Farmer Thorstein went to find Gudrid and woke her, bidding her cross herself and pray God to help her. 'Thorstein Eiriksson has spoken to me, that he wants to see you, but it is for you to decide what course you will take, for I cannot direct you one way or the other.' 'It may be', she replied, 'that this wondrous event is intended as one of those things which are to be stored in our hearts for ever; yet I trust that God's keeping will stand over me. And under God's mercy I will risk speaking with him; for I cannot escape, if I am fated to suffer hurt. I have no wish for him to haunt us further—and that, I suspect, is the alternative.'

So Gudrid went now and found her Thorstein, and it seemed to her that he was weeping. He spoke certain words quietly in her ear, so that she alone heard them; but what he did say [H. *adds* so that everyone heard] was that those men would be truly blest who kept their faith well, for salvation and mercy attended upon it; though many, he added, kept their faith ill. 'Nor is that a good usage which has obtained here in Greenland since the coming of Christianity, to lay men down in unconsecrated [557. consecrated] ground with only a brief service sung over them. I want to be borne to church, and those others likewise who have died here; but I want Gardar to be burnt on a pyre as soon as possible, for he is the cause of all the hauntings which have taken place here this winter.' He spoke to her further of her own affairs, declaring that her future would be a notable one. He bade her beware of marrying a Greenlander, and urged her too to bestow their money upon the church, or give it to the poor; and then he sank back for the second time.

It had been the custom in Greenland, ever since the coming of Christianity, that men were buried on the farms where they died, in unconsecrated [557. consecrated] ground. A stake would be set up, leading from the breast [H. *adds* of the dead], and in due course, when clergy came that way, the stake would be pulled up and holy water poured into the place, and a service sung over them, even though this might be a good while later.

The bodies [H. *adds* of Thorstein Eiriksson and the rest] were borne to the church at Eiriksfjord, and services sung over them by the clergy. Later Thorstein died, and his entire estate passed to Gudrid. Eirik took her into his own home, and looked after her and hers well.

v

Living in the north of Iceland, at Reynisnes in Skagafjord (the place is now called [Stad]), was a man known as Thorfinn

Karlsefni, the son of Thord Horse-head. He was a man of good
family and very well-to-do. His mother's name was Thorunn.
Thorfinn was a trader overseas, and had the name of a good
merchant. One summer Karlsefni fitted out his ship with Greenland in mind. Snorri Thorbrandsson from Alptafjord decided to
go with him, and they had forty men with them. A man by the
name of Bjarni Grimolfsson, a Breidafjord man, and another
named Thorhall Gamlason, an Eastfirther, made their ship ready
the same summer as Karlsefni, proposing to sail to Greenland,
and they too had forty men aboard. They put to sea with these
two ships as soon as they were fitted out. There is no record of
how long they were at sea, but this can be said, that both ships
made Eiriksfjord in the autumn. Eirik and other of the settlers
rode to the ships, and they promptly started a brisk buying and
selling. The skippers invited Eirik [557. Gudrid] to help himself
to anything he liked from among their wares; and Eirik showed
himself no less generous in return, for he invited the two ships'
crews to come and spend the winter with him at Brattahlid. The
merchants accepted this offer, off they went with Eirik, and their
goods were now transferred to Brattahlid, where there was no
lack of fine big storehouses to keep them in. [H. *adds* Nor was
there a noticeable lack of anything else they needed]. The merchants had a very good time at Eirik's over the winter.

But as the time wore on towards Yule Eirik came to look less
cheerful than was his habit. So one day Karlsefni came and had a
word with him. 'Is something the matter, Eirik? I can't help
thinking you are rather more silent than you were. You are treating
us with great hospitality, and we feel bound to repay you to the
best of our means and ability. So tell me now the reason for your
low spirits.'

'You have been kind and gracious guests,' replied Eirik, 'and it
does not so much as enter my mind that you have treated me other
than perfectly. [H. What troubles me rather is whether once you
find yourselves in other parts it will be noised abroad how you
never spent a poorer Yule than this now coming in, when Eirik
the Red was your host at Brattahlid in Greenland.]'

'That will not be so,' Karlsefni assured him. 'On board our
ships we have malt and meal and corn, and you are welcome to
help yourself to anything you please, and prepare a feast as
splendid as your ideas of hospitality would have it.'

Eirik accepted this offer, and a Yule feast was now prepared, and one so choice and costly that men thought they had rarely seen such high living [H. *adds* in a poor country].

Then after Yule Karlsefni put to Eirik a proposal for Gudrid's hand, for as he saw it this lay in Eirik's competence, and he thought her a beautiful and accomplished lady. Eirik answered yes, he would welcome his suit—she deserved a good match, he said. 'And it is likely that she will be fulfilling her destiny,' were she given to him. He had heard nothing but good of Karlsefni, he said. His proposal was now put to her, she declared herself content with whatever Eirik decided for her, so without more ado the match was made, the feast augmented, and the wedding held. There was great and merry entertainment at Brattahlid the winter through, with much playing of board-games and story-telling, and many things to comfort and cheer the household.

This same winter long discussions took place at Brattahlid. Karlsefni and Snorri resolved to go and find Vinland, and men debated this a good deal. The upshot was that Karlsefni and Snorri fitted out their ship, meaning to go and find Vinland in the summer. Bjarni and Thorhall resolved to make the journey with their ship and the crew which had served with them. There was a man by the name of Thorvald, a son-in-law [*sic*] of Eirik the Red. Thorhall was nicknamed the Hunter; for a long while now he had been out on hunting expeditions with Eirik in the summers, and had much business in his charge. He was tall of stature, dark and ogreish, was getting on in years, of difficult disposition, taciturn and of few words as a rule, underhand and offensive of speech, and always busied to a bad end. He had had little truck with the Faith since it came to Greenland. Thorhall had hardly a friend to his name, yet Eirik had long been accustomed to consult with him. He was aboard ship with Thorvald and his crew, for he had an extensive knowledge of the unsettled regions. They had that same ship which Thorbjorn had fetched to Greenland. They resolved to go along with Karlsefni and his men, and for the most part they were Greenlanders who went. They had a hundred and sixty men on board their ships. They then sailed away for the Western Settlement and for Bjarneyjar, Bear Isles. From Bjarneyjar they sailed with a north wind, were at sea two days, and then found land. They rowed ashore in boats and explored the country, finding many flat stones there, so big that a

19. THE VINLAND VOYAGE, I

Leaving Brattahlid. View down Eiriksfjord (Tunugdliarfik).

20. THE VINLAND VOYAGE, 2

Promontorium Winlandiæ, Cape Bauld, the northern extremity of Newfoundland, seen from the Strait of Belle Isle. In the

pair of men could easily clap sole to sole on them. There were many arctic foxes there. They gave the land a name, calling it Helluland, Flatstone Land. Then they sailed with a north wind for two days, when land lay ahead of them, with a great forest and many wild animals. Off the land to the south-east lay an island, where they found a bear, so called it Bjarney, Bear Island. But the land where the forest was they called Markland, Wood Land.

Then when two days were past they sighted land, and sailed to the land. Where they arrived there was a cape. They beat along the coast and left the land to starboard; it was an open harbourless coast there, with long beaches and sands. They put ashore in boats, came across the keel from a ship, so called the place Kjalarnes, Keelness. Likewise they gave a name to the beaches, calling them Furdustrandir, Marvelstrands, it was such a long business sailing past them. Then the land became bay-indented, and towards these bays they headed their ships.

It happened when Leif was with king Olaf Tryggvason, and he commissioned him to preach Christianity in Greenland, that the king gave him two Scots, a man named Haki, and a woman Hekja. The king told Leif to make use of these people if he had need of fleetness, for they were fleeter than deer. These people Leif and Eirik provided to accompany Karlsefni. So when they had sailed past Furdustrandir they put the Scots ashore, ordering them to run into the region lying south, spy out the quality of the land, and come back before three days were past. They were so attired that they were wearing the garment which they called 'bjafal': this was so put together that there was a hood on top, it was open at the sides and sleeveless, and buttoned between the legs, where a button and loop held it together; while for the rest they were naked. They cast anchor and lay there this while, and when three days were past they came running down from the land, and one of them had grapes in his hand and the other self-sown wheat. Karlsefni said they appeared to have found a choice, productive land. They took them on board ship and went their ways until the land was indented by a fjord. They laid the ships' course up into this fjord, off whose mouth there lay an island, and surrounding the island strong currents. This island they called Straumsey [H. Straumey]. There were so many birds there that a man could hardly set foot down between the eggs. They held on into the fjord, and called it Straumsfjord [H. Straumfjord], and here they carried their goods off the ships and made their preparations. They had brought all sorts of livestock with them, and looked around at what the land had to offer. There were mountains there, and the prospect round was beautiful. They paid no heed to anything save exploring the country. There was tall [*or* abundant] grass there. They spent the winter there, and a hard winter it proved, with no provision made for it; they were in a bad way for food, and the hunting and fishing failed. Then they went out to the island, hoping it would yield something by way of hunting or fishing or something drifted ashore. But small store of food was there, though their stock did well there. So now they prayed to God, that he should send them something to eat, but their prayers were not answered as quickly as they craved. Thorhall disappeared, and men set off to look for him; this continued for three whole days. On the fourth day Karlsefni and Bjarni found him on the peak of a crag, staring up at the sky, with both his eyes and mouth and nostrils agape, scratching and pinching himself, and reciting something. They asked him why he had come to such a place. It was none of their business, he retorted, and told them not to look so dumbstruck; he had lived long enough, he said, not to need them troubling their heads over him. They urged him to return home with them, which he did. A little later a whale came in; they hurried to it and cut it up, yet had no notion what kind of whale it was. Karlsefni had a wide knowledge and experience of whales, but for all that did not recognize this one. The cooks boiled this whale and they ate of it and were all taken ill of it, at which Thorhall came forward and said, 'Was it not the case, that Red Beard proved a better friend than your Christ? This is what I get for the poem I made about Thor my patron. Seldom has he failed me.' But the moment men heard this, no one would make use of the food; they threw it over the cliff, and committed their cause to the mercy of God. And then they were enabled to row out fishing, and there was no shortage of provisions. In the spring they went up into Straumsfjord and got supplies from both sources, hunting on the mainland, eggs in the breeding grounds and fishing from the sea.

Now they talked over their expedition and made plans. Thorhall the Hunter wished to proceed north by way of Furdustrandir and Kjalarnes and so look for Vinland, but Karlsefni wished to travel south along the coast, and east of it, believing that the land which lay further south was more extensive, and it seemed to him wiser to explore in both directions. So now Thorhall began making ready out by the islands, and there were not more than nine men going with him, for the rest of their company went with Karlsefni. And one day, when Thorhall was carrying water to his ship, he took a drink, and chanted this poem:

> 'They told me, wartrees bold,
> This land held, once we found it,
> Such drink as men ne'er drank of;
> My curse then—all men hear it!
> This sucking at the bucket,
> This wallowing to spring's welling,
> Fine work for helm-god's war-oak!
> No wine's passed lips of mine.'

Later they put to sea, and Karlsefni saw them out past the islands. Before they hoisted sail Thorhall chanted a verse.

> 'Back sail we now where beckon
> Hands of our own Greenlanders;
> Have steed of seabed's heaven
> Search out the streams of ocean:
> While here these brisk sword-stirrers,
> This precious country's praisers,
> On Furdustrand far-stranded,
> Boil whale for wambling bellies.'

Afterwards they parted company and sailed north by way of Furdustrandir and Kjalarnes, and wished to beat to westward there. They met with a storm and were shipwrecked off Ireland, where they were badly beaten and enslaved. It was then Thorhall lost his life.

VI

Karlsefni sailed south along the land with Snorri and Bjarni and the rest of their company. They journeyed a long time till they reached a river which flowed down from the land into a lake and so to the sea. There were such extensive bars [557. islands] off the mouth of the estuary that they were unable to get into the river except at full flood. Karlsefni and his men sailed into the estuary, and called the place Hop, Landlock Bay. There they found

self-sown fields of wheat where the ground was low-lying, and
vines wherever it was hilly. Every brook there was full of fish.
They dug trenches at the meeting point of land and high water,
and when the tide went out there were halibut in the trenches.
There were vast numbers of animals of every kind in the forest.
They were there for a fortnight enjoying themselves and saw
nothing and nobody. They had their cattle with them.

Then early one morning when they looked about them they
saw nine [H. a great multitude of] skin-boats, on board which
staves were being swung which sounded just like flails threshing
—and their motion was sunwise.

'What can this mean?' asked Karlsefni.

'Perhaps it is a token of peace,' replied Snorri. 'So let us take a
white shield and hold it out towards them.'

They did so, and those others rowed towards them, showing
their astonishment, then came ashore. They were small [H. dark],
ill favoured men, and had ugly hair on their heads. They had big
eyes and were broad in the cheeks. For a while they remained
there, astonished, and afterwards rowed off south past the headland.

Karlsefni and his men built themselves dwellings up above the
lake; some of their houses stood near the mainland, and some near
the lake. They now spent the winter there. No snow fell, and
their entire stock found its food grazing in the open. But once
spring came in they chanced early one morning to see how a
multitude of skin-boats came rowing from the south round the
headland, so many that the bay appeared sown with coals, and
even so staves were being swung on every boat. Karlsefni and
his men raised their shields, and they began trading together.
Above all these people wanted to buy red cloth [H. *adds* in return
for which they had furs to offer and grey pelts]. They also wanted
to buy swords and spears, but this Karlsefni and Snorri would
not allow. They had dark unblemished skins to exchange for the
cloth, and were taking a span's length of cloth for a skin, and this
they tied round their heads. So it continued for a while, then
when the cloth began to run short they cut it up so that it was no
broader than a fingerbreadth, but the Skrælings gave just as much
for it, or more.

The next thing was that the bull belonging to Karlsefni and his
mates ran out of the forest bellowing loudly. The Skrælings were

terrified by this, raced out to their boats and rowed south past the headland, and for three weeks running there was neither sight nor sound of them. But at the end of that period they saw a great multitude of Skræling boats coming up from the south like a streaming torrent. This time all the staves were being swung anti-sunwise, and the Skrælings were all yelling aloud, so they took red shields and held them out against them. [H. *adds* The Skrælings ran from their boats and with that] they clashed together and fought. There was a heavy shower of missiles, for the Skrælings had warslings too. Karlsefni and Snorri could see the Skrælings hoisting up on poles [H. a pole] a big ball-shaped object [H. *adds* more or less the size of a sheep's paunch], and blue-black in colour, which they sent flying [H. *adds* from the pole] inland over Karlsefni's troop, and it made a hideous noise where it came down. Great fear now struck into Karlsefni and all his following, so that there was no other thought in their heads than to run away up along the river [H. *adds* for they had the impression that the Skræling host was pouring in upon them from all sides. They made no stop till they came] to some steep rocks, and there put up a strong resistance.

Freydis came out-of-doors and saw how they had taken to their heels. 'Why are you running from wretches like these?' she cried. 'Such gallant lads as you, I thought for sure you would have knocked them on the head like cattle. Why, if I had a weapon, I think I could put up a better fight than any of you!'

They might as well not have heard her. Freydis was anxious to keep up with them, but was rather slow because of her pregnancy. She was moving after them into the forest when the Skrælings attacked her. She found a dead man in her path, Thorbrand Snorrason—he had a flat stone sticking out of his head. His sword lay beside him; she picked it up and prepared to defend herself with it. The Skrælings were now making for her. She pulled out her breasts from under her shift and slapped the sword on them, at which the Skrælings took fright, and ran off to their boats and rowed away. Karlsefni's men came up to her, praising her courage. Two of Karlsefni's men had fallen, and four [H. a great many] Skrælings, but even so they had been overrun by sheer numbers. They now returned to their booths [H. *adds* and bandaged their wounds], puzzling over what force it was which had attacked them from the land side. For now it looked to them as though there had been only the one host, which came from the boats, and that the rest of the host must have been a delusion.

Further, the Skrælings had found a dead man whose axe lay beside him. One of them [H. *adds* picked up the axe and cut at a tree with it, and so they did one after the other, and thought it a great treasure, and one which cut well. Afterwards one of them set to and] cut at a stone, the axe broke, and then he thought it useless because it could not stand up to the stone, so threw it down.

It now seemed plain to Karlsefni and his men that though the quality of the land was admirable, there would always be fear and strife dogging them there on account of those who already inhabited it. So they made ready to leave, setting their hearts on their own country, and sailed north along the coast and found five Skrælings in fur doublets asleep near the sea, who had with them wooden containers in which was animal marrow mixed with blood. They felt sure that these men would have been sent out from that country, so they killed them. Later they discovered a cape and great numbers of animals. To look at, this cape was like a cake of dung, because the animals lay there the nights [557. winters] through.

And now Karlsefni and his followers returned to Straumsfjord [H. *adds* where there was abundance of everything they had need of]. It is some men's report that Bjarni and Freydis [H. Gudrid] had remained behind there, and a hundred men with them, and proceeded no farther, while Karlsefni and Snorri had travelled south with forty men, yet spent no longer at Hop than a bare two months, and got back again that same summer. Then Karlsefni set off with one ship to look for Thorhall the Hunter, while the rest of their party stayed behind. They went north past Kjalarnes, and then bore away west, with the land on their port side. There was nothing but a wilderness of forest-land [H. *adds* to be seen ahead, with hardly a clearing anywhere]. And when they had been on their travels for a long time, there was a river flowing down off the land from east to west. They put into this rivermouth and lay at anchor off the southern bank. It happened one morning that Karlsefni and his men noticed up above the clearing a kind of speck as it were glittering back at them, and they shouted at it. It moved—it was a uniped—and hopped down to the river-bank off which they were lying. Thorvald Eirik the Red's son was sitting by the rudder, and the uniped shot an arrow into his guts. He drew out the arrow. 'There is fat round my belly!' he said. 'We have won a fine and fruitful country, but will hardly be allowed to enjoy it.' Thorvald died of this wound a little later. The uniped skipped away and back north, and Karlsefni and his men gave chase, catching sight of him every now and again. The last glimpse they had of him, he was leaping for some creek or other. Karlsefni and his men then turned back. [557. It happened one morning Karlsefni and his men noticed up above a clearing a kind of speck as it were glittering back at them. It moved—it was a uniped—and hopped down to where they were lying [*scil.* Karlsefni and] Thorvald Eirik the Red's son. Then said Thorvald: 'We have won a fine country.' The uniped then skipped away and back north, and shot an arrow into Thorvald's guts. He drew out the arrow and 'There is fat round my belly!' he said. They gave chase to the uniped, catching sight of him every now and again, and it looked as if he was getting away. He leaped out to a creek.] Then one of the men sang this ditty:

> Men went chasing,
> I tell you no lie,
> A one-legger racing
> The seashore by:
> But this man-wonder,
> Curst son of a trollop,
> Karlsefni, pray ponder,
> Escaped at a gallop.

Then they moved away and back north, believing they had sighted Einfætingaland, Uniped Land. They were unwilling to imperil their company any longer. They proposed to explore all the mountains, those which were at Hop and those they [*scil.* now] discovered. [H. They concluded that those mountains which were at Hop and those they had now discovered were one and the same (range), that they therefore stood directly opposite (in line with?) each other, and lay (*or* extended) the same distance on both sides of Straumfjord.]

They went back and spent that third winter in Straumsfjord. There was bitter quarrelling [H. *adds* on account of the women], for the unmarried men fell foul of the married [H. *adds* which led to serious disturbances]. Karlsefni's son Snorri was born there the first autumn and was three years old when they left.

[H. When they sailed from Vinland] they got a south wind and reached Markland, where they found five Skrælings, one of them a grown man with a beard, two women, and two children. Karlsefni captured the boys but the others escaped and sank down into the ground. These boys they kept with them, taught them their language, and they were baptized. They gave their mother's name as Vætilldi, that of their father as Uvægi. They said that kings ruled over Skrælingaland, one of whom was called Avalldamon and the other Valldidida. There were no houses there, they said: the people lodged in caves or holes. A country lay on the other side, they said, opposite their own land, where men walked about in [H. lived who wore] white clothes and whooped loudly, and carried poles and went about with [H. carried] flags. They concluded that this must be Hvitramannaland [H. *adds* or Ireland the Great].[1] And now they came to Greenland and spent the winter with Eirik the Red.

But Bjarni Grimolfsson was carried into the Greenland [H. Ireland] Sea and came into wormy waters, and before they knew it the ship grew worm-eaten under them. They talked over what plan they should adopt. They had a tow-boat which was coated with seal-tar, and it is common knowledge that the shell-worm does not bore into timber which is coated with seal-tar. The voice of the majority was to man this boat with as many of the men as she would take. But when it came to the point, the boat would not take more than half the ship's company. Then Bjarni proposed that they should go into the boat, but go by lot, and not by rank. But every living soul wanted to go into the boat, and she just could not take them all, which was why they adopted this plan of transferring men from ship to boat by lot. And the way the lot fell out, it fell to Bjarni to go into the boat, and roughly half the crew with him.

So those who had drawn lucky transferred from ship to boat.

[1] Further to Hvitramannaland: 'He [Ari Masson] was driven off course to Hvitramannaland, which some call Ireland the Great. It lies west in the ocean, near Vinland the Good. It is reckoned six days' sail west from Ireland. Ari failed to get away again and was baptized there. The first to tell of this was Hrafn the Limerick-farer, who had spent a long time at Limerick in Ireland. According to Thorkel Gellisson, Icelanders who had their information from Thorfinn earl of Orkney report that Ari had been recognized in Hvitramannaland but failed to get away. He was held in high regard there (*Landn.* S. 122).' Another who failed to escape from this entirely mythical country was Bjorn, champion of the Breidavik men and lover of Thurid, he 'who was a closer friend to the housewife at Froda than to her brother the priest at Helgafell'. See *Eyrbyggia Saga*, cap. 64.

When they had got into the boat, a young Icelander who had been Bjarni's shipmate, called out: 'D'you mean to leave me here, Bjarni?'

'That is the way of it,' replied Bjarni.

'This', said he, 'is not what you promised me when I followed you from my father's house in Iceland.'

'I see nothing else for it,' said Bjarni. 'But answer me, what do you suggest?'

'I suggest we change places. That you come here, and I go there.'

'So be it,' replied Bjarni. 'For I see you are greedy for life, and think it a hard thing to die.'

Then they changed places. This man went into the boat, and Bjarni aboard ship, and men reckon that Bjarni perished there in the wormy sea, and those men who remained on board with him. But the boat and those who were in her went their ways till they reached land [H. *adds* at Dublin in Ireland], where they afterwards told this story.

Two summers later Karlsefni returned to Iceland, and Snorri [H. Gudrid] with him, and went home to his place at Reynisnes. His mother considered he had made a poor marriage and did not stay in the same house with them that first winter. But once she found Gudrid to be so remarkable a woman, she returned home, and they lived happily together.

The daughter of Karlsefni's son Snorri was Hallfrid, the mother of bishop Thorlak Runolfsson. Karlsefni and Gudrid had a son whose name was Thorbjorn, whose daughter's name was Thorunn, mother of bishop Bjorn. There was a son of Snorri Karlsefni's son by the name of Thorgeir, the father of Yngvild, mother of bishop Brand the first.

And that is the end of this saga.[1]

---

[1] In place of this last sentence Hauk Erlendsson supplies a genealogy leading to himself: Steinunn too was a daughter of Snorri Karlsefni's son, she who was married to Einar the son of Grundar-Ketil, son of Thorvald Krok, son of Thorir from Espihol. Their son was Thorstein Ranglat, who was father of that Gudrun whom Jorund from Keldur married. Their daughter was Halla, mother of Flosi, father of Valgerda, mother of Herra Erlend Sterki, father of Herra Hauk the Lawman. Another daughter of Flosi was Thordis, mother of the lady Ingigerd the Mighty, whose daughter was the lady Hallbera, abbess of Reynisnes at Stad. Many other distinguished people in Iceland are descended from Karlsefni and Gudrid, who are not catalogued here. God be with us. Amen.

8

Karlsefni's Voyage to Vinland

THE *Hauksbók* VERSION OF PART OF THORFINN
KARLSEFNI'S EXPEDITION TO VINLAND

THEN after Yule Karlsefni put before Eirik a proposal of
marriage for Gudrid, for as he saw it this lay in Eirik's competence. Eirik gave him a favourable answer, reckoning she must
follow her fate, and that he had heard nothing but good of
Karlsefni. So that was how it ended: Thorfinn married Gudrid,
the feast was augmented, their wedding held and drunk to, and
they spent the winter at Brattahlid.

There were long discussions at Brattahlid, that men ought to go
and find Vinland the Good, and it was the general opinion it
would be found a good and fruitful country out there. And so it
came about that Karlsefni and Snorri fitted out their ship to go
and find that country in the spring. The man Bjarni and his fellow
Thorhall, who have already been mentioned, went with them in
their own ship. There was a man by the name of Thorvard, who
was married to Eirik the Red's natural daughter Freydis, who
went along with them, together with Eirik's son Thorvald, and
[that other] Thorhall who was nicknamed the Hunter. He had
been with Eirik a long time now, acting as hunter for him in the
summers, and during the winters as his bailiff. He was a big,
strong, dark and ogreish man, taciturn, but when he did speak
abusive, and he was always advising Eirik for the worse. He was
a bad Christian, but he had a wide knowledge of the unsettled
regions. He was on board ship with Thorvard and Thorvald
(they had that same ship which Thorbjorn Vifilsson had fetched
to Greenland). In all they had a hundred and sixty men when they
set sail for the Western Settlement and from there to Bjarney,
Bear Isle. From there they sailed south for two days and then

sighted land. They launched their boats and explored the country-side, finding huge flat stones there, many of them twelve ells across. There were large numbers of arctic foxes there. They gave the land a name, calling it Helluland. Then they sailed onwards for two days and changed course from south to south-east, and found a land heavily forested, with many wild animals. Offshore to the south-east lay an island. They killed a bear on it, so called the island Bjarney, Bear Island, and the land Markland.

From here they sailed south along the land for a long while till they came to a cape. The land lay to starboard; there were long beaches and sands there. They rowed ashore and found there on the cape the keel from a ship, so called the place Kjalarnes. The beaches they called Furdustrandir, Marvelstrands, because it was such a long business sailing past them. Then the land became bay-indented, and into one of these bays they headed their ships.

King Olaf Tryggvason had given Leif two Scots, a man named Haki, and a woman Hekja, who were fleeter than deer. They were on board Karlsefni's ship, and once they had sailed past Furdu-strandir they put the Scots ashore, ordering them to run across country southwards to spy out the quality of the land, and come back before three days were past. They were wearing the garment which they called 'kjafal': this was so put together that there was a hood on top, it was open at the sides and sleeveless, and but-toned between the legs with a button and loop; while for the rest they were naked. They waited there a while, and when the Scots came back the one had a bunch of grapes in his hand and the other an ear of new sown [*sic*] wheat; so with that they went back on board ship and afterwards sailed on their way.

They sailed into a fjord off whose mouth there lay an island surrounded by strong currents. So they called this island Straumey. There were so many eider-duck on the island that a man could hardly take a step for the eggs. The place itself they called Straumfjord, and here they carried their goods off the ships and made their preparations. They had brought all sorts of live-stock with them, and the country round was very fine. They paid no heed to anything save exploring the country; they spent the winter there, but made no provision for this all the summer; the hunting and fishing failed, and they were in a bad way for food. Then Thorhall the Hunter disappeared. Before this they had prayed to God for food, but their prayers were not answered as quickly as their needs craved. They were looking for Thorhall three whole days, and found him where he was lying on the peak of a crag, staring up at the sky with his mouth and nostrils both agape, and reciting something. They asked him why he had gone to such a place, but he told them that was none of their business. They urged him to return home with them, which he did. A little later a whale came in. They went to it and cut it up, yet never a man of them knew what kind of a whale it was. Once the cooks had boiled it, they ate and were all taken ill of it. Then said Thorhall, 'Red Beard proved a better friend now than your Christ. This is what I get for the poem I made about Thor my patron. Seldom has he failed me.' But the moment they heard this, they disposed of the entire whale into the sea and committed their cause to God. With that the weather improved, enabling them to row out to sea fishing, and from then on there was no shortage of provisions, for there was hunting of animals on the mainland, eggs in the island breeding grounds, and fish from the sea.

The story now goes that Thorhall wished to proceed north by way of Furdustrandir to look for Vinland, whereas Karlsefni wished to travel south along the coast. Thorhall began making ready out by the island, and they were not more than nine men all told, for all the rest of the company went with Karlsefni. And when Thorhall was carrying water to his ship and had taken a drink of it, he chanted this poem [See p. 181: They told me, etc.].

When they were ready they hoisted sail. This time Thorhall chanted [See p. 181: Back sail we now, etc.].

After this they sailed north by way of Furdustrandir and Kjalarnes, and wished to beat to westwards, but met with a west wind and were shipwrecked in Ireland, where they were beaten and enslaved, and Thorhall lost his life, according to what traders have reported.

9

The Story of Einar Sokkason

Einars Þáttr Sokkasonar
also called
Grænlendinga Þáttr

I

THERE was a man named Sokki, the son of Thorir, living at Brattahlid in Greenland. He was highly esteemed and popular with all. His son's name was Einar, a man of high promise. Father and son had great authority in Greenland, and stood head and shoulders above other men.

On a given occasion Sokki had a Thing summoned, at which he announced that he did not wish their land to remain bishopless any longer, but wanted all his compatriots to make a contribution from their means so that a bishop's see could be established—a proposal to which all the franklins assented. Sokki asked his son Einar to undertake the necessary journey to Norway. He was the fittest person, he told him, to carry out this mission. So Einar said he would go, just as his father wished, and took with him a big supply of ivory goods and walrus hides to push his case with the chieftains.

They arrived in Norway, and it was Sigurd Jerusalem-farer who was king there at the time. Einar came to have audience with the king; he eased his case forward by means of gifts, and afterwards set out his aims and intention, petitioning the king to help him, so that he might get what he was asking for to meet his country's need. The king agreed that this would indeed be a fine thing for Greenland.

Then the king summoned before him a certain man named Arnald, who was a good clerk and well fitted to be a teacher of

God's word. The king bade him address himself to this task for God's sake and his, the king's, prayers. 'And I will send you to Denmark with my letters and seal, to have audience with Ozur archbishop of Lund.' Arnald replied that he was not much tempted to undertake this; first on his own account, in that he was ill fitted for it; second, because of parting with his friends and family; and third, because he would have to deal with such a cantankerous people. The king's counter to this was that the greater the trials he suffered at men's hands, the greater would be his merit and reward. Arnald confessed he could not find it in his heart to refuse the king's prayer—'But if it is ordained that I accept the sacred office of bishop, then I want Einar to swear me this oath, that he will help and uphold the rights of the bishop's see and those properties which are given to God, and chastise those that trespass against them, and be the defender of all things that pertain to the see.' The king said he should do this, and Einar agreed to undertake it.

So now the bishop-elect went to see archbishop Ozur, and put his business before him, and the king's letters too. The archbishop welcomed him warmly; they came to know each other's mind, and once the archbishop could see that this was a man in every respect fit for high office he consecrated Arnald as bishop [1124], and parted with him handsomely. Arnald then returned to the king who received him warmly. Einar had brought with him from Greenland a bear which he presented to king Sigurd, and in return gained honour and the king's esteem.

Later they set off in one ship, the bishop and Einar, while Arnbjorn the Norwegian together with such other Norse men as desired to go out to Greenland made ready in a second. Next they sailed to sea, but the wind was not over-helpful to them, and the bishop and Einar came in at Holtavatnsos under Eyjafjall in Iceland. At that time Sæmund the Learned was living at Oddi; he went to meet the bishop and invited him to his home for the winter, and the bishop was grateful, and said he would accept. Einar spent the winter under Eyjafjall.

The story goes that when the bishop rode from the ship with his men, they stopped for a rest at some farm or other in the Landeyjar. They were sitting in the open air when out came an old woman with a wool-comb in her hand. She walked up to one of the men, and, 'Eh, buckie,' she said, 'wilt fasten the tooth in my comb?' He took it, saying yes he would, took a riveting-hammer out of a bag, and did a job which pleased the old lady very much. Now this man was none other than the bishop, for he could turn his hand to anything, and this story has been related of him for the proof it gives of his humility.

He spent the winter at Oddi, where he and Sæmund hit it off well together. There was no news of Arnbjorn and the others, so the bishop and Einar concluded he must have reached Greenland. Next summer they left Iceland and came to Greenland, to Eiriksfjord, where they were given a cordial welcome, but to their great surprise could still get no news of Arnbjorn. Several summers passed, then it was generally agreed that they must have perished. The bishop established his see at Gardar and transferred himself there. Einar and his father were his mainstay, whilst they of all their fellow-countrymen stood highest in favour with the bishop.

II

There was a Greenlander by the name of Sigurd Njalsson who of an autumn often went off fishing and hunting in the Wilderness: he was a master of the seaman's art. There were fifteen of them all told, they reached the glacier Hvitserk in the summer, and had come across some human cooking-places and signs of catches too.

'Which would you rather do,' Sigurd asked them, 'turn back or go on? There is not much of the summer left. On the other hand our catch has been a poor one.'

His shipmates said they would rather turn back. It was a dangerous business, they contended, sailing these big fjords under the glaciers.

He admitted that was true. 'Yet something tells me the bigger part of our catch lies ahead, if we can only lay hands on it.'

They said the decision must be his. They had trusted to his guidance for a long time now, they said, and everything had gone well. He admitted that his own inclination was to press ahead, so that was what they did. There was a man by the name of Steinthor on board their ship. He now struck in, saying: 'Last night I had a dream, Sigurd, a dream I will describe to you. For as we were threading this big fjord here, it seemed to me I got in amongst some precipices and yelled out for help.' Sigurd said the dream was none too good. 'So don't go spurning at what can help you, and landing yourself in such a hole that you can't keep your mouth shut.' For Steinthor was a very headstrong, heedless sort of man.

As they headed up the fjord Sigurd asked: 'Am I right in thinking there is a ship in the fjord?' Yes, they said, there was. Great news would come of this, said Sigurd. They held on towards it up the fjord, and could see that the ship had been beached in a river-mouth and covered over. She was a big sea-going vessel. Next they went ashore, and saw a hall there, and a tent close by. For a start, said Sigurd, they had best pitch their own tent. 'The day is coming to a close, and I want everyone to stay quiet and watchful.' In the morning they walked across and looked the place over. Near them they could see a block of wood: stuck in it was a pole-axe, and there was a man's corpse close by. Sigurd reckoned this man had been chopping wood and had collapsed for hunger. With that they walked to the hall, where they saw another corpse. This one, reckoned Sigurd, had stayed on his feet as long as he could. 'They must have been the servants of those who are inside the hall.' For an axe lay beside this one too. 'I think it a wise precaution,' said Sigurd, 'to break open the hall and let the stench of the bodies which are inside clear off, and the foul air which has been gathering there this long while. And mind, everybody, to keep out of its way, for there is nothing more certain than that it will bring on such sickness as is utterly destructive of man's being. Though it is unlikely the men themselves will do us any harm.'

Steinthor said it was silly to give themselves more trouble than there was call for, and as they were breaking open the hall he walked in at the door. As he came out Sigurd got a look at him. 'The man is all changed!' he said. And at once he began to yell and run off, with his comrades in pursuit of him, and leapt into a fissure in a crag where no one could get at him, and perished there. His dream had come only too true for him, said Sigurd.

Afterwards they broke open the hall, following Sigurd's instructions closely, and got no hurt by it. Inside the hall they saw dead men and a lot of money. Said Sigurd: 'As I see it, it will be best for you to clean the flesh off their bones in these boilers they had. It will be easier then to move them to church. Most likely this will be Arnbjorn, for this second fine ship standing here on the shore, I have heard tell she was his.' She was a vessel with a

21. DRANGAR, EIRIK THE RED'S FIRST HOME IN ICELAND

22. BRATTAHLID, EIRIK THE RED'S HOME IN GREENLAND

The stone walls in the foreground are those of the third,
early thirteenth-century church.

23. CHRISTIAN GRAVE AT SANDNES, GREENLAND

The skeletons of a man, woman, and child, with a small wooden cross between them.

figurehead, coloured, and altogether a treasure. But the merchant-ship was badly broken underneath, and in Sigurd's opinion was by now good for nothing. So they took out her bolts and nails, then burned her, and took a loaded transport out from the Wilderness, the tow-boat too, and the vessel with a figurehead. They got back to the settlement and found the bishop at Gardar. Sigurd told him of their adventures and the finding of the money. 'So far as I can see,' he said, 'the best thing that can happen to this money is for it to accompany their bones, and so far as I have any say in the matter, that is how I want it to be.' The bishop assured him that he had acted well and wisely, as everyone agreed. There was a lot of money and valuables along with the bodies, and the bishop described the ship with her figurehead as a great treasure. Sigurd said of that too that it would be best if it went to the see for the good of their souls. The rest of the goods those who had found them divided among themselves in accordance with the law of Greenland.

But when news of these events reached Norway it came to the ears of a nephew of Arnbjorn's named Ozur. There were other men as well who had lost kinsmen of theirs aboard that ship and felt entitled to inherit their money. They made a voyage to Eiriksfjord, where men came down to the shore to meet them; they started buying and selling, and later were found lodgings in men's homes. Skipper Ozur went to Gardar where the bishop lived, and spent the winter there. There was a second merchant-ship up in the Western Settlement at this same time, belonging to a Norwegian, Kolbein Thorljotsson; while yet a third ship was under the command of Hermund Kodransson and his brother Thorgils. They had a substantial body of men with them.

During the winter Ozur had a talk with the bishop, how he had come out to Greenland expecting to inherit after his kinsman Arnbjorn. He asked the bishop to arrange for the inheritance to be paid over both in respect of himself and the rest of them; but the bishop contended he had received the money in accordance with the law of Greenland relative to this kind of mishap; he had not done this, he said, of his own initiative, and he maintained that it was only right and proper that the money should go for the good of the souls of those who had been its owners, and to the church where their bones were buried. It was shabby, he said, to claim the money now. After this Ozur would not stay another

14

day at Gardar with the bishop; he went off to join his crew, and they stuck close together, all of them, over the winter.

In the spring Ozur prepared a lawsuit for the Greenlanders' Thing. This Thing was held at Gardar, the bishop was in attendance along with Einar Sokkason, and they had a strong body of men. Ozur attended too, together with his shipmates. Once the court was set up Einar marched into court with a strong force, and said he thought they would have endless trouble dealing with foreigners in Norway if this was to be the course of events out in Greenland. 'We want to have the law that obtains here!' And when the court went into procession, the Norwegians failed to get anywhere with their case and had to withdraw. Ozur did not like this at all. He felt he had won humiliation for his pains, not money; so what he resorted to was this: he went to where the coloured ship was standing, and cut two strakes out of her, one on each side, upward from the keel. After which he went off to the Western Settlement, where he met Kolbein and Ketil Kalfsson, and told them how things stood. Kolbein agreed that he had been treated shamefully, but what he had resorted to, that was not so good either, he said.

Said Ketil: 'I strongly advise you to move up here to us, for I have heard that the bishop and Einar act hand in glove together. You will never be able to cope with the bishop's plots and Einar's power of action, and we had best all stand together.'

He agreed that was probably the most useful thing they could do. One of the merchants' party there was Ice-Steingrim. Ozur now returned to Kidjaberg, where he had been before.

The bishop grew very angry when he learned that the ship was ruined. He summoned Einar Sokkason before him, and this is what he told him: 'The time has now come for you to make good those oaths you swore when we left Norway, to punish any affront to the see and its possessions on those that wrought it. I hereby declare Ozur's life forfeit, for he has ruined what rightly belonged to us, and in every respect treated us with contempt. There is no concealing that I do not like things the way they are, and I shall brand you a perjurer if you do nothing about it.'

'It is not a good thing to have done, lord bishop,' Einar agreed, 'yet some will say there is excuse of a kind for Ozur—he has suffered so heavy a mulcting—even though these men might not easily contain themselves when they laid eyes on those splendid treasures which had belonged to their kinsmen, yet could not secure possession of them. Indeed, I hardly know what line to take here.'

They parted coolly, and the bishop's face was eloquent of his displeasure. But when folk went to the church anniversary and feast at Langanes, the bishop put in an appearance with Einar at the feast. A lot of people had come along for the service, and the bishop sang mass. Ozur was one of those who attended, and was standing by the south side of the church against the church wall, and talking to him was a man named Brand Thordarson, one of the bishop's servants. He was urging him to give way to the bishop. 'For then,' he said, 'I believe all will end well, but as it is the outlook is bleak.' Ozur said he just could not find it in his heart to do that, he had been treated so badly, and they went on arguing the ins and outs of it. Then the bishop and the rest of them left the church for the house, and Einar joined in the procession. But just as they arrived at the hall doors Einar broke away from the party and went off to the churchyard all on his own, seized an axe from the hand of one of the worshippers and walked south round the church, to where Ozur stood leaning on his axe. He instantly struck him his death-blow, then walked back indoors, where by now the tables had been set up. Einar took his place at table opposite the bishop, without saying a word.

Then Brand Thordarson walked into the room and up to the bishop, and, 'Have you heard the news, lord bishop?' he asked.

Not a thing, said the bishop. 'And what have you to report?'

'A man has just dropped down dead outside.'

'Who did it?' asked the bishop. 'And who was the victim?'

Brand said there was a man near him who could tell him all about it.

'Einar,' asked the bishop, 'have you caused Ozur's death?'

'Quite right,' he replied. 'I have.'

'Such deeds are not right,' said the bishop. 'Yet this one is not without its justification.'

Brand asked that the body should be washed and a service sung over it. There was plenty of time for that, replied the bishop, and men sat to table, taking their time over everything, and indeed the bishop appointed men to sing over the body only when Einar pressed for it, urging that this should be done in a way which was seemly and proper. The bishop said that in his opinion it would be the properer course not to give him church burial at all. 'However, at your request he shall be buried here at a church which has no resident priest.' Nor would he appoint clergy to sing over him before his body was laid out.

'Things have taken a sharp turn now,' said Einar, 'and in no small measure through your contriving. There are a lot of violent men concerned in this, and in my opinion a lot of trouble is heading our way.'

The bishop said he hoped they would be able to stave off all such violence, and offer arbitration and a just solution of the case, so long as it was not pursued in a violent way.

III

The news spread and the merchants came to hear of it. 'My guess was not far out,' said Ketil Kalfsson, 'that this would cost him his head.'

There was a kinsman of Ozur's whose name was Simon, a big, strong man; and Ketil said it was probable, if Simon acted in character, that he would not be overlooking the slaughter of Ozur his kinsman. Simon's comment was that this was not the occasion for big talk.

Ketil had their ship made ready. He sent men to see skipper Kolbein and had him briefed with the news. 'And tell him this, that I am going to prosecute Einar in court, for I know the law of Greenland and am quite prepared to handle these people. Besides, we have a strong force of men, if it comes to trouble.' Simon said he was prepared to take his lead from Ketil, and afterwards set off to find Kolbein, and informed him of the killing and of Ketil's message, that they should join forces with those from the Western Settlement and attend the Greenlanders' Thing. He would certainly come if he could, said Kolbein; he would like the Green-landers to discover that it did not pay to go killing their men. Ketil immediately took over the lawsuit from Simon and set off with a fair body of men, ordering the merchants to follow quickly after. 'And bring your goods with you.' The moment he received this message Kolbein took action, ordered his mates to come to the Thing, and explained that they had now so strong a following that it was doubtful that the Greenlanders could encroach on their rights. And now Kolbein and Ketil met and laid their heads together—and each of them a man to be reckoned with. They set off, had a foul wind, but kept moving ahead: they had a big body of men, though as it happened fewer than they had expected. And now men came to the Thing.

Sokki Thorisson had come there too. He was a shrewd sort of man, old by now, and was often appointed to arbitrate in men's lawsuits. He went to see Kolbein and Ketil to tell them he wished to seek for an atonement. 'I want to offer myself as an arbitrator between you,' he said, 'and though I have stronger ties with Einar my son, still I shall act in the case in such a way as will seem pretty fair to myself and to other reliable and sensible men.' Ketil said he thought they would be all for pressing their case to its conclusion. Still he did not entirely rule out the idea of a settlement. 'But we have been treated monstrously, and it has never been our way to let our rights go by default.' Sokki said he thought they would not stand an even chance if it came to a fight, besides which it remained to be seen, he said, whether they would get any more satisfaction even though he, Sokki, was not their judge and arbitrator.

The merchants went into court and Ketil put his case against Einar. Said Einar: 'It will make news everywhere if they overbear us in this case.' And he marched to the court and broke it up, so that they could not proceed with their business. 'It still stands,' said Sokki, 'that offer I made for a reconciliation and to arbitrate in the case.' But Ketil said he thought that any further compensation he awarded would serve no purpose now. 'Einar's lawlessness in this case remains unaffected.' And with that they parted.

The reason why the merchants from the Western Settlement had not put in an appearance at the Thing was that they got a head wind there when they were ready with their two ships. But at midsummer there was to be an arbitration made at Eid, and now these merchants made their way down from the west and lay off a certain headland, where they all met together and held a conference. Kolbein swore it should not have come so near a settlement had they all been there together. 'But now I think it best for us all to attend this meeting, and with all the resources we can muster.' And that was the way of it: they went off and into hiding in a certain hidden bay a short distance from the bishop's see.

It happened at the see that they were ringing for his mass just as Einar Sokkason arrived. When the merchants heard this, they said it was paying Einar great honour that the bells should be rung to greet him. It was a scandal, they said, and were furious at it. But, 'Don't be upset by it,' said Kolbein, 'for it might well turn out that before evening falls this could change to a funeral knell.'

Now Einar and his men came and sat down on a bank there. Sokki laid out the articles to be valued and those items which were intended as compensation. Said Ketil: 'I want Hermund Kodransson and myself to price these articles.' It should be so, said Sokki. Ozur's kinsman Simon was prowling round with a scowl on his face while the price of the articles was being settled. And now an ancient coat of plate-mail was brought forward. 'What an insult,' cried Simon, 'offering such rubbish in payment for a man like Ozur!' He dashed the mail-coat to the ground and marched up to the men who were sitting on the bank, and the minute the Greenlanders saw this they sprang to their feet and stood facing downhill against Simon. And now Kolbein moved up outside them as they all turned forward, then slipped in at their rear, and it was at one and the same moment he got behind Einar's back and cut at him with his axe between his shoulders and Einar's axe lighted on Simon's head, so that they both suffered a mortal wound.

'It is only what I expected,' said Einar, as he fell.

Then Einar's foster-brother Thord rushed at Kolbein, intending to cut him down, but Kolbein swerved out of his way, jabbing with his axe-horn, and catching him in the throat, and Thord was killed instantly. With that battle was joined between them; but the bishop sat down alongside Einar, and he breathed his last on the bishop's knees. There was a man by the name of Steingrim who said they must stop fighting, please; he walked in between them with certain others, but both sides were so mad that he had a sword whipt through him in a twinkling. Einar died up on the bank by the booth of the Greenlanders. By this time there were many men badly wounded, and Kolbein and his party got down to their ship with three of their men killed, and afterwards got themselves across Einarsfjord to Skjalgsbudir, where the merchant-ships were lying and being busily made ready for sea.

There had been a bit of a brawl, commented Kolbein. 'And I can't help thinking the Greenlanders will be no better pleased now than before.'

'It was a true word you spoke, Kolbein,' said Ketil, 'that we should hear a funeral knell before we got away, and I believe that Einar's dead body is being carried to church.'

Kolbein agreed that he was not without some responsibility for this.

'We can expect the Greenlanders to launch an attack on us,' said Ketil. 'I think it best for our people to carry on loading as hard as they can, and for everyone to stay aboard ship by night.'

Which is what they did.

IV

Sokki was deeply distressed by what had happened, and canvassed for help if it came to a fight. Living at Solarfjall was a man named Hall, very level-headed and a good farmer. He was on Sokki's side, and was the last to come in with his following. He said to Sokki: 'This plan of yours, using small boats to attack big, looks most unpromising to me, when you consider the welcome I feel sure they will have prepared for us. Another thing, I don't know how far this muster of yours can be relied on. Those worth their salt will all give a good account of themselves, true, but the rest will be more for hanging back, so your leaders will all get knocked on the head, and our case end up worse than it started. So it seems to me only wise, if there is to be a fight, that everybody now swears an oath that he will either die or conquer.'

At these words of Hall's a good deal of their courage seeped out of them. 'Yet we cannot let it drop,' said Sokki, 'while the case remains unsettled.'

Hall replied that he would try for a peaceful settlement between them. He called out to the merchants, asking: 'Shall I have peace to come over and see you?' Kolbein and Ketil called back that he should, so he went across to them and argued the need to get the case settled after such great and dire events. They declared themselves ready for either alternative, war or peace, just as the others pleased; all these evils, they argued, had come about through the Greenlanders. 'But now that you are showing such goodwill, we pledge our word that you shall compose the issue between us.' He said he would arbitrate and judge in the light of what seemed to him most right, like it as they might, either party. Next, this was put to Sokki, who likewise agreed to Hall's jurisdiction. The merchants must carry on day and night with their preparations to leave, and they stressed that nothing would satisfy Sokki except that they should be out and away at the earliest possible moment. 'But if they dawdle over their preparations and mortify me so, then it is certain they shall have no redress if they are caught.'

On that note they parted, and a place was fixed on for the announcement of the award. 'Our sailing arrangements are not getting on at all quickly,' said Ketil, 'while supplies are running out fast. I suggest we look round for provisions. I know where there is a man living who has any amount of food, and I think it only sense to go and find him.' They said they were all ready, and later hurried ashore one night, thirty of them in a group, all armed. They reached this farm, but it was completely deserted. Thorarin was the name of the farmer living there. 'My suggestion has not turned out so well,' said Ketil, whereupon they turned away from the farm and down the path towards the ships. There was a bushy place they passed. 'I feel drowsy,' said Ketil. 'I am going to sleep.' This was not exactly prudent, they held, but all the same down he lay and went to sleep, while they sat watching over him. A little later he woke up. 'Matters of some moment have been revealed to me,' he told them. 'How would it be if we were to pull up this clump which is under my head here?' They pulled up the clump, and down below it was a big cave. 'To start with, let us take a look what sort of provisions are here,' said Ketil. They found sixty carcases there, twelve eighty-pound weights of butter, and any amount of dried fish. 'It is a good thing,' commented Ketil, 'that I have not led you on a fool's errand.' And they went down to the ship with their plunder.

Now time wore on to the peace-meeting, and both sides turned up to it, both merchants and Greenlanders. Hall made this announcement: 'This is my award between you, that I want Ozur's killing to cancel that of Einar; but because of the disparity between the two men outlawry shall follow for the Norwegians, so that they get neither food nor shelter here. In addition, the following killings shall be held equal: franklin Steingrim and Simon, Krak the Norwegian and Thorfinn the Greenlander, Vighvat the Norwegian and Bjorn the Greenlander, Thorir and Thord. Which still leaves one of our men unpaid for, Thorarin by name, a man with helpless folk dependent on him. He must be paid for with money.'

Sokki said the award was a bitter disappointment to him and his fellow Greenlanders, when men were paired off in such fashion; but Hall was firm that his verdict should stand even so, and it was on those terms they parted.

The next thing, in swept the ice and all the fjords were frozen. It was a pleasing thought to the Greenlanders that they might lay hands on them if they could not get away by the appointed time, but at the very end of the month all the ice swept out, the merchants got away from Greenland, and that was their parting.

They reached Norway. Kolbein had brought a white bear from Greenland and went with this creature into the presence of king Harald Gilli, and presented it to him, and held forth before the king about what cruel treatment the Greenlanders had meted out, slandering them greatly. But later the king heard a different story and thought that Kolbein had been pitching him a lot of lies, so no bounty followed in respect of the bear. After that Kolbein took sides with Sigurd Shamdeacon, attacked the king in his chamber, and gave him a wound [1136]. But later, as they were on their way to Denmark and crowding sail, with Kolbein in the tow-boat and the wind blowing hard, the boat was torn adrift and Kolbein was drowned. But Hermund and the others came to Iceland to the land of their fathers.

And that is the end of this saga.

APPENDIXES

Appendixes

I. *NJÁLA:* GREATEST OF SAGAS

To begin with, *Njála* is the picture of an age. Just as *War and Peace* includes within its world not only the Bezukhovs, the Rostovs, the Bolkonskis and the Kuragins, but peasant, soldier, clerk and seamstress, Berthier and Kutuzov, Czar and Emperor, and even Platon Karataev's dog, so *Njála* has room not only for Njal and his sons and for such southern families as are their enemies and friends, but for all the leading men of Iceland too, Snorri Godi, Gudmund the Mighty, Skapti Thoroddsson, and further afield for the kings and earls of Norway, Denmark, Orkney and Ireland; for hucksters, beggarwomen, farmers and sailors, and even for the hound Sam whose dying howl announced Gunnar's approaching doom. There are some twenty-five fully-drawn characters, and these are surrounded by scores of shrewdly delineated lesser persons who between them give us the very feel of the great days of the Republic. Nor is the picture one of a confined society. If the young Icelanders are farmers' sons, they are many of them peasant princes who have rubbed shoulders with kings and noblemen and louted to none of them. The heartland of the saga is Iceland, from the deep rifts of Thingvellir to the southern ice-sheet; but its events reach out over northern and western Europe. Paradoxically, it is the more Icelandic for its awareness of the world outside. The heartland shows truer against the wide horizons.

It follows that *Njála* is a full book. The main theme is never suspended: the burning of Njal, all that preceded it and all that was fated to follow, these are before us from the opening sentences to the last. But this sequence of cause and event is enriched by much else. For *Njála*'s massive certainty thrives on a shimmering interplay of yea and nay, of hopes raised and poised and raised again, then dashed. How easily Gunnar might have lived. How easily the slaying of Hoskuld could have been compounded. At how many points the tragic action seems to be arrested, and might

be averted. 'If only,' we say, 'if only——'. For this is life itself
moving before us, the moment hardly to be determined when the
casual hardens into certainty. In another dimension *Njála* is the
saga of law *par excellence*; it is rich in constitutional history; and
the story of the conversion to Christianity is amply presented.
Law, the Constitution, and the change of faith are essential to the
private histories of the characters. *Njála* is not an historical thesis
which needs human protagonists; it is a work of realistic fiction
which uses history with superb skill for its own creative purposes.
Its ultimate concern is with something which transcends historical
fact or tradition—and that is human destiny. So the old religion
and the new are needed, and prophecy and the supernatural,
together with ingredients noble and mean, wise and foolish,
important and petty, and sometimes ambiguous. These are
presented directly through human beings, their thoughts, motives,
and actions. For the most part the saga is heroic or tragic, yet
from time to time the note may be homely or comic; the pointing
and counterpointing is most delicate. What men do, and why they
do it, and what happens to them—these are the problems cogi-
tated and the issues displayed. *Njála* proceeded not only from a
skilled hand but from a richly-stored mind. Its author was learned
in earlier saga generally; he was well versed in historical records,
both genealogical and narrative, native and foreign; the lawbooks
he had at his fingers' ends, and his knowledge of patristic and
other religious literature was extensive. To this book learning he
could add a wealth of oral tradition whose volume and variety
we are only now coming to appreciate.

His main concern, we have said, was with human destiny. The
hero of the first third of the saga is Gunnar, one of the noblest
men that ever lived in Iceland. It was his fortune (and misfortune)
to marry the beautiful, spoiled, and trouble-bent Hallgerd. 'She
had lovely hair, and was so richly-tressed that she might hide
herself in it; but she was prodigal and fierce.' Many men had died
because of her, this perilous maiden who grew worse after
marriage; and Gunnar was the dearest sacrifice to her imperious
and enigmatic temper. She involved him against his will in so
many feuds that eventually two-score of his enemies besieged him
in his house. Only his wife and mother were with him, but he
held them off till his bowstring was cut through. It was now
that he asked for two locks of his wife's long hair, to twist into a

new string; and it was now with her snake-tongue that she tauntingly denied him his request. Soon he was dead, after one of the unforgettable defences in heroic literature; but Hallgerd lived on to embroil the sons of Njal still deeper in a new feud which would lead to an even more destructive climax.

Njal was Gunnar's best friend, an older man with a houseful of turbulent sons, including the troll-ugly, homicidal Skarphedin. Time and again he was able to save Gunnar from the disasters in which Hallgerd's pride and greed engulfed him. He was a wise and peace-loving man, loyal and magnanimous, at once blest and racked by his ability to read into the future. Not that he was a blind fatalist: men, he knew, had their choice of action, but that choice once made Njal knew what must follow. Thus he foresaw Gunnar's death if he would not accept his banishment abroad, and the moment came when he foresaw his own. The most unbearable of all the burdens laid on him by his wisdom and foresight was when his son Skarphedin came home to tell him that he had killed his foster-brother Hoskuld.

'Bitter news this,' says Njal, 'and bad to hear, for indeed this grief touches me so close that I think it would have been better to lose two of my sons and have Hoskuld live.'

'It is some excuse for you', says Skarphedin, 'that you are an old man. It is only to be expected it would touch you close.'

'No less than my age', says Njal, 'is the fact that I know better than you what will follow.'

'What will follow?' asks Skarphedin.

'My death,' says Njal, 'and my wife's death, and the death of all my sons.'

The duty of vengeance for Hoskuld fell upon Flosi, and because he was a man of heroic mould he discharged it. But even at the burning itself he sought to spare all save the slayers of Hoskuld. He calls the women and children and all the servants out to safety, and they go. Then, as the hall blazes, he begs Njal to come out too.

'I have no wish to come out,' answers Njal, 'for I am an old man and little fitted to avenge my sons, and I will not live my life in shame.'

Then Flosi spoke to Bergthora [Njal's wife]: 'Come out, lady, for I would not for anything burn you here indoors.'

'I was given to Njal young,' said Bergthora, 'and it was my promise to him that we should share the same fate.'

And so, their destiny accepted, as Gunnar and Flosi had

accepted theirs, they perish by fire, and all their sons, fierce and terrible men, perish too. Yet the burning of Bergthorshvoll, as Flosi only too well knew, was 'a great, ill deed' which could solve nothing. The balances sway anew, and now it is Kari, Njal's son-in-law, whose infant son had also died in the fire, who inherits the sacred and inalienable duty of a bloody revenge. For years Kari hunted down the burners, in Iceland and abroad. All other men took atonement in time, but he took none. Atonement came in the end when his ship was wrecked on the coast near Svinafell. He reached Flosi's home in the storm, a helpless man seeking safety, and as he came inside the house his foe knew him and sprang up to meet him, and kissed him, and set him down in the high seat by his side. And we know that all the vast orchestration of the saga has been leading to this last clear note of reconciliation. Only one thing remains to be told: how Flosi died. Long years later he sailed to Norway for house-timber, and was late putting to sea when he returned. 'People warned him that his ship was not seaworthy, but Flosi replied that she was good enough for a doomed old man.' Somewhere between Norway and Iceland she went down with all hands. 'And there I end the Saga of the Burning of Njal.'

II. THE ONLY KING WHO RESTS IN ICELAND

[These two chapters from *Ólafs Saga Helga* recount the last stages of king Olaf's dealings with his enemy and kinsman Hrœrek, one of the five kings of Uppland. Olaf captured all five, took the tongue from one, the eyes from Hrœrek, and the others he banished. After that he never let Hrœrek out of his sight, though he treated him well enough. However, Hrœrek in all his moods was constant for revenge, and before our portion of his story opens had attempted both assassination and escape.

The Icelander Thorarin Nefjolfsson is known not only for his unsuccessful attempt to reach Greenland with king Hrœrek, but for a famous crossing from (Stad in) Mœr in Norway to Eyrar (i.e. Eyrarbakki) in the south-west of Iceland. He covered the distance of about 730 nautical miles in four days and four nights, the fastest recorded run.]

84

It happened on Ascension day [15 May 1018] that king Olaf went

24. SWORDS

The viking's chief weapon. *Left*, beautiful and deadly, the Lodingen sword, from Lofoten, Norway.

25. THE SANDNES CHRIST

to high mass. The bishop walked in procession round the church, leading the king, and when they came back to the church the bishop led the king to his seat in the north of the choir. As usual king Hrœrek was seated next to him. He had his face under his over-cloak. When king Olaf had sat down king Hrœrek put his hand on his shoulder and felt it. 'Fine clothes you wear now, kinsman,' said he. 'This is a high festival,' replied king Olaf, 'held in remembrance of Jesus Christ's ascension to heaven from earth.' 'I am not quite clear,' said king Hrœrek, 'what you tell me about Christ, so that I can keep it safe in mind. Much of what you tell me seems none too credible, though to be sure many wonders happened in the old days.'

When mass had begun king Olaf stood up, raised his hands above his head and bowed towards the altar, and his cloak fell back from off his shoulders. King Hrœrek sprang up quick and hard and struck at king Olaf with a knife of the kind called 'rytning'. The blow came on the cape by the shoulders as the king was bending forwards; the clothes were badly cut, but the king was unwounded. When king Olaf knew of this assault he sprang forward on to the floor. King Hrœrek struck at him a second time with the knife, but missed him. 'Are you fleeing then, Olaf Digri,' he cried, 'from me, a blind man?' The king ordered his men to seize him and lead him out of the church, which was done.

Following this incident king Olaf was urged to have king Hrœrek killed. 'It is pressing your luck hard, king, to keep him about you and spare him, whatever mischief he gets up to. Day and night his one thought is to take your life, while once you let him out of your sight we see no one who will keep so close an eye on him that there will be no chance of his escaping. And if he gets loose he will promptly raise an army and do great harm.'

'What you say is true enough,' replied king Olaf. 'Many a man has got his death for less provocation than Hrœrek's. But I am loth to tarnish the victory I won over the Upplanders' kings, when in a morning I caught them all, and seized their kingdoms in such fashion that I need not be the death of a single one of them, for they were all my kinsmen. At the moment I find it hard to tell whether Hrœrek will put me in a position where I must have him killed or not.'

Hrœrek had put his hand on king Olaf's shoulder to find out whether he was wearing a mail shirt.

15

85

There was a man called Thorarin Nefjolfsson, an Icelander whose family lived up north, not of high birth, but full of sense and wise conversation, and ready to speak his mind in the highest company. He was a great traveller and had spent much time in foreign parts. Thorarin was very ugly, and the main cause of this was the deformity of his limbs. His hands were big and ugly, and his feet were far worse.

Thorarin was staying in Tunsberg when the events just narrated took place. He and king Olaf were not unacquainted. At the time Thorarin was fitting out the merchant ship he owned, for he proposed sailing to Iceland in the summer. King Olaf had Thorarin as his guest for a few days and had plenty to talk to him about. Thorarin slept in the royal quarters. Early one morning it happened that the king was awake while the others in the room were asleep. The sun had just risen, and it was quite light indoors. The king could see how Thorarin had stuck one of his feet out from under the bedclothes. He studied the foot for a while, then those in the room woke up.

'I have been awake some time,' the king told Thorarin, 'and have seen a sight well worth seeing, a man's foot so ugly that I cannot think there is an uglier in this town.' And he told the others to take a look, whether it appeared that way to them; and all who looked vowed that it was so.

Thorarin understood very well what they were talking about. 'There are few things,' he replied, 'whose match you cannot hope to find, and it is very probable that is the case here too.'

'For my part,' said the king, 'I am convinced that so ugly a foot just cannot be found, no, even if I have to bet on it.'

'I am willing to bet you I shall find an uglier foot here in the town,' said Thorarin.

'Then let the one proved right claim anything he likes of the other,' said the king.

'So be it,' replied Thorarin, and stuck his other foot out from under the bedclothes. It was no whit handsomer than its fellow, and its big toe was missing. 'See for yourself, king, another foot, which is uglier to the extent that one of its toes is missing. I have won the bet.'

'No, no,' said the king, 'the other foot is uglier to the extent that it has five nasty toes, and this only four. So I have a claim to make of you.'

'Dear are the king's words,' said Thorarin. 'And what claim are you making?'

'This,' said he, 'that you carry king Hrœrek to Greenland and hand him over to Leif Eiriksson.'

'I have never been to Greenland,' replied Thorarin.

'If you have not,' said the king, 'then it is high time a traveller like you did.'

At first Thorarin made little answer in the matter, but when the king kept pressing his request he did not entirely evade the issue, but said this: 'I will let you hear, king, the demand I had it in mind to make, had our bet been won by me. It was this: I wanted to ask for a place among your men. And if you grant me that, it will be all the more my duty not to dawdle over what you ask of me.'

The king agreed to this and Thorarin became his retainer. He saw to his ship, and when he was ready to sail took charge of king Hrœrek. As he took leave of king Olaf he asked the king: 'Now should it turn out, sire, as is not improbable and happens often enough, that we cannot complete the Greenland passage but must run for Iceland or some other land, how shall I part with this king to your satisfaction?'

'If you come to Iceland,' said the king, 'you must deliver him into the hands of Gudmund Eyjolfsson or Skapti the Lawspeaker or some other chieftain who wishes to accept my friendship and the tokens that go with it. But if you are driven to other lands lying nearer home, then so arrange matters that you know for sure Hrœrek will never return alive to Norway. But do this only if you see there is nothing else for it.' ·

When Thorarin was ready and had a good wind he sailed the whole outer course away beyond the islands, and north of Lidandisnes stood out to sea. For a while he did not get a good wind, but made it very much his business not to come to land. He sailed south of Iceland, then knew where he was, and so west of the land into the Greenland sea. There he got great storms and heavy seas, and late in the summer came to Iceland, to Breida-fjord. Thorgils Arason was the first man of any importance to come to them, and Thorarin told him of king Olaf's message, his offer of friendship and the tokens relating to the taking over of king Hrœrek. Thorgils showed himself friendly in return, inviting king Hrœrek to his house, where he stayed with Thorgils for the winter. But he did not like it there, and asked Thorgils to have him conveyed to Gudmund. He seemed to have heard, he said, that at Gudmund's was the most splendid style of living in Iceland, and it was to him he had been sent. So Thorgils did as he asked and provided men to convey him to Gudmund at Modruvellir. Gudmund gave him a good welcome because of the king's message, and it was there he spent his second winter. Then he liked it there no longer, so Gudmund found him a place to live at a little farm called Kalfskinn, where there were very few people, and there he spent his third winter. And ever since he lost his kingdom, he said, that was where he liked being best, for there he was held the first man by all. The following summer Hrœrek took the sickness which brought him to his death, so it is said he is the only king who rests in Iceland.

III. UNGORTOK THE CHIEF OF KAKORTOK

[This splendidly bloodthirsty tale, together with its illustrations by the Greenlander Aron of Kangeq, is reproduced from Henry Rink, *Tales and Traditions of the Eskimo*, Translated from the Danish by the Author, London, 1875, pp. 308–17].

It once happened that a kayaker from Arpatsivik came rowing up the firth, trying his new bird-javelin as he went along. On approaching Kakortok, where the first *Kavdlunait* [plural of *kavdlunak*, foreigner, Norseman] had taken up their abode, he saw one of them gathering shells on the beach, and presently he called out to him, 'Let us see whether thou canst hit me with thy lance.' The kayaker would not comply, although the other continued asking him. At last, however, the master of the place, named Ungortok [Ungor=Yngvar?], made his appearance, and said, 'Since he seems so very anxious about it, take good aim at him;' and soon the kayaker sent out his spear in good earnest, and killed him on the spot. Ungortok, however, did not reproach him, but only said, 'It certainly is no fault of thine, since thou hast only done as thou wast bidden.' When winter came, it was a general belief that the Kavdlunait would come and avenge the death of their countryman; but summer came round again; and even two summers passed quickly by. At the beginning of the third winter, the same kayaker again rowed up to Kakortok, provided with the usual hunting tools, bladder and all. This time he again happened to see a Kavdlunak gathering shells, and somehow he took a fancy to kill him too. He rowed up towards him on that side where the sun was shining full upon the water, and launching his spear at him, killed him at once, upon which he returned home unobserved, and told how he had done away with one of the Kavdlunait. They reproached him with not having let their chief know of this; and the murderer answered them, 'The first time I only killed him because I was asked over and over again to do so.' Some time after this occurrence, a girl was sent out to draw water in the evening; but while she was filling the pail, she noticed the reflection of something red down in the water. At first she thought it to be the reflection of her own face; but turning round, she was horrified at seeing a great crowd of Kavdlunait. She was so confounded that she left the pail behind, and hurried into the house to tell what had happened. At the same time the enemies posted themselves in front of the door and the windows. One of the inmates instantly ran out, but was soon killed with an axe, and cast aside. They were all dispatched in this way: only two brothers remained unhurt. They happily escaped out on the ice. The Kavdlunait, however, soon caught sight of them, saying, 'Those are the last of the lot; let us be after them;' and at once began the pursuit. The leader now said, 'I am the quickest of you; let me start after them;' and he followed them out on the ice, where the speed of the brothers had been greatly reduced owing to the younger one having got new soles to his boots, which made them slippery, and caused him often to lose his footing. At length they reached the opposite shore, and Kaisape, the elder, succeeded in climbing the icy beach; but the younger fell, and was quickly overtaken. Ungortok cut off his left arm, and held it up before his brother, saying, 'Kaisape! as long as thou livest thou won't surely forget thy poor brother.' Kaisape, who was not armed, could render him no assistance, but quickly took to his heels. He crossed the country for Kangermiutsiak, where his father-in-law was living. Here he remained all winter, and was presented with a kayak. In summer he kayaked southward to learn some magic lay that had power to charm his enemies. He again wintered at Kangermiutsiak; but when the summer came round he went away to the north, in order to find himself a companion. At every place he came to, he first inquired if there happened to be a couple of brothers, and then he went on to examine the inside fur of their boots to see whether they had any lice in them; and he travelled far and wide before he found two brothers, of whom the younger one was altogether without lice. This one he persuaded to assist him, and made him return with him to Kangermiutsiak. He was now very intent on catching seals; and of all he caught he had the hairs removed from the skins, which were then used for white skins. This done, he went out in search of a large piece of driftwood, and at last found one to suit his purpose. He now proceeded to excavate it with his knife until it was all hollow like a tube, and made a cover to fit tightly at one end; and both sides he furnished with little holes, for which he also made stoppers of wood. Being thus far ready, he first put all the white skins inside the hollow space, shut it up at the end with the cover, and likewise closed the little side holes. He then put it down into the water, upon which all the kayakers joined in towing it down the inlet to Pingiviarnik, where they landed it; and having got out the skins, attached strings to them, then hoisted and spread them like sails, so that the boat came to have the appearance of a somewhat dirty iceberg, the skins being not all alike white. The people now got in: it was pushed off from land, and Kaisape gave the order, 'Let the skins be spread!' This was accordingly done; and the people on shore were astonished to see how very like it was to an iceberg floating slowly along. Kaisape, who wanted to take a survey of the whole from shore, said to the crew, 'Now ye can take the boat out yourselves, while I step ashore to have a look at it.' When he beheld the work of his hands, he was well pleased with it, and ordered the boat to land again. The skins were all spread out to dry in the sun; and when this had been done, he remarked that he had not yet forgotten his brother. They were now ready to go to Kakortok and have their revenge, but for some time they were obliged to station themselves at Arpatsivik, awaiting a favourable wind to carry them up the inlet. When the fair wind had set in, the firth gradually filled with broken bits of ice of different form and size. Now was the time for Kaisape to spread all sail and get in. Several boats followed in his wake, but the crews landed a little north of Kakortok to gather fagots of juniper; while Kaisape and his helpmates, well hidden in the hollow wood, and keeping a constant look-out through the peep-holes, drifted straight on towards the house. They saw the Kavdlunait go to and fro, now and then taking a look down the inlet. Once they distinctly heard it announced, 'The *Kaladlit* [plural of kalâlek, a Greenland Eskimo] are coming:' upon which they all came running out of the house; but when the master had reassured them, saying, 'It is nothing but ice,' they again retired; and Kaisape said, 'Now, quick! they won't be coming out for a while, I think.' They got out on shore; and, well loaded with juniper fagots, they all surrounded the

12.

house. Kaisape filled up the doorway with fuel, and then struck fire to it, so that all the people inside were burned; and those who tried to make their escape through the passage were also consumed. But Kaisape cared little for the people in general; his thoughts all centred in Ungortok; and he now heard one of his helpmates exclaiming, 'Kaisape! the man whom thou seekest is up there.' The chief had by this time left the burning house through a window, and was flying with his little son in his arms. Kaisape went off in pursuit of him, and approached him rapidly. On reaching the lake, the father threw his child into the water that it might rather die unwounded. Kaisape, however, not being able to overtake his antagonist, was forced to return to his crew. Ungortok ran on till he reached Igaliko, and there established himself with another chief named Olave. On finding that Kaisape would not leave him at peace there, he removed to the head of the firth Agdluitsok, where he settled at Sioralik, while Kaisape established himself at the outlet of the same firth. The following summer he again left in pursuit of Ungortok, who, however, succeeded in getting to the coast opposite the island of Aluk. Kaisape traced him right along to the north side of the same island, where he took up his abode; and he now consulted the East-landers with regard to some means of killing Ungortok. At last one stood forth, saying, 'I will get thee a bit of wood from a barren woman's boot-shelf, out of which thou must shape thine arrow.' Having pronounced some spell upon it, he handed it over to Kaisape, who acknowledged the gift saying, 'If it comes true that this shall help me, I will be bound to give thee my aid in hunting and fishing.' He now went on making as many arrows as could be contained in a quiver fashioned out of a sealskin; and last of all, he added the precious charmed one, and then with his helpmates left for the great lake in front of Ungortok's house, where Kaisape stuck all the arrows in the ground at a certain distance from each other; and finally also the charmed one. He let his companion remain below by the lake, and cautiously mounted some high hills by himself, from whence he could see Ungortok striding to and fro outside his house. He heard him talk to himself, and mention the name of Kaisape. However, he resolved to await the coming of night to carry out his purpose. In the dusk he stole away to the house, and looked in at the window, holding his bow ready bent. Ungortok was passing up and down as swiftly as a shadow, on account of which it was impossible for him to take a sure aim. He therefore levelled his bow at Ungortok's wife, who lay sleeping with a baby at her breast. Ungortok, hearing a noise, gave a look at his wife, and perceived the arrow sticking fast in her throat. Meantime Kaisape had quickly run back to the margin of the lake to fetch another arrow, while Ungortok sped after him with uplifted arm holding the axe that had formerly killed his brother in readiness for himself. Kaisape launched his second arrow at him, but Ungortok escaped it by falling down and making himself so thin that nothing but his chin remained visible; and before long Kaisape had spent all his arrows, without having hit his mark. Ungortok broke them in twain, and threw them into the lake. But at last Kaisape caught hold of the charmed arrow, and this went straight through the protruding chin down into the throat. As Ungortok did not, however, expire immediately, Kaisape took flight, but was shortly followed by the wounded Ungortok. Kaisape had been running on for a good long while, when all of a sudden he felt

13.

his throat getting dry, and fell down totally exhausted. Remembering Ungortok, however, he soon rose again, and running back to see what had become of him, found his dead body lying close by. He now cut off his right arm, and holding it up before the dead man, repeated his own words, 'Behold this arm, which thou wilt surely never forget!' He also killed the orphan child; and taking the old Eastlander with him, he travelled back to Kangermiutsiak, where he sustained the old man, whose bones, according to report, were laid to rest in that same place.

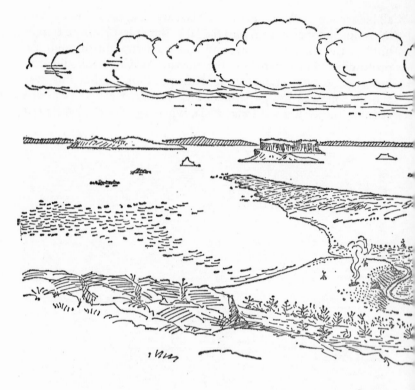

A panorama sketch by Thórhallur Vilmundarson, redrawn by Hallċ
excavation site into Épaves Bay. The author of the sketch has ɾ
of the presumed scene *c.* A.D. 1000. In the background (*left*) is the coċ
background (*right*) is Cape Bauld. Out in Sacred Bay is Great Sacɾ

IV. STRAUMFJORD IN VINLAND

The most important recent contributions to the case for northern
Newfoundland's being regarded as Promontorium Winlandiæ,
and for Karlsefni's Straumfjord (557 Straumsfjord) being most
profitably sought in the area of Sacred Bay, are these: Captain
W. A. Munn's booklet, *Wineland Voyages*, 1914 (several times
reprinted till 1946, the edition I have used); V. Tanner, *De gamla
nordbornas Helluland, Markland och Vinland. Ett rsföök till lokaliser-*

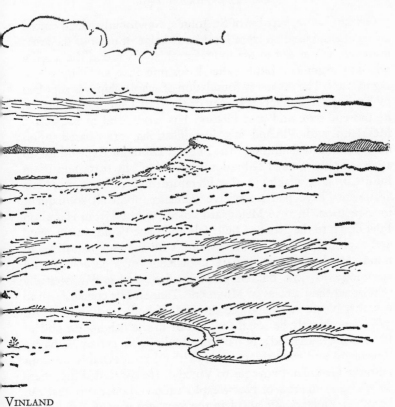

VINLAND

...tursson, showing Black Duck Brook flowing past Ingstad's 1962
...empted a reconstruction of the ruins, but offers a generalized picture
...Labrador, with Belle Isle (*centre*) at the entrance to the Strait. In the
...and (*left*), then Little Sacred Island (behind Warrens Island).

ing av huvudetapperna i de isländska Vinlandsagorna, Budkaveln, No. 1,
Åbo, 1941, and the same author's *Outlines of the Geography, Life and
Customs of Newfoundland-Labrador* (*the eastern part of the Labrador
Peninsula*), Acta Geographica 8, No. 1, Helsinki, 1944; Helge
Ingstad, *Landet under Polarstjernen* (original title *Landet under
Leidarstjernen*, Oslo, 1959), Copenhagen, 1960; Jørgen Meldgaard,
Fra Brattalid til Vinland, Naturens Verden, Copenhagen, December,
1961; various contributions to the Danish, Norwegian, and
Icelandic press since October 1961.

Captain Munn, a native of St. John's, Newfoundland, advanced an argument based on close local knowledge of most of the areas involved. It was not in the more formidable sense of the word a scholarly argument, but is valuable for reference, and most pleasing in itself. The necessary foundation of scholarship was supplied by Tanner's monumental survey of the East Labrador peninsula, its present state and past history. His work, and in respect of Markland and Vinland his identifications, are 'Based upon observations made during "the Finland-Labrador Expedition" in 1937 and "the Tanner Labrador Expedition" in 1939, and upon information available in the literature and cartography.' His arguments have had a decisive influence upon all subsequent investigation. In 1956 Meldgaard sailed the coast from Hamilton Inlet down to the Strait of Belle Isle and Cape Bauld, and camped and explored at many points ashore, with the saga narratives in mind. He brought an expert knowledge of archaeology and ethnology to bear on the problems involved and powerfully reinforced the theories of Munn and Tanner. His conclusion too was that Norse ruins and the site of Leifsbudir and Straumfjord might confidently be sought within or in the neighbourhood of Pistolet Bay. Ingstad's book was an admirable survey of Norse Greenland and everything to do with it, so inevitably he dealt with the Greenland voyages to Vinland. He concluded that there were two main areas of Norse exploration and discovery that can be called Vinland: Vinland I in the northern part of Newfoundland, Vinland II down in Massachusetts and Rhode Island. In 1960 and 1961 Ingstad made extensive journeys along the coasts of Quebec, Newfoundland, and Labrador, seeking evidence of Norse settlements. With Anne Stine Ingstad he found what they judged to be early Norse dwellings in Épaves Bay, less than a mile south of Lance-aux-Meadows. Here, thought Ingstad, was the site of Leifsbudir, and in the summer of 1962 extensive excavations were carried out there. His investigations continue.

The results are challenging and likely to prove conclusive. There are many ruins of ancient dwellings on both sides of the mouth of Black Duck Brook. Some of these belonged to a people of Stone Age Culture, in all probability the Dorset Eskimo, who have left behind them the usual detritus of flints, lamps, weapons, and the like, as well as fireplaces and cooking pits. In addition there are various houses which may be European in origin, a fire-pit and a furnace for extracting iron from bog-ore, with their attendant charcoal, slag, clay, bits of iron, one piece of bronze, anvil and hearth. Certainly men who could work in iron have lived by Black Duck Brook. What awaits a final proof is that they were Norsemen of the early eleventh century. The first C-14 (Carbon) tests on the 'iron age' material are said to be favourable to a date *c*. A.D. 1000. The cairns found in the area have been examined for runic inscriptions without result.

The clearest and fullest account of the Ingstad expedition of 1962 so far to appear has been published in the form of two articles in *Lesbók Morgunblaðsins*, 30 September and 14 October 1962, written by one of its members, Professor Thórhallur Vilmundarson of the University of Iceland. They summarize the finds, describe the Sacred Bay countryside minutely with reference to the saga-narratives, and reinforce an earlier article in *Morgunblaðið*, 19 November 1961, with a cogent presentation of the literary, historical, and geographical case for seeking the Promontorium Winlandiæ, and Karlsefni's headquarters at Straumfjord, in northern Newfoundland. Vinland as a geographical term would be the continuing stretch of coastline and country from the Promontorium to the furthest point south reached by the Norsemen, right down to New England. As with Greenland and, to a lesser extent, Iceland, we need not assume that the Norsemen had a close knowledge of the entire area.

Finally, this seems the place to note Captain Carl Sølver's reconstruction of the Skalholt map 'in proper proportion to degrees of longitude and on Mercator's principles'. On the Skalholt map thus re-ordered the distance from Herjolfsnes in Greenland to Cape Bauld at the extremity of Promontorium Winlandiæ is 640 sea miles on a course S 50 W. On a modern map it is 622 sea miles on a course S 40 W, a remarkably close correspondence (*Vestervejen*, Copenhagen, 1954, p. 97. The reconstructed map is on page 59 there).

V. TEXTS AND EDITIONS

1. *Íslendingabók*
Íslendingabók, or *Libellus Islandorum*, 'The Book of the Icelanders', was written by Ari Thorgilsson the Learned (1067/8–1148),

probably between 1122 and 1125, and certainly before 1133. It appears to be the revision of an earlier work of his written for the bishops then holding office in Iceland, and is a concise, indeed severely condensed, history of Iceland from the Settlement to his own day, critical, accurate, based on reliable sources of information, and much concerned with chronology. Its faults are a certain arbitrariness of subject matter and lack of proportion between its parts, but these were inherent in Ari's design and purpose. It richly deserves the praises heaped upon it from the earliest times to our own day as an indispensable sourcebook of Icelandic (and in one of its chapters Greenlandic) history and the oldest sustained narrative prose in any Scandinavian language. It is preserved in two transcripts of the seventeenth century, and despite the lateness of this date preserved with care and accuracy. The best edition is by Halldór Hermannsson, *The Book of the Icelanders* (*Íslendingabók*), *Edited and Translated with an Introductory Essay and Notes*, Islandica XX, New York, 1930.

2. Landnámabók

Landnámabók, 'The Book of the Landtakings *or* Settlements', as its name implies, is a schematized record of the colonization of Iceland. It preserves a wealth of information regarding some 400 of the principal settlers, usually telling where they came from, where they took land, what happened to them, and through what descendants and what vicissitudes their families persisted. The settlements are dealt with in an orderly progress clockwise round the island. Its matter is for the most part as entertaining as it is useful, for along with genealogical and historical fact it offers us anecdote, folktale, contemporary belief and superstition. It is possible, but not proven, that Ari Thorgilsson, the author of *Íslendingabók*, was also the author of an original, no longer extant, *Landnámabók*. If he was, he was helped in his undertaking by Kolskegg the Learned (who died before 1130), who wrote about the settlements in east and south-east Iceland, and no doubt by many informants whom he met either on his travels or at public assemblies. Even if he was not its author, it is generally agreed that his writings or *schedulæ* (for he wrote more than *Íslendingabók*) were important for its compilation. The five versions of *Landnámabók* now extant date from the thirteenth to the seventeenth century, and derive from the lost version prepared by

Styrmir the Learned (*c.* 1170–1245), the so-called *Styrmisbók* of
c. 1225. The relationship of *Styrmisbók* to the assumed *Landnámabók* of Ari cannot be determined. The two complete but far from
identical versions of *Landnámabók* preserved from medieval times
are those of Sturla Thórðarson (*Sturlubók*), most likely written
between 1260 and 1280, and Hauk Erlendsson (*Hauksbók*), written
some time before Hauk's death in 1334. The third medieval
version, *Melabók*, survives in a few fragments only, though rather
more of it can be recovered from the seventeenth-century *Þórðarbók*, which was compiled by Síra Thórður Jónsson of Hitardal
(d. 1670) from *Melabók* when it was less defective than it is now
and Björn Jónsson's *Skarðsárbók*, in its turn compiled from
Sturlubók and *Hauksbók*.

The relationship between the different versions of *Landnámabók*
is still less than clear, despite the studies of Björn M. Ólsen and
Jón Jóhannesson's *Gerðir Landnámabókar*, Reykjavík, 1941. But
the purposes of the present volume are unquestionably best
served by a reliance on the version prepared by the famous
thirteenth-century historian Sturla Thórðarson, and on Hauk's
enlarged version, based as he tells us that was on *Sturlubók* and
Styrmisbók. The standard edition of *Landnámabók* is that of Finnur
Jónsson, Copenhagen, 1900, 1921, and 1925; the most recent
that of Einar Arnórsson, Reykjavík, 1948. The best edition of
Skarðsárbók is by Jakob Benediktsson, Reykjavík, 1958. My own
selection owes much to Jón Helgason's *Fortællinger fra Landnámabók*, Copenhagen, 1951. *Landnámabók*'s account of Eirik the
Red has been excluded because its entire substance will be known
from the opening sections of *Grœnlendinga Saga* and *Eiríks Saga
Rauða*.

3. *Grœnlendinga Saga* and *Eiríks Saga Rauða*

Grœnlendinga Saga is preserved in the form of three interpola-
tions relating to Eirik the Red, his son Leif, and the Greenlanders,
inserted in the 'Large' Saga of king Olaf Tryggvason, itself preserved in *Flateyjarbók*, an extensive codex written down in the last
decades of the fourteenth century. Of the source of these chapters
(that is, from what manuscript their scribe Jón Thórðarson
copied them) we know nothing. The age of *Grœnlendinga Saga*, as
opposed to the age of the codex in which it is preserved, has
been the subject of much inquiry. It has been ascribed to the

fourteenth century, to various decades of the thirteenth, and even to the end of the twelfth. The strongest argument for an early date has been offered by Jón Jóhannesson (the end of the twelfth century in *Aldur Grænlendinga Sögu*, 1956, p. 158, or the beginning of the thirteenth, *Íslendinga Saga* I, 1956, p. 126).

Eiríks Saga Rauða, which is sometimes called *Þorfinns Saga Karlsefnis* (*Þórðarsonar*), is preserved in two vellum manuscripts and five seventeenth-century manuscripts which derive from these. The vellums are AM 544 4to, which is part of the big codex *Hauksbók* [*H*] made before 1334 for Hauk Erlendsson and already referred to as containing Hauk's version of *Landnámabók*; and AM 557 4to [557], sometimes called *Skálholtsbók*, of the fifteenth century. They tell the same story, in the same order of events, but with frequent and sometimes considerable differences of wording. This is because *H*, in part written out by Hauk himself, is a deliberate 'improvement' of its original, whereas 557 comes from a pen which far from seeking to improve it is not even concerned to do it justice, and as a consequence abounds in gaucheries and inadvertencies. Considered as literature then, the *H* version outshines 557, but as Sven B. F. Jansson has demonstrated in his comprehensive study (*Sagorna om Vinland* I, Lund, 1944), 557 despite the late date of the manuscript in which it is preserved is beyond all doubt an earlier and more authentic version of *Eiríks Saga Rauða* than its polished rival.

Eiríks Saga Rauða must have been composed after 1263, if we trust to the reference in the concluding genealogy of both *H* and 557 to 'bishop Brand the first', which is intelligible only in a context of bishop Brand the second (of Holar 1263–64), and if we further believe that its opening chapters were taken from Sturla Thórðarson's recension of *Landnámabók*. It is, however, possible that the reference to bishop Brand is a late addition, and that there was an older version of *Eiríks Saga Rauða* known to and used by Sturla, so the dating cannot be certain. On grounds of style and composition the saga has been held by different judges to be of both the first and the last quarter of the thirteenth century. Of recent authorities Matthías Thórðarson, *Eiríks Saga Rauða* (Íslenzk Fornrit IV), Reykjavík, 1935 (reissue of 1957), pp. lxxxiv–v, places it in the first third of the century, and Stefan Einarsson, *A History of Icelandic Literature*, New York, 1957, p. 138, hesitantly in the first quarter; Sigurður Nordal, *Sagalitteraturen* (Nordisk

Kultur VIII B), Copenhagen, 1952, pp. 244 and 248–49, lists it among sagas written 1230–80; Halldór Hermannsson, *The Vinland Sagas*, New York, 1944, p. viii, subscribes to the general view that 'our Saga was written in the latter half of the thirteenth century', as does Jón Jóhannesson in those works of his already cited.

Probably we should conclude that the version of the saga from which *H* and 557 derive was written not long after 1263, but that this was not necessarily the original *Eiríks Saga Rauða*. *Grœnlendinga Saga* appears to be not of later date than *Eiríks Saga Rauða*, and might indeed be earlier, for it either knows nothing of or completely disregards the tradition stemming from Gunnlaug Leifsson's Life of Olaf Tryggvason that Leif Eiriksson discovered Vinland. Instead it grants the honour of the discovery to Bjarni Herjolfsson, while giving Leif a more convincing role as Vinland's first explorer. Nothing is gained by exalting either saga at the expense of the other, but *Grœnlendinga Saga* is assuredly a very important document indeed. Both sagas seem to be put together from older and partly oral tradition, *Eiríks Saga Rauða* somewhere on Snæfellsnes, and *Grœnlendinga Saga* possibly in Skagafjord. They do not derive from a common original; and while the possibility that the author of *Eiríks Saga Rauða* used a detail or two from *Grœnlendinga Saga* cannot be ruled out, it seems safer to conclude that the two sagas were written independently and in ignorance of each other. That the author of *Grœnlendinga Saga* described the Leifsbudir area largely in terms of Karlsefni's Hop was not because he had read *Eiríks Saga Rauða*, but because he filled a deficiency in his own sources from tradition associated with Karlsefni. Had he known *Eiríks Saga Rauða* he would have used it more fully and more skilfully, and differently.

For *Grœnlendinga Saga* I have used the text, and in the matter of the narrative relating to Leif's conversion and evangelism the arrangement, of Halldór Hermannsson, *The Vinland Sagas*, 1944. In the case of *Eiríks Saga Rauða* I have translated 557, at the same time presenting the significant variants of *H*. On occasion in contexts not affecting the narrative or argument of this book where 557 makes less than full sense or is the victim of its scribe I have felt free to resort to *H* without indication, and inevitably any save a literal translation must obscure scores of minor differences of expression. I have used the parallel texts of 557 and

H in Sven B. F. Jansson's *Sagorna om Vinland*, and consulted at all times Halldór Hermannsson, *The Vinland Sagas*.

4. *Einars Þáttr Sokkasonar*

In this soberly told short saga we get a good look at life in Greenland in the second and third decades of the twelfth century. It is preserved in *Flateyjarbók*, and has been translated from Matthías Thórðarson's text in *Íslenzk Fornrit* IV, pp. 273–94 (where it is entitled *Grænlendinga Þáttr*).

VI. BIBLIOGRAPHICAL NOTE

A thoroughgoing bibliography of the Atlantic voyages and settlements would be an enormous compilation, beyond the scope and intention of this book. In general, sources and authorities have been named in their context, and the books now listed are by way of supplement.

The sagas relating to Iceland, Greenland, Vinland, will be found in the three series, *Íslenzk Fornrit*, Reykjavík, 1933—; *Altnordische Saga-Bibliothek*, Halle, 1891–1929; and *Íslendinga-sagnaútgáfan*, Reykjavík, 1946–50. The standard edition of the Annals is still Gustav Storm's *Islandske Annaler indtil 1578*, Christiania, 1888. All known material relating to Greenland was collected in the three volumes of *Grønlands Historiske Mindesmærker* (*GHM*), Copenhagen, 1838–45. These and the relevant volumes of *Meddelelser om Grønland* (*MGr*), Copenhagen, 1878—, are indispensable to the study of Norse Greenland. Of periodicals and series the following are particularly rewarding: the *Saga-Book* and other publications of the Viking Society for Northern Research, London; *Skírnir*, Reykjavík; *Islandica*, Ithaca, New York; while the two encyclopedias, *Nordisk Kultur*, Copenhagen, 1931–56, and *Kulturhistorisk Leksikon for nordisk Middelalder*, Copenhagen, 1956—, are repositories of authoritative information.

Authors and books which I have not always had occasion to mention adequately in my footnotes are: Vigfusson and Powell, *Origines Islandicæ*, I and II, 1905; Knut Gjerset, *History of Iceland*, 1922; Sigurður Nordal, *Íslenzk Menning*, I, Reykjavík, 1942; G. Turville-Petre, *Origins of Icelandic Literature*, 1953; Jón Jóhannesson, *Íslendinga Saga*, I and II, Reykjavík, 1956–58; Knut Gjerset,

History of the Norwegian People, I and II, 1927; Andreas Holmsen *Norges Historie fra de eldste Tider til 1660*, Oslo, 1961 edition; Poul Nørlund, *Viking Settlers in Greenland and their Descendants during five hundred years*, 1936; Helge Ingstad, *Landet under Polarstjernen*, Copenhagen, 1960; Fridtjof Nansen, *In Northern Mists. Arctic Exploration in Early Times*, I and II, 1911; T. D. Kendrick, *A History of the Vikings*, 1930; Shetelig and Falk, *Scandinavian Archaeology*, 1937; and for the Vinland voyages, A. M. Reeves, *The Finding of Wineland the Good*, 1895; W. Hovgaard, *The Voyages of the Norsemen to America*, New York, 1914; G. M. Gathorne-Hardy, *The Norse Discoverers of America*, 1921; Einar Haugen, *Voyages to Vinland*, New York, 1942.

The Maps

Note 1. The routes shown on Maps 2, 4, and 5, whether they indicate the sea voyages of the Norsemen or the coastal progress of the Eskimo, are approximate only. In the case of the former, even where the old sailing directions have been preserved, detail is usually lacking.

Note 2. Map 2 owes much to the series of maps of Norse Greenland in Lauge Koch, *The East Greenland Ice*, Meddelelser om Grønland 130, Copenhagen, 1945. Map 3 could not have been prepared without the guidance of C. L. Vebæk's 'Topografisk Kort over Østerbygden. Med Nordbonavne for Kirker og Vigtigste Fjorde', 1952. Map 4 is based on a sketch-map of Jørgen Meldgaard's, in *Fra Brattalid til Vinland* (Naturens Verden, December, 1961).

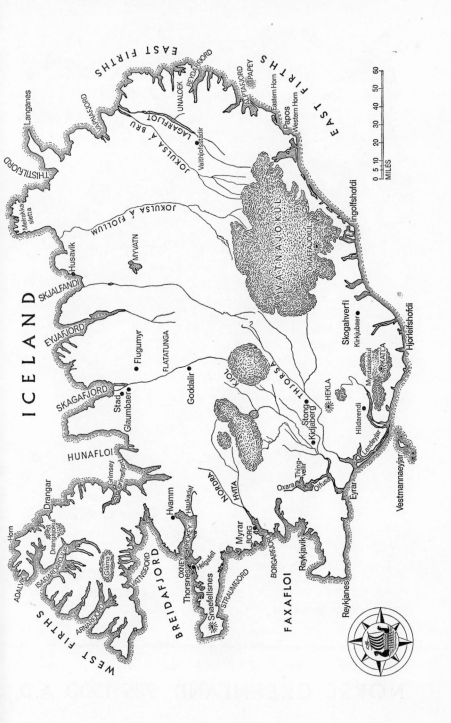

ICELAND

EAST FIRTHS

EAST FIRTHS

Langanes

THISTILFJORD

VAPNAFJORD

BORGARFJORD

REYDAFJORD

UNALOEK

VATTAFJORD

PAPEY

Eastern Horn

Papos

Western Horn

JOKULSA A BRU

LAGARFLJOT

Valthjofsstadir

Melrakka
sletta

JOKULSA A FJOLLUM

Ingolfshofdi

MYVATN

VATNAJOKUL

Husavik

SKJALFANDI

ORAEFAJOKUL

EYJAFJORD

Skogahverfi

Kirkjubaer

Hjörleifshofdi

Flugumyr

FLATATUNGA

Goddalir

KJOL

THJORSA

Mydalsjokul

KATLA

SKAGAFJORD

Stad

Glaumbaer

HEKLA

Stong

Kicjaberg

Hildarendi

HUNAFLOI

Drangar

Drangajokul

Grimsey

Grimsfjord

NORDRA

HVITA

Thing-
vellir

Oxara

Olfusa

Landeyjar

Eyrar

Horn

ADALVIK

SAERFJORD

Glama

VATNSEORD

Hvamm

Haukadal

Bredken

OXNEY

Thorsnes

Helgafell

Myrar

BORG

STRAUMFJORD

Reykjavik

Vestmannaeyjar

ARNAFJORD

BREIDAFJORD

Snaefellsnes

FAXAFLOI

Reykjanes

WEST FIRTHS

60
50
40
30
20
10
5
0
MILES

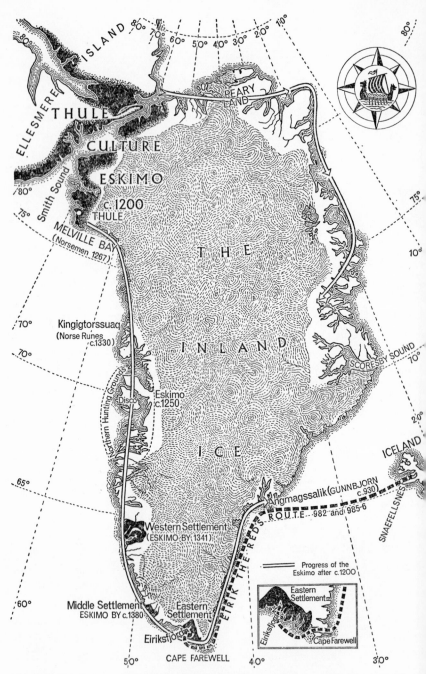

NORSE GREENLAND 985-1500 A.D.

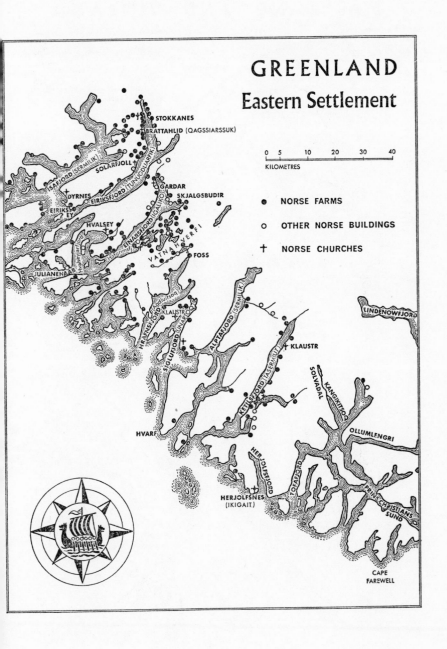

GREENLAND
Eastern Settlement

```
0    5    10        20        30        40
KILOMETRES
```

● NORSE FARMS

○ OTHER NORSE BUILDINGS

† NORSE CHURCHES

STOKKANES
BRATTAHLID (QAGSSIARSSUK)
ISAFJORD (SERMILIK)
SOLARFJOLL
DYRNES
EIRIKSFJORD (TUNUGDLIARFIK)
EIRIKS EY
GARDAR
SKJALGSBUDIR
HVALSEY
EINARSFJORD (IGALIKO)
VATNAHVERFI
FOSS
JULIANEHAB
KLAUSTR
SIGLUFJORD (UNA)
ALFTAFJORD (SERMILIK)
KLAUSTR
KETILSFJORD (TASERMIUT)
SOLVADAL
KANGIKITSO
LINDENOWFJORD
HVARF
OLLUMLENGRI
HERJOLFSFJORD
HERJOLFSNES (IKIGAIT)
TOFAFJORD
PRINS CHRISTIANS SUND
CAPE FAREWELL

MARKLAND AND VINLAND

Main route to VINLAND (Leif, Thorvald, Karlsefni).

Probable route of Thorvald and Karlsefni north-west from Leifsbudir-Straumfjord

Ⓔ Indicate the approximate position
Ⓘ of the native ESKIMO and INDIAN population c. 1000 A.D.

Cape Harrison

Ⓔ

Ⓔ

Ⓔ

Ⓔ

Hamilton Inlet

THE STRAND

Cape Porcupine

0 10 20 30 40 50 60 70 80 90 100

MILES

Ⓘ

Ⓘ English River

SANDWICH BAY

North West River

LAKE MELVILLE

Ⓘ

Goose Bay

Ⓘ

LABRADOR

Ⓔ

Ⓔ

ALEXIS RIVER

ST. LEWIS RIVER

Battle Harbour

Ⓔ

BELLE ISLE

ST. AUGUSTINE RIVER

Pistolet Bay

Sacred Bay

Great Sacred Island

Cape Bauld

Ⓘ

QUEBEC

Ⓘ

STRAIT OF BELLE ISLE

THORVALD'S MEN

Ⓔ HARE BAY

Ⓔ

Ⓔ

Ⓔ

LITTLE MECATINA RIVER

Ⓘ

Ⓔ

Ⓔ

NEWFOUNDLAND

Ⓘ

Ⓘ

WHITE BAY

KARLSEFNI AND SNORRI

Ⓘ

Ⓘ

Index

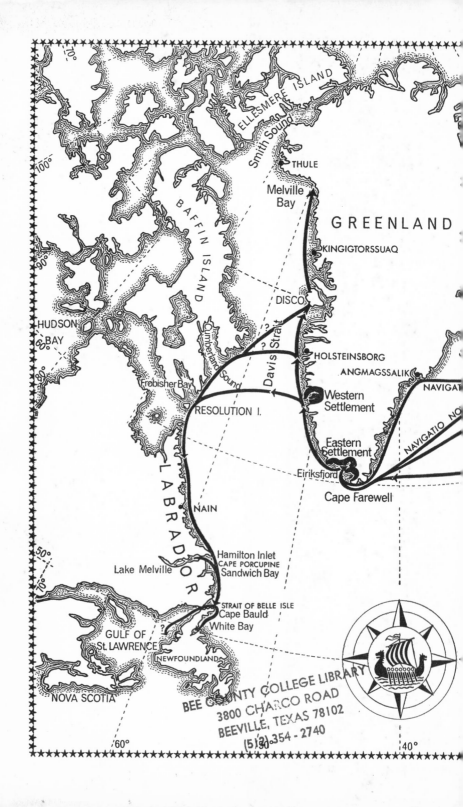

THULE

Melville
Bay

GREENLAND

ELLESMERE ISLAND

Smith Sound

KINGIGTORSSUAQ

BAFFIN ISLAND

DISCO

HUDSON
BAY

HOLSTEINSBORG

ANGMAGSSALIK

Cumberland Sound

Davis Strait

NAVIGAT

Frobisher Bay

Western
Settlement

NAVIGATIO NO

RESOLUTION I.

Eastern
Settlement

L A B R A D O R

Eiriksfjord

Cape Farewell

NAIN

Hamilton Inlet
CAPE PORCUPINE
Sandwich Bay

Lake Melville

STRAIT OF BELLE ISLE
Cape Bauld
White Bay

GULF OF
St. LAWRENCE

NEWFOUNDLAND

NOVA SCOTIA